ABINGDON
PREACHER'S
ANNUAL
1991

ABINGDON PREACHER'S ANNUAL 1991

COMPILED AND EDITED BY

John K. Bergland

ABINGDON PRESS
Nashville

ABINGDON PREACHER'S ANNUAL 1991

Copyright © 1990 by Abingdon Press

This book is printed on acid-free paper.

ISBN 0-687-00567-1
ISSN 1047-5486

Scripture quotations, unless otherwise noted, are from the Revised Standard Version of the Bible, copyright 1946, 1952, 1971 by the Division of Christian Education of the National Council of Churches of Christ in the USA. Used by permission.

Those noted GNB are from the *Good News Bible*—Old Testament: Copyright © American Bible Society 1976; New Testament: Copyright © American Bible Society 1966, 1971, 1976. Used by permission.

Those noted JBP are from *The New Testament in Modern English*, by J. B. Phillips. Copyright © 1972 by J. B. Phillips.

Those noted KJV are from the King James Version of the Bible.

Those noted NASB are from the New American Standard Bible, © The Lockman Foundation 1960, 1962, 1968, 1971, 1972, 1973, 1975, 1977. Used by permission.

Those noted NIV are taken from the *Holy Bible: New International Version*. Copyright © 1973, 1978, 1984 by the International Bible Society. Used by permission of Zondervan Bible Publishers.

Those noted TLB are from *The Living Bible*, copyright © 1971 by Tyndale House Publishers, Wheaton, IL. Used by permission.

MANUFACTURED IN THE UNITED STATES OF AMERICA

To Barbara, my lovely wife, steady encourager, and the shock absorber in our household

□

Bob, my strong son, who is also my colleague in the ministry, a devoted friend, and able companion

□

Peggy, my wonderful daughter, who is my boldest critic, most loyal advocate, and an adventuresome partner in work and play

□

Mildred, my sainted mother, who has prayed for me without ceasing and from whom I learned to love the scriptures

CONTENTS

□

SECTION II:

SERMON RESOURCES

SECTION III:
INDEXES

PREFACE

☐

Preaching has long been the central task of ministry. The scriptures also hold a primary place in the life of the church. This book is intended to help ministers preach the Sunday lessons throughout the year.

Persons who have been "set apart" by the church for the specialized ministry of Word, Sacrament, and Order face an awesome task. The year stretches before them as an unending procession of services. Every Sunday morning demands that once again the minister be prepared to preach, to pray, and to lead the church in Christian worship. The *Abingdon Preacher's Annual* provides a starting place. Use it week-in and week-out.

Use this book with confidence. Turn to it with the expectation that it can help you in the search for information concerning the Christian calendar, the lectionary, and special seasons. It offers suggestions for worship and some fine examples of other ministers' sermons and prayers. Our purpose has been to provide a book that can strengthen the plans and individual gifts and graces of each pastor.

The *Abingdon Preacher's Annual* primarily follows the Sunday lessons of *The New Common Lectionary*. Therefore, the sermons begin with a text. The text finds you instead of your finding the text. The move from text to sermon is as varied as are commentaries on the text. This book does not presume a pattern for the preparation of sermons. It does, however, provide for each Sunday:

1. The assigned texts, Old Testament, Epistle, and Gospel for each Sunday.

2. A brief description of the central theme, story, or message of each lesson.

3. A section about "Interpretation and Imagination."

4. A sermon for each Sunday.

5. Call to worship, prayers, and hymns for each Sunday.

13

The "interpretation and imagination" material will provide idea starters, insights, information, illustrations, and preferences.

The sermons are from a broad representation of ministers, both geographically and denominationally. Some are well known and preach to large congregations and to international audiences. Some are more hidden in their place of preaching. All intend to be faithful servants of the word.

Offertory sentences and funeral texts may be found in the second section of this book. That section also includes a helpful outline of the lectionary lessons for the year, prepared by the Reverend Bob Bergland. This very useful overview of the whole year helps a preacher to plan each Sunday with easy awareness of the texts and themes that will follow. The important question of biblical authority is addressed in an article titled "Infallibility and Authority" by Dr. Thomas Langford, a distinguished professor at Duke Divinity School.

I am indebted to the ministers who have written sermons and prayers for this book. I wish that each reader could know the charisma of many of these preachers. Properly considered, their sermons are not limited by the confining dimensions of a printed page. Each of these preachers is a wonderful Christian friend, and the gathering of their material has brought the joy of old friendships renewed and the excitement of new ones.

I am indebted to those who have further strengthened my hand for this task: my secretaries, Marcia Moritz, Lisa Bryant, and Emma Faircloth; typists Katherine A. Straghan and Debra Sepp; my son, Bob Bergland, a United Methodist pastor and chairperson of The Conference Work Area on Worship, has helped with numerous suggestions and resources.

My colleague and friend Dr. Edwin Burtner taught homiletics for many years at United Theological Seminary in Dayton, Ohio. He used to say, "There is no single way to prepare to preach. Each of us must go to Jabbok ford and wrestle alone." May the God of Jacob and the God of our Lord Jesus Christ bless you and name you among those who preach the Word of God.

John K. Bergland
Pentecost 1989

14

SECTION I

□

FIFTY-TWO SUNDAY SERMONS

JANUARY 6

□

Epiphany

Epiphany means "manifestation" and suggests a theme of light—light to the nations.

To discover how to be human now,
Is the reason we follow the Star.
(W. H. Auden, "Three Wise Men")

The Sunday Lessons

The Psalm: Psalm 72:1-14.

Isaiah 60:1-6: When the exiles were returning to Jerusalem, the prophet Isaiah wrote poems about the radiance of that restored city. "Your light has come; the glory of the Lord has risen upon you." Nations will come to that light. Camel caravans will bring gifts of gold and frankincense to celebrate God's presence.

Ephesians 3:1-12: Paul was in prison. He had preached that Gentiles were partakers of the promise and that God's grace was for them, too. This angered the Judaizers, but the darkness of human bigotry did not discourage the apostle called "to preach to the Gentiles the unsearchable riches of Christ."

Matthew 2:1-12: Wise men (magi) came from the east, asking, "Where is he who has been born king of the Jews?" They had seen his star and followed it to Bethlehem, where they found the Christ child and worshiped Him. Herod, the king, was troubled by reports that a baby, destined to be king, had been born.

Interpretation and Imagination

For centuries, the Jewish people had waited for a Savior. Their scriptures had prophesied his coming. Their worship heralded the promised Messiah. Yet, when the Christ child was born, they

17

did not recognize him. The chief priests and scribes, who quoted their cherished texts to King Herod, told about the coming of an anointed one, but they did not seek him.

Herod, who was king of the Jews, liked to be called Herod the Great. He had left his mark on Jerusalem and throughout Israel. As a devout Jew, Herod would never sacrifice a pig; yet, this ruthless tyrant had killed his own sons. The saying went abroad that it was better to be Herod's pig than Herod's son. With wonderful irony, Matthew portrays a well-placed king as one who is uncertain, compared to pagan magi. He shows a powerful and ruthless ruler, losing his kingdom to the might and right of the newborn Christ child.

Stars are lesser witnesses than are prophets and scriptures. Gentiles appear late in the drama of salvation history. But one star, shining a bit brighter, and gentile kings from far away places reveal and discover that the glory of God is with us.

The glory of God is like that. It surprises. It's manifestations mix meaning with mystery. The late Carlyle Marney was once asked if he knew anything about the glory of God. He answered, "Most times it sneaks up from behind and grabs you."

That may be the way Christmas comes to you. Twelve days later, in a celebration of Epiphany—"little Christmas" some call it—in the Christmas of the Gentiles, in a light that shines for all people. The searchers fail to find the one whom they seek, but some are led to the presence of One who seeks them.

THE MAGI MOMENT

Matthew 2:1-12

A SERMON BY HEATHER MURRAY ELKINS

The text for the day is Matthew's account of the Magi, but the context for us is post-Christmas. It's over. It has happened, and now these figures appear bearing gifts just when we've trashed the last of the ribbons and wrappings. What is the point of celebrating their late arrival? Most of us haven't a clue that Christmas itself is a late arrival on the liturgical scene. East is east, and west is west. Why split the gospel between them? But the text presses on our context for a second chorus. We, like the Magi, arrive late at the party. We Gentiles are grafted onto the story. Their question reminds us not to presume a prominent place at the table or in the church: "Where is he who is born king of the Jews?"

A family decided to make a journey like that of the Magi. But there was no doubt about it: *They were lost.* They were also late, but that could wait. The lostness was the critical factor. Of course, the lack of precise directions could have been their first clue that this would not be a quick trip in any sense of the expression. There was a main road, and there was an unmarked road, and then there was a field, and somewhere in the field was something called "the village," and in the north corner of the village was a family who had a name, but no address. "But, you needn't worry," said the stay-at-home guide. "There will be someone waiting for you. They know you're coming." That "someone waiting" determined that they go.

It had not been a willing journey. Someone else had decided to sponsor a needy family for Christmas. Someone else had gathered up oranges, apples, bread, crayons, books, blankets, and a bureau. Someone else had decided that the destination was the Yaqui Indian migrant camp, and the someone else who knew the way had just arrived on the doorstep to say he couldn't go. So, in place of a well-planned piece of Christmas charity, with a truck and a driver and plenty of time and daylight, there was an overstuffed station wagon driven by someone who hated to ask for directions. Packed in between the cartons were the rest of the family, who hated getting lost and being late for the Christmas Eve program. Only a dim sense that this was part of the real meaning of Christmas kept the car on the road. Like the unwise Magi, they set off looking for someone without the assistance of a star or a sign.

They found the road and the village, and maybe the north corner, but that was it. They couldn't find the someone they were sent to find, the someone who was waiting. They certainly weren't alone; people were everywhere, peering in the windows and pressing around them. Perhaps, in the daylight, the urgent poverty that pressed and pulled on them would have produced pity. But in the darkness, in the confusion and the unknowing, it bred fear.

No Christmas illusion could survive this razor's edge of existence. They were accustomed to the nips and tucks of a teacher's salary, but this was different. They drove between hovels of cardboard and rusty sheets of tin. They circled shoeless men. The fiery sparks from burning oil drums flickered in the eyes of the children. They understood without saying so that the children of the poor were children to fear. What good was the tree tied to the roof of the car? It was needed for fuel, not for tinsel. What good were the books that showed lives the children standing in the firelight could not afford to imagine? What good was their good will? A falling star, no more, deepening the darkness and adding the cruelty of wishing.

The childish tension of a missed Christmas program was overwhelmed by the recognition that in this tableau were no tender poses. Not only had the Magi not arrived, but even God was missing from the scene. No lullabies about mangers here; orange-crate walls did little to shut out the whine of the wind. In place of toddlers reaching to touch pretty Jesus, dirty, fierce hands tore a doll to pieces as they struggled for possession of it.

The family retreated to the car to reconsider their mission. Their random charity was causing chaos. So they drove on, looking for a place to deliver the goods and depart. How wise the chimney approach appeared on Santa's part. How necessary the star had been. Wisdom was not enough to know how to deliver gifts of frankincense or oranges. They circled the village, looking for a sign. Then it came and stopped them right in their tracks. Over the doorway of a shelter made of cardboard and scraps hung a blanket.

Someone had moved the blanket to peer out at the sound of their passing. The light from inside reached into the darkness. A very rough, modern interpretation of scripture occurred: And when they saw the star, they rejoiced exceedingly with great joy. They stopped, got out, and being glad it was almost over, walked into wonder or mystery or whatever word you use when awe gets under your skin.

Someone was waiting. This was the place. They knew it. It was more than the light that spread from a handmade stove to the faces of the children. It was more than a graceful mother, grateful for the odds and ends of Christmas; more than the inarticulate, hand-pumping father who returned carrying trash to burn for heat. It was even more than the newborn baby sleeping in a cardboard box on the dirt floor. Perhaps it was the parallel, too obvious for tears, between the ancient story of straw and light and swaddling clothes. Or perhaps it was the sheer relief that here modern Magi could be forgiven as givers instead of takers. But in that light, for whatever reason, the Magi moment came.

The discarded bureau became a baby's bed and a treasure chest and a table. Bringing the tree had been a last-minute decision, and the oranges were tied with ribbons and hung for decoration. Secondhand clothes provided a fashion show with eager models and audience. The smaller children put bows in their hair and danced to their own inner rhythm. Songs in at least three known languages were tried on and passed around. Names were exchanged, and it was revealed that the mother's name was Maria; they had made an appropriate choice. Epiphanies leave little to chance.

The parting came late and with reluctance. Promises were made, but the future was shadowed by the threat of principalities and powers. The "holy" family were migrants, Yaquis, illegal refugees from oppression, who could not be acknowledged for political reasons. They knew the weight of Herod's hand. They knew what it meant to flee for the sake of the children. Like their ancient counterparts, they took flight into "Egypt," and under the watchful eyes of overseers, set up camp. They picked the crops and emptied the fields. When they were paid, they braced themselves for the bulldozers that would come and level their sheds, their village, and their fragile sense of home. A return visit would confirm their prophetic dread. The cold light of winter would reveal only an empty field swept clean of the life of this night. But for this moment, this Magi moment, the treasures—in Paul's words, "the unfathomable riches of Christ"—had been opened. "The mystery which for ages had been hidden in God who created all things" had been brought to light—starlight. This is enough light for any Magi to travel by.

Now, at the story's conclusion, comes a confession. I have shared with you a family heirloom, a treasure that is passed from hand to hand each year. It is a handmade story about a true time. My father, my mother, and my sisters made that journey to the Yaqui home. My father, my mother, and my sisters, not me. Like the last of the Magi, I had chosen to stay behind. I was to be Mary in the Christmas play and decided not to risk what I knew to be an impossible errand. I was, in fact, waiting smugly at home, ready to reproach them for missing Christmas, only to discover I was the one who got lost.

Christ had not arrived in the middle of the marvelous program. He had hidden, waiting to be found behind a migrant blanket. I missed him. You may run the same risk sitting here, hearing this. Somewhere in the world, someone is waiting, and if you don't go looking, if you won't risk getting lost and being late, then you will miss your Magi moment. Instead of seeing what happens, you will be left with only the story. But if that happens—when it happens—you will discover as I have discovered and as Paul once discovered, sometimes the story is light enough for the way. To us, "the very least of all saints," this grace will be given "to preach to the Gentiles the unfathomable riches of Christ." On Epiphany, that story comes with a gift: the sacrament of Christ's table.

On communion plates used in the early church, there was engraved a star, the wise men's star. It was placed there to show that now the star leads those who would be wise to Christ's presence here. Come. It's time for the journey. Someone is waiting. Come and receive what is more precious than gold, more fragrant than frankincense. Follow the star. Receive him here at the table. Here in the starlight are the gifts of God for the people of God. And when the star moves from here into the world, follow it. It will surely lead you to the place where the Child of God is waiting.

Suggestions for Worship

Call to Worship:

Minister: Rejoice, for God has sent the Messiah.

People: **Let the mountains bring peace to the people.**

Minister: May righteousness rule from sea to sea.

People: **Let justice come down like rain.**

Minister: May mercy endure as long as the sun shall last.

People: **Let truth outlive the moon.**

Minister: Arise, shine, for the light has come.

Morning Prayer: Holy One, light of light, you have revealed yourself in your gift Emmanuel. Like the Magi, we come seeking the Child of God. Like the Magi, we have followed our faint glimmers to the One who is the light of the world. Here we offer our gifts, made of trash and treasure. We lay before you lives that need your refiner's fire. We relinquish our memories that they may be drained of their bitterness. We open our feelings so that they may absorb the fragrance of your forgiveness. Light of light, shine in our hearts and lead us to where the Christ is waiting. This we ask for the sake of the world, ourselves, and your Son. Amen.

Suggested Hymns: "Arise, Shine Out, Your Light Has Come"; "Hope of the World"; "Go, Tell It on the Mountain."

Pastoral Prayer: Hope of the world, holy, loving God, accept what we will offer in love to your Son. We give only what is already your own. Through him, with him, in him lives all that we would give. But here, on the clean straw of this hour of prayer, we lay that to which we have a claim: broken dreams and days, battered wills and bodies, minds both tangled and unraveled. We kneel, knowing what we have been. In Christ's eyes, let us see what we will be. Let us rise with strength, knowing that he holds our lives in his hands, and in that strength, from that knowing, may we startle the world with the confidence of our hope and the generosity of our love. Amen.

JANUARY 13

□

First Sunday After Epiphany (Baptism of the Lord)

Christ's glory was manifest at his baptism. The waters of baptism also remind us of the creative power of God.

The Sunday Lessons

The Psalm: Psalm 29.

Genesis 1:1-5: Darkness covered the surface of a formless and empty earth. Then the winds of God blew across the chaos. God said, "Let there be light." Then it was the morning of the very first day.

Acts 19:1-7: Christian disciples at Ephesus had been baptized with John's baptism of repentance, but they had not heard of the Holy Spirit. Paul placed his hands on them and "the Holy Spirit came upon them."

Mark 1:4-11: John the baptizer was preaching a baptism of repentance and forgiveness. Jesus came from Nazareth in Galilee to Judea and was baptized in the Jordan. Verses 9-11 witness to Jesus' unique relationship with God—"my beloved Son." *Beloved* means "chosen."

Interpretation and Imagination

Sometimes we leave early—before the final buzzer, before the last hymn, before anyone else leaves the party. Watching a drama on television, a woman switched channels, saying, "I hate sad endings." Worried about a possible traffic jam, a father had the family watch the fireworks finale from the car.

Some persons are that way about salvation history. They leave right after baptism. They embrace a theology that expects Christ to provide an early escape from the sin, grief, and pain of this life.

The lectionary suggests that the reading stop at verse 11, but don't neglect the words that follow the baptismal account: "The Spirit immediately drove him out in the wilderness" (vs. 12). In the larger context of Mark's Gospel, it is plain that the good news is about suffering. The servant style is never denied or modified.

Note how Mark's Gospel portrays Christ as the One who engages the world and its sickness, evil, and sin. At the beginning of this Gospel, Christ meets the baptist with the camel-skin clothes, and he wades into the waters that wash away sin. Coming out of those waters, he is called "beloved Son." The word *son* is used throughout Mark. Near the end a centurion speaks the name as the Christ hangs dead on the cross: "Truly this man was the Son of God."

What is the ultimate conclusion, the omega point of salvation history? The perfect transformation of the world? A sudden eschatological victory over evil? Our removal to a safe place prepared for us? Not in Mark's gospel.

The beginning and the end, the alpha and the omega, center in Jesus Christ, the Son of God and his cross.

AN END TO CONFUSION

Genesis 1:1-5; Mark 1:4-11

A SERMON BY H. GRAY SOUTHERN

Announcements often confuse rather than inform. Well meaning church bulletin announcements tell you that, "At the conclusion of Sunday's service, Mrs. Jones will lay an egg on the altar" or "All those desiring to become 'Little Mothers' should meet with the pastor after the service in his study" are the types of things that amuse. But errors in announcements cause enormous problems. On one New Year's Day, the TV announcer said that "the 'Tonight Show' has been cancelled; the 'Tomorrow Show' will be seen tonight, and the 'Today Show' will be seen tomorrow." It took a newspaper article to explain the confusion. If you want to see more confusion, just watch someone try to decide between two favorite desserts.

Many of us are confused about many things. When I was a child, I thought that by the time persons were as old as I am now, they would understand everything. But I don't. And those of you who are twice my age—and older than that—are quick to say that things will get no better. There is uncertainty about life and its meaning, whom to trust, what to do, how to love, and how to communicate with those you do love. All too much confusion exists.

"And there went out to [John] all the country of Judea, and all the people of Jerusalem; and they were baptized by him in the river Jordan, confessing their sins" (Mark 1:5). The people came out to John, heard his preaching, and confessed themselves to be confused. They were searching for ways to succeed and for ways to find love. John preached about God and how God would take some of their confusion away. God would give them grace through a mighty messenger who would calm them and inspire them. This messenger would come and give them the Holy Spirit: a gift from God that would give them peace and strength.

The people were so glad about John's message that many of them were baptized. They were thankful that God cared enough to help them figure out how to live. They were baptized as a sign of their acceptance of John's message, a message of hope and peace, a message that promised an end to their confusion about life.

Jesus came forward to see his cousin John, who was baptizing in God's name by the river Jordan. Jesus knew that John was baptizing those people who wanted God to give them purpose, people who wanted an end to confusion about how to live their lives, and people who believed in God's power to bring order out of chaos. Jesus was one of those people who knew God's power, and he was baptized. God marked Jesus as the One who could bring order to all people on earth.

That means something very clear for us. If we want order and peace in our lives, we must fill our lives up with an understanding and love for Jesus. Jesus Christ teaches us about those things of which we can be most certain. Christ teaches us clearly about God, who always watches over us and who is always with us in the Holy Spirit.

Everybody told me how easy it is to sail. And true, in the textbooks, it is a fairly simple idea. But on the water, where there are currents and eddies, along with charts to read and a lot of lines and sails and a tiller to worry about, everything gets confusing. Eventually, you get things organized. You find a marker in the distance. You get the sails up, catch the wind, and off you go. Just when you think you have the hang of it, a sudden gust of wind blows, and everything is upset. Or a storm comes and nothing works and you get confused, probably along with being angry because nothing is working the way you want it to work.

Learning to live is a lot like learning to sail. Just remember how hard it was to grow up. You get things fairly well together, decide on what you're going to do, and start. Then something happens. An unexpected surprise blows into your life, and everything is upset. Or a bad blow comes and nothing works and you get confused and probably angry. Sometimes people just do not know what they want or how to get it. The pain and confusion experienced by people like that is beyond calculation. Where is an end to that confusion?

Whether you are on a sailboat or trying to get through the day, the solution is the same. God marked the solution when Jesus was baptized. Jesus taught us about God and God's love. When you lose sight of Jesus, you are in as much trouble as sailors are when they get off course and lose sight of their marker. Neither the sailors nor you know where to go. Without Christ as the central reference of your life, confusion reigns. With Christ in the center of your life, you will know what to do.

If you are confused about what to do, ask God and ask yourself what you think Jesus would do in this situation. Listen for the Holy Spirit. God will speak to you just as God spoke to Jesus after his baptism. You may not hear a voice, but you should do as you are led. Confusion will end. You will have peace. That peace will certainly feel better than the indecision or confusion that you knew.

Confusion is part of being human. If you are ever confused, then ask for the love of Christ and the leadership of God's Holy Spirit to come into your life and give you an end to confusion. God will do it.

Let us pray: God of life and freedom, we celebrate your revelation of Jesus as the Christ who brings us to you. Help us when we are confused and do not know what to do. Make us new in Jesus Christ, who is Lord forever. Amen.

Suggestions for Worship

Call to Worship:

Minister: The time is fulfilled.

People: The kingdom of God is at hand! Believe in the gospel!

Prayer of Confession: God of grace and glory, you order this world and our lives, showing us your power over all life. We confess before you that often we neglect our baptismal vows: that we neglect your worship, in public and in private, that we are too often slow to renounce evil, that we forget your ways. Forgive us our sin and fill us with the power of the Holy Spirit that we might live righteous lives.

Hear us, too, we pray, as we confess before you our abuse of our neighbors . . . (*pause*). Move us to find their pardon and yours, for we pray through the One whom you claimed as your beloved Son, Jesus Christ our Lord. Amen.

Suggested Hymns: "Jesus Shall Reign"; "Blessed Assurance"; "Glorious Things of Thee Are Spoken."

Pastoral Prayer: Eternal God, you made us and this world, brought beauty out of chaos and brought order into our lives. Give us your grace that we might become new people. For what you have done in creating us, and for what your son, Jesus, did in redeeming us, and for your Spirit which sustains us, we praise you.

Lord, as your face moved across the waters and your Spirit breathed order and life into us, so come into our lives, we pray. Give us order and calm when we are confused. Give us certainty about how we are to live and love one another and you. Change our lives as we should be changed into your daughters and sons.

God, our redeemer, we thank you for all those who preach the gospel and teach its truth. Especially we thank you for those who teach us, your servants. Bless their work and give them inspiration. Guide us to support and care for them as best meets their needs. Teach us to be as glad for their work and success as we are for our own.

Lord, you heal our hearts, minds, and bodies whenever we turn to you. Give your healing power to those we name, remembering . . . and those in our hearts. Care for those who are confused, especially the aged, the sick, the frightened, and the poor.

God, sovereign over us all, order and calm our troubled world, we ask. Guard and guide our president and our governor, that they and all our leaders, will so order our world that we might live in peace and justice with one another.

For these gifts we thank you, Almighty God, in the name of Jesus Christ, whom you bless and by whom you bless us, teaching us to pray and to say: (recite the Lord's Prayer).

JANUARY 20

□

Second Sunday After Epiphany

Witnesses who were asked to tell what they had seen and heard echoed the invitation of Christ: "Come and see."

The Sunday Lessons

The Psalm: Psalm 63:1-8.

I Samuel 3:1-10 *or* 20: The Lord's call to Samuel is mistaken by the boy to be a call from the blind Eli, whom he was serving. Three times Samuel hears the voice until Eli says, "If he calls you, you shall say, 'Speak, Lord, for thy servant hears' " (v. 9). God's call to Samuel was a call to be a prophet.

I Corinthians 6:12-20: Some members of the Corinthian church were engaging in sexual relationships with temple prostitutes. They excused their conduct with the gnostic view that Christianity was separate from the world of flesh and blood: "All things are lawful for me" (v. 12). Paul argues that both body and soul belong to Christ and that the "body is a temple of the Holy Spirit within you. . . . So glorify God in your body" (vv. 19-20).

John 1:35-42: Two of the baptist's disciples, hearing him refer to Christ as "the lamb of God" (v. 36), leave him to follow Jesus. They ask, "Where are you staying?" (v. 38). Jesus answers, "Come and see" (v. 39). Andrew found Simon and said, "We have found the Messiah" (v. 41). Phillip spoke of Christ to Nathaniel, who questioned, "Can anything good come out of Nazareth?" (v. 46). "Come and see," Phillip said. They will see more. "You will see heaven opened" (v. 51).

Interpretation and Imagination

"Follow me" is an invitation that seems simple enough. It is a directive: "If you will follow, follow!"

Yet, there is much more in this call of the first disciples: (1) It is a call that causes them to leave their boats and nets and the good life symbolized by the phrase "under the fig tree"; (2) it is a call to forsake other religious devotion such as the sect led by John the Baptist and Judaism (Nathaniel); (3) the invitation is given not only by Jesus but also by his witnesses (the baptist, Andrew, Phillip); and (4) response to the call is directly related to seeing and knowing. John recognized the Christ. Jesus could see the character of Simon Peter and Nathaniel and could foresee their destiny as disciples. The disciples saw in nearsighted ways and were promised new visions from heaven.

If the gnostics erred in believing that religion only had to do with the heavenly, modern religious thought has erred in its belief that the flesh and blood realities of society and politics are the confining walls of God's realm. Science and technology, with their passion for the immediate, may tempt us to ignore the transcendent, but they will not satisfy our deepest hungers. There's a hunger that a Big Mac can't satisfy and a thirst that is unquenched by Gatorade.

The text addresses every visual reality. Come and see where I am staying! If the church loses perspective in the physical world, we may unwittingly cause distortions in secular society. Come and see the man from Nazareth! Rude dialect and a lack of culture made the place seem ordinary and overlooked. Come and see heaven opened! To see the objective, physical world clearly is a step toward a vantage point for seeing beyond it into the mysteries of heaven.

Look at the rainbow beyond. Come and see the man from Nazareth—and see heaven.

DO YOU KNOW WHAT I HEARD?

John 1:35-42

A SERMON BY H. GRAY SOUTHERN

Why do you believe? All of us came to have faith in different ways, ways as distinctive as we are. But all of us came to have faith by means of a few common denominators. First, God was at work in us to give us the Holy Spirit so that we would believe. Everyone who believes has that Holy Spirit, God within us, to testify to us that we are God's and that God is ours. Second, people witnessed with their lives. Most important, someone told you about Jesus. Good example is not enough: the reason for that example must be explained. To witness means to talk about and to live out our love of Jesus Christ.

Andrew met Jesus and wanted to stay with him. Andrew found out that Jesus had wonderful things to give. "We have found the Messiah" (John 1:41). In Jesus, Andrew saw the Christ and knew him to be the one person who really understood and would tell us about God. Then Andrew brought Peter to Jesus. Or, more accurately, Andrew's *words* brought Peter to Jesus.

There are many reasons to talk about Jesus, but let's talk about the reason why we might not witness. First, people, meaning the speaker and the hearer, are embarrassed. If we are honest, many of us will confess that we are embarrassed to talk about our faith. Even though there is a time and a place for everything, somehow the time and place to talk about our faith never come—unless, of course, we are here at church, where it is safe to talk about "religious things." In its more extreme form, that sort of embarrassment comes from not wanting to look like a Bible-banger, the sort of person who will convert you whether you like it or not by banging you over the head with a great big copy of the Scriptures or whatever else it takes. Many people have confused a simple explanation of why they believe in Jesus with hard-core arm-twisting tactics. Some people will tell you that talking about faith is sort of like talking about politics or sex: It is in poor taste. The answers to our embarrassment are several. Remember that there are many things that you do not discuss with total strangers. I was taught to respect myself and my family enough not to discuss our business with just everybody I met. But I was also taught that there is indeed a time and a place to discuss almost everything, including the most intimate details of my life. We must choose when it is appropriate to talk about Jesus. God's expectation is that we will at some time talk about our faith with the people around us. If we do not share our faith with them, we have abused them as much as, if not more than, we would have if we badgered them with it.

Besides, you're not such a good Christian yourself, are you? If you don't have all the answers, who are you to start talking about God? Well, look at Andrew. He didn't know everything that there was to tell about Jesus. He had only just met Jesus at the tenth hour, about four o'clock in the afternoon, and had spent that one evening with him. Notice that Andrew didn't try to tell Peter everything Jesus had said. Andrew just told Peter that he understood Jesus to be the Messiah. Andrew did not have to prove anything to Peter. Andrew only had to talk about what he believed, what he knew and no more. Evidently something else—or someone else—was there, too, working in Peter's heart. That someone was God. If you have ever been afraid to talk about your faith, and most of us are, remember that it's not up to you to convert anybody. God converts. Now, God may use you and your words or witness about Jesus, but it is God and God alone who will convert people. The preacher didn't convert you, God did; the Sunday school teacher didn't convert you, God did; even your mother, good as she was, didn't convert you, God did. And so, it will be God who converts the people with whom you talk. You don't have to worry about it.

Whom do you talk to? Do you have to go preach on the street corner? Well, do that if you want, but the person preaching on the street corner doesn't know me and so can't really care about me. But if people I know—a member of my family, a member of my church, a friend—share their faith with me, I will be changed. The people with whom we are to share our faith are the people God puts in our lives. The people with whom we are to share our faith are the people with whom we live, with whom we work, with whom we play cards, with whom we go to parties. They are the people who really matter to us, and we must really matter to them. Figure it this way: If you can eat with someone, sleep with someone, tell jokes and laugh with someone, why don't you share the rest of your intimate self and tell that person what you believe? People want to hear from us as much as we would like to hear from them. Andrew shared his newfound faith with his brother, the man with whom he worked. Andrew did not go out to the front yard and start to preach to strangers. Andrew *talked* with his own family first. Samuel did not run out of the church and start knocking things out of people's hands in an effort to tell them about his experience with God. He did tell Eli, the man he worked for, about what God had done. Whom do you talk about God with? Start with people you know.

But why bother? In our country only 58 percent of our citizens are professing Christians who belong to churches; only one-half of that number attend worship or church three times a month. What that effectively means is that three-fourths of the population of the United States is not churched and seems to profess no faith in Christ as Lord. Those of us here at worship are the exception, not the rule. That was hard for me to believe at first. I rationalized that I'm a pastor and that I spend a lot of time with church people. But that was a cop-out. I started to calculate, and I could come up with the names of thirty people I know fairly well who are not professing Christians and who wonder about what to believe. They need to hear my faith.

The other reason to share your faith is that sharing it will make you see what you have. The Holy Spirit has put within each of us knowledge and belief in God and in God's Son, Jesus Christ. That knowledge lifts us up, gives us God in whom to trust, and it makes us glad. Telling that story of good news will only remind us of what we have. I am never so glad to speak my faith as after a funeral or a divorce or some other grief has hit someone, and I have been there to speak the words of God's grace. In the midst of speaking that good news, I am reminded again of what God has given me: good news of peace and life. Then I know that I, too, with you, am called by God as were Andrew and Samuel to tell others about life and joy and peace as I know them through Jesus Christ our Lord.

Let us pray: Almighty God, we thank you for the gift of faith that you have put in our lives. Help us to talk about you with others so that they can have the same joy we have found in you. Give us your mind and heart now to think of that one person with whom we need to share your Son's gospel (*pause*). Help us to speak to that person, for his or her sake, and for the sake of Jesus Christ, who came for that person and for us all. Amen.

Suggestions for Worship

Call to Worship:

Minister: O magnify the Lord with me;

People: Let us exalt his name together!

Minister: For with you is the fountain of life,

People: **In your light we see our light now and for
evermore!**

Prayer of Confession: God, you are the Light of the world. In
your light, we see our lives and know our poverty. Forgive us, we
pray, for our silence and hesitancy in speaking for you. Pardon
our haste to be quiet about your wondrous works done in us.

All-seeing God, you know our lives, our hearts, and our
thoughts. Pardon us for the wrongs we have done in quietness
and calm. Forgive us our secret prides and selfish desires.
Inspire us to share love and kindness with others that we might
live in peace with them all the days of our lives.

Lord of all life, you have equipped us with strength and spirit.
Pardon our willingness to give your work to others. Remind us of
our place in your church and your kingdom and strengthen us by
our knowledge of you that we might truly know you and the light
of peace who is Jesus Christ, our Lord. Amen.

Suggested Hymns: "Ye Servants of God"; "I Love to Tell the
Story" or "We've a Story to Tell to the Nations"; "Go, Tell It on
the Mountain."

Pastoral Prayer: God, our Lord, you gave us the Christ to be our
Savior. You redeem us from our sins by his power and his cross.
You raise us to life through his death and resurrection. And you
give us faith in you. For that light and its loving hope that our
faith gives us, we thank you. Inspire in us true faith and hope,
give us the promise of your company always, and guide us to be
your holy people, for the sake of Jesus Christ, our Lord.

God, your Son became our servant, and you lifted him up. We
pray for your servants in your church, especially for our
missionaries . . . and for all those whom they serve. Strengthen
them with the Holy Spirit and cause the light of their witness to
enlighten all those around them. Inspire all your people to serve
you better and make us mindful of our mission to serve in our
place. Make us bold to witness to you and for Christ Jesus. Make
us timid and quiet when we should hold our tongue. And guide
our words so that those we know and those we love and we

ourselves might discover anew the power of Jesus Christ, the Light of the world.

God of light and peace, enlighten those who suffer with the certain hope of your love. Inspire those who care for them with your peace. Heal them according to your will. We pray for those who are cold and needy and for those who suffer in mind and spirit. Remember those who are addicted to drugs and other substances, robbing their lives of your grace. Answer our needs with your love and open our minds to what you are doing for us in Jesus Christ, our Lord.

Hear us as we pray for ourselves and those we love: For hearing us and for answering us, we praise you, O God. We know that you answer our needs and delight in our love. And we remember, too, that Jesus Christ taught us to pray and to say together: (recite the Lord's Prayer).

JANUARY 27

□

Third Sunday After Epiphany

Their livelihood (fishing) became an avocation when the disciples heard the call to follow. Contracts with this world all have termination dates. The world is passing away. The lessons call for repentance.

The Sunday Lessons

The Psalm: Psalm 62:5-12.

Jonah 3:1-5, 10: Jonah, a narrow-minded nationalistic prophet who hated the Ninevites, wanted nothing to do with a warning of judgment. After he ran away and the storm at sea and the belly of the fish: "The word of the Lord came to Jonah the second time, saying, 'Arise, go to Nineveh, that great city, and proclaim to it the message that I tell you' " (vv. 1-2). When Nineveh repented, God did not destroy the city. Jonah's preaching of repentance relates to the Gospel lesson.

I Corinthians 7:29-31 *or* 35: "The form of this world is passing away" (v. 31). Paul responded to the Corinthians' questions about marriage and sexual conduct and concluded with a discussion about divided interests. "The appointed time has grown very short; from now on let those . . . who deal with the world [be] as though they had no dealings with it" (vv. 29, 31).

Mark 1:14-20: John's arrest and the beginning of Jesus' ministry in Galilee are the historical context for announcing, "The kingdom of God is at hand" (v. 15). The kind of repentance and belief that benefits citizens of that kingdom is shown in the response of the disciples. Hearing "Follow me and I will make you become fishers of men" (v. 17), they immediately left their nets and followed him."

Interpretation and Imagination

When Harvard was founded in 1636, the stated purpose for each student was that "the main end of his life and studies" be to know God and Jesus Christ, "which is eternal life." Currently among universities, colleges, and technical schools, there is discussion about useful and useless education. The difference has to do with rewards in the bread and butter sense of personal income.

To Harvard's credit, the core curriculum prescribed in recent years included one course in philosophy that intends to help students "think systematically about such issues as justice, obligation, personal responsibility, citizenship, friendship." But the change at Harvard reflects the changing values in education motivated by an industrialized and materialistic society. Profits have become primary.

Now we are warned "there is no such thing as free lunch" in the ecological world. Toxic waste, acid rain, and depleted energy sources combine to ward off "social cost accounting." In theological terms, one would speak of "the judgment of God."

Jonah warned of impending doom. Paul reminded the Corinthians that the relationships and businesses of this world are fleeting. When our Lord spoke about the kingdom of God, he called for repentance. Repentance is more than a change of mind. It is a radical reordering of priorities and allegiance. The disciples "repent and believe," as they leave boat, net, and family to follow.

CALLED TO FOLLOW

Mark 1:14-20

A SERMON BY ROBERT M. TERHUNE

The Japanese use a picturesque expression to describe a statement that's been heard so often that people do not really listen closely to it anymore. They say that you have heard it so much you've developed calluses on your ears. Perhaps many of us have developed calluses on our ears in regard to this passage from the Gospel of Mark. We've heard it quoted and expounded so much that we consciously or unconsciously feel we've heard all that needs to be said about it.

I challenge you today, however, to listen anew, with fresh, uncallused ears to the call of Jesus to his disciples. Hear his words not as a past, but as a present call and recognize what he expects of those he summons to be his disciples.

We are told in verse 14 that "after John [the Baptist] was arrested, Jesus came into Galilee, preaching the gospel of God." This marks the beginning of Jesus' public ministry. It is noteworthy that he went first to Galilee, for that area was known as "Galilee of the Gentiles." The fact that Jesus' ministry began in Galilee, that his first disciples were called there, speaks of a gospel that is not only for the Jews but for the Gentiles as well, and it is for us.

We listen carefully to the first address given by a person assuming public office, sensing that it will reveal something of his intentions and character. Jesus' first words as he embarked on his public ministry convey both power and purpose: "The time is fulfilled, and the kingdom of God is at hand; repent, and believe in the gospel" (v. 15). The "time" the prophets had foretold from centuries before, when God would visit his people to bring salvation, to bring his reign—that time had come.

In Jesus the Christ, God came into our time and space and reached forth his hand of love and healing, forgiveness, and salvation. In Jesus, the kingdom of God is always "at hand." God's reign in each of our lives becomes a possibility. But the opportunity to choose God's reign is set in time. Each one of us must accept or reject the offer as it is given. Jesus' calling of his first disciples is a clear demonstration of that reality.

Passing along the Sea of Galilee, Jesus saw two fishermen at work, Simon and Andrew by name. He called out to them: "Follow me, and I will make you fishers of men." He called, and continues to call, ordinary people to follow him. It was not to the elite, as the world designates the elite, that Jesus extended his first invitation to become his disciples. It was to common, ordinary folk.

What potential did Jesus see in those fishermen? Certainly it was not their education. Perhaps it was the quality that is lacking in those who consider themselves well-educated—the ability to be taught or, more precisely, the *humility* to be taught. We who think of ourselves as highly educated are often self-satisfied and view ourselves in the role of teacher rather than student. The recognition of inadequacy and the willingness to be taught are the characteristics of a follower of any discipline.

The early Christian disciples were called disciples of "The Way." In Japan, one practices Judo, the way of self-defense; Ochado, the way of tea; Shodo, the way of the brush, or calligraphy. They are called "the way of" because they require lifelong commitment to a master, a lifelong commitment to a teacher. These are not passing hobbies, but require serious, daily commitment to pattern yourself after the master teacher. Being a disciple demands patience, persistence, and endurance—not popular qualities in our throwaway culture in which often the response to difficulty is giving up or running away.

It was no mistake that Jesus chose fishermen to be his first disciples. Have you ever gone fishing? Fish are finicky. Sometimes they bite, and sometimes they don't. Even if you fish by net, you can't always be sure of a good haul. But if you're a fisherman, you go out just the same, day in and day out. That requires patience, persistence, and endurance.

Follow me, and I will make you fishers of men. It is a call with a purpose: Learn from me how to catch others for God's kingdom. We are to follow, and he will make us into fishers of people. That is the promise. That is the order or procedure. We follow; he makes. He does not expect us to know how to do the work he has for us without his teaching.

Follow me—it is not only an invitation, but it is also a command from one with authority. I do not think that those first disciples fully knew who Jesus was when they accepted his call, obeyed his call, and followed him. But as they obeyed him, he revealed himself to them in response to their obedience. In their relationship to him, he gave them of himself, his Spirit, and that indwelling of Jesus in their hearts caused them to become true disciples, to become remade in God's image for God's purposes—to become fishers of men.

Jesus is calling you and me today to follow him, to model him, to be filled with his power to bring hope and love to our world. Are we willing to answer that call?

ROBERT M. TERHUNE

Suggestions for Worship

Call to Worship:

Minister: It is for God alone that my soul waits in silence.

People: He is my rock and my salvation.

Minister: God has spoken, and we have heard that power belongs to God.

People: And to our sovereign God belongs steadfast love.

Prayer of Confession: O God, you know that we live in the midst of temptation and evil. Conflict and confusion threaten our lives and contradict our baptism. In our frailty, we cannot stand alone. Through the saving power and redeeming love of your beloved Son, save us and help us, we pray. Amen.

Suggested Hymns: "All Praise to Thee, for Thou, O King Divine"; "Jesus Calls Us"; "Only Trust Him."

Pastoral Prayer: "May we who are pilgrims, conscious of life's varying scenes, learn by faith, our Father, to cling to Thee.

We know that Thou wilt be in the future as Thou hast been in the past. We know that Thou wilt lead us on through all the tomorrows as Thou hast led us through the yesterdays. We know that Thou wilt not let us go, even when we, in willful neglect and indulgence, try to wander from Thy way.

As we set our faces toward the new year, we know full well that it will bring many changes. The old must give place to the new. Time does not stand still, nor the world cease from its turning. Wilt Thou give to us the courage and fortitude of mature men and women that will enable us to stand upon our faith, as the spirit of the living Lord shall give us strength. In Thy strong name we pray. Amen." (Peter Marshall, *The Prayers of Peter Marshall*)

FEBRUARY 3

□

Fourth Sunday After Epiphany

The authority of the Christ over evil and sin is clearly set forth in the Gospel lesson. We also recall the authority of Moses.

The Sunday Lessons

The Psalm: Psalm 111.

Deuteronomy 18:15-22: Moses predicts the coming of a prophet who will speak with the same authority he had. "The Lord your God will raise up for you a prophet like me" (v. 15). This prophet will speak only what the Lord commands him to say.

I Corinthians 8:1-3: Some Corinthian Christians were eating food that had been sacrificed to idols. Paul notes that an idol has no real existence: "There is . . . one Lord, Jesus Christ, through whom are all things and for whom we exist" (v. 6). Food does not commend one to God. Paul concludes: "If food is a cause of my brother's falling, I will never eat meat" (v. 13).

Mark 1:21-28: In the synagogue at Capernaum, Jesus rebuked an unclean spirit, saying, "Be silent, and come out of him!" (v. 25). This follows the choosing of his disciples and is the first act in Jesus' ministry recorded by Mark. The people were amazed and said, "With authority he commands even the unclean spirits, and they obey him" (v. 27).

Interpretation and Imagination

He met his match that day, and people still talk about it. Until that time, he controlled everything. He had the money. He had the muscle. No one challenged his opinions, much less his decisions. Though often wrong, he was never in doubt.

The one who changed all that came to the community to teach

school: a rather small and unspectacular woman whose strength of character was not immediately apparent. There were no particular incidents that mounted a challenge or marked a conflict. Quiet confidence and steady resolve that were nurtured by a devotion to all that is good and true simply changed the whole community and the town boss, too——like leaven changes the lump.

There's a confidence in Mark's Gospel that gives birth to faith and joy. It begins with an exorcism that proclaims the overthrow of sin and death.

One hardly expects such influence from one born in a stable, a refugee child in Egypt, a poor carpenter from an obscure village. Christ came to Capernaum without academic credentials, economic influence, or military power. Yet, even the powers of all that is evil and destructive yielded to him.

The movie *The Exorcist* portrayed the confrontations between good and evil as being dramatic and bone chilling. Contemporary images of exorcisms, often gleaned from television preachers, picture an evangelist hero "commanding" the demon to come out. There is an authority that confronts evil in more silent ways. Summed up in the earliest of Christian creeds, it's the affirmation, "Jesus is Lord!"

NURSING MOTHERS AND TATTOOED HANDS

Isaiah 49:14-18

A SERMON BY H. MICHAEL BREWER

Let's set the stage: The time is five centuries before the birth of Jesus Christ. The place is Babylon. The people are Jews, captives of the Babylonians, unwilling sojourners in a land far from Jerusalem. The Holy City itself lies in ruins. Its walls were demolished by the Babylonians, and the Temple was looted and burned. The people are almost convinced that God has forgotten and forsaken them. Their worship is full of sad songs and laments. They cannot understand the tragedy that has swept them away, or why God is so distant. "The Lord has forsaken us," they weep. "Our Lord has forgotten us."

But in the midst of the weeping and wailing, one man stands up and denounces their foolish talk of being Godforsaken. He is a prophet, and he speaks for the Lord. His words of comfort are among the most moving passages in the Bible. From beginning to end, the Scriptures echo with assurances of God's love, but seldom do they achieve the depth and power of Isaiah 49:14-18. At this moment of tragedy, the prophet is not concerned with words of judgment or warnings of coming wrath. His purpose is to convince the people of God's love for them.

He begins by drawing a picture of the most profound of human love: a mother with her nursing child. Mother love is at the roots of human existence, a reality that cuts across time and culture. To be sure, fathers also love their children, but there is an undefinable specialness in the relationship between a mother and her child. Mother love brings to mind that long-suffering love that refuses to give up on wayward children.

"Can a woman forget her suckling child?" asks the prophet, "or show no compassion upon the son of her womb?" God's love is like that, but even more constant, more enduring, more selfless. Some mothers do abandon their children and let their love wither away. Not God. He is completely faithful. Think about the depth of love that never lets go, never dries up even when we rebel. God's love for us is as unflagging as it is unearned. Why, the best of mothers would abandon her hungry newborn long before God would turn away from his people.

Have you ever tied string around your finger in order to remember something? I have. It really works. Throughout the day, each time you glance at your hand you are reminded by the string. The string is constantly in sight whether you are cooking or sawing or turning pages or changing channels. The prophet says that God has carved our likeness on the palms of his hands so as never to forget us. To put it another way, we are tattooed on God's palms.

My father has tattoos on his arms, souvenirs of his younger and wilder days. I used to be fascinated by those tattoos. One is a skull with a snake coiled about it. Another shows a dagger with a ribbon draped over it. On the ribbon is my father's name—and they misspelled his name! Can you imagine that? For thirty-five years, my dad has worn a tattoo with his name spelled wrong. I guess it could be worse. Some fellows tattoo the names of sweethearts on their chests and end up marrying some other girl. One thing about tattoos, when you've got them, you've got them for good. Even the best surgical techniques rarely succeed in removing tattoos. My father's tattoos have faded a little over the years, but they are still clear, and he will carry them to the day he dies.

The prophet says that we are tattooed on our Creator's hands. We are carved in God's own flesh for all time as a constant and eternal reminder of his love for us. It would be easier for my dad to wash off his tattoos than it would be for God to stop loving us.

This is a very human way of talking about God. We know that God has no tattoos, or even hands. But talking this way makes God's love visible to us, as visible as string around a finger or tattoos on palms or nails through hands on a cross.

The prophet in Babylon lived five hundred years too early to speak to his despairing people about Jesus Christ. Yet, the same love that is pictured here in Isaiah is the love that became human in Jesus, the love that led our Savior to a cross, the love that sustains us today.

I wish I could find the words to speak as powerfully here and now as the prophet did back in Babylon. I pray that none of us will ever find ourselves in the same dire straits as did the exiled Jews, but we still need to be assured that God is faithful and that God's love is unfailing. We may never lose our homes, our country, or our faith, but we do face the quiet disasters and personal tragedies that make life hard to bear sometimes: broken relationships, tedious jobs, illness, family strife, and financial uncertainty. And casting a pall over every joy is the inevitability of death for those whom we love and for ourselves.

But we are not forsaken! We are not forgotten! The highest human love pales before God's love for us. The most enduring human reminders are insignificant before God's faithfulness to us. The seas will dry up and the stars will plummet from the sky before God will stop loving us. The heavens and earth will pass away like a breath on a frosty morning, but God's love will remain. Nothing can steal that love from us, not national disaster or personal crisis or evil powers or persecution or even death. A mother might lay aside her baby, but God will not desert us.

This passage began with an aching lament and ends with a promise of joy to come. The prophet says: Lift up your eyes and look around you. Look beyond the houses and streets of Babylon. Look to a day when Jerusalem will be rebuilt and her walls raised up. She will gather her people like a bride gathers her jewelry. The streets will be thronged, and the city will overflow.

Walled cities and growing populations don't speak much joy nowadays, so let's translate this into our lives. This promise was given as much to us as it was to the Jewish refugees: Lift up your eyes, people, and look beyond the doubts and fears that beset us all around. Look to a city that awaits us, a city whose streets are filled with people who love God and have given their lives to him. There are no walls, for no evil can enter that place, and no lamps, for God is the light of that city. There is no death there, no tears or pain or mourning. That city is our city, and God will dwell among us and cherish us with undying love. Then, as now, God's love will be deeper than the carvings in his own flesh and more tender than a mother's love for her nursing child. Praise God! Amen.

Suggestions for Worship

Call to Worship:

Minister: The fear of the Lord is the beginning of wisdom.

People: All who follow his commandments will walk in truth.

Minister: All that God does is faithful and just.

People: He has set his people free; to him belongs eternal praise.

Opening Prayer: O God of mercy and truth, set us free from the bondage of all evil and sin and give us the liberty of wisdom and the fullness of life revealed in Jesus Christ, our Lord, to whom be glory forever. Amen.

Hymns: "The Battle Hymn of the Republic"; "Jesus! the Name High over All"; "God of Love and God of Power."

Pastoral Prayer: Almighty God, you are the author and finisher of all things. Your authority is from the beginning and remains to the end. At your word light pushed back the darkness and everthing that is was made. You called Moses and gave him the power of your law. You sent your Son, Jesus, and gave him the authority of your own presence. All the forces of evil must yield to your sovereignty.

Your love is patient, O God. Your grace seems vulnerable; yet, it never is. Your power is made perfect in weakness, and your strength has come to us in the gentleness of a carpenter from Nazareth.

Hear us as we pray. Many of us are conflicted. The demon voices of our age have taken our dreams and shouted down our hopes. Our hearts are lonely, our bodies tired. Our minds are insensitive to truth. Our sins still follow us.

We have come to praise you, O Christ, and we ask you now to take our lives and so order them that a small part of your goodness and radiant love may be found in this time and place. Through Jesus Christ, our Lord, Amen.

FEBRUARY 10

□

Last Sunday After Epiphany (Transfiguration Sunday)

We are called to the mountain—the mountain of law and vision, God's holy hill of truth.

The Sunday Lessons

The Psalm: Psalm 50:1-6.

I Kings 2:1-12a: Three times, the loyalty of Elijah's postulant Elisha was tested. Beyond the Jordan, Elijah was taken away in a chariot of fire and a whirlwind. Then Elisha's wish, "a double share of your spirit" (v. 9), was realized.

II Corinthians 4:3-6: Paul writes about "the light of the knowledge of the glory of God in the face of Christ" (v. 6). This reference to the transfiguration is linked with the apostles's own preaching. Those who are blinded by this world cannot behold the glory.

Mark 9:2-9: Words first spoken at his baptism were heard again on the Mountain of Transfiguration. God confirms, "This is my beloved Son; listen to him" (v. 7). Moses and Elijah, two men associated in both Jewish and Christian belief with the beginning of a new age, appear with Jesus. They disappeared into heaven, and Christ, alone now, started down the mountain to a suffering world.

Interpretation and Imagination

Pioneers traveling west climbed the last mountain and then saw the great Pacific. A Holy Land tour guide said, "From this mountain you can see the merging of three continents, Africa Asia, and Europe." On Sinai, Moses saw the backside of God. Beyond Jordan, Elisha saw Elijah leave in a chariot of fire. On the

Mountain of Transfiguration (some say Mt. Hermon; tradition claims Mt. Tabor), Peter and the others saw the glory of Christ. Mark's Gospel saw his suffering.

Hugh Anderson, in discussing verse 13 (suffer many things and be treated with contempt) writes, "No easy glory . . . the verse links the divinely willed fate of 'Elijah' in the person of John the Baptist with the divinely willed fate of the Son of Man."

In your spiritual pilgrimage to this holy mountain, what do we see? A confusing story that doesn't fit into twentieth-century perspective in any real way and leaves one discussing legends, visions, and the historical? A theophany that tells about men seeing God? A glory in Christ that overshadows the greatest lawgiver and the greatest prophet? A wonderful spiritual light that shines brighter than all the others to push back the darkness? If this is all we see, we are nearsighted. The gospel is veiled.

Mark would have us see that the Son of God, the only mortal who really has it right, is on his way to a cross where he will bear the hurt, shame, loneliness, and death brought on by the sins of our world. Blinded by this world, many see nothing. Dazzled by the glory, others see only the possibility of shrines and temples. And the words of Christ keep echoing. "You have eyes to see. Won't you see?"

TRANSFIGURED

Mark 9:2-9

A SERMON BY HEATHER MURRAY ELKINS

And six days later, Jesus took with Him Peter and James and John, and brought them up to a high mountain by themselves. And He was transfigured before them. (MARK 9:2 NASB)

Transfigured—part of a past tense verb in a past tense story. So connected are word and story that the dictionary lists this passage from Mark as the example of this word's meaning. It's an association worn smooth by the slow circle of the Gospel season. Transfiguration Sunday, the last of the light of Epiphany. Lent is on hand, with its purple shadows and somber themes. We cover the altar with white, perhaps rubbing absent-mindedly at the spots of wax left by the candles of Advent. Despite the Gospel's caution about the limits of laundry "exceedingly white, as no launderer on earth can whiten them," we make a mental note: "Clean for Easter." We must be prepared. At the conclusion of this service, we will fold up the edges of the garment of the altar, stained by wax and magic gifts, and send it to the cleaners. We want to be ready for what happens next.

We know what's next. The crowds, the confusion, Passion, and Pilate. There will be a shadow of the cross and the sharp edges of betrayal and thorns. We know what will happen next. We know, but they didn't. Neither the big fisherman nor the sons of thunder were prepared for what happened on the mountain. *Transfiguration* was not a word in their vocabulary, not a dictionary definition. They were transfixed, pierced by this unexpected light. They were impaled, made motionless by his change in appearance, the company he kept, and a command too direct to doubt; "This is my beloved Son; listen to him" (Mark 9:7).

They were not prepared for what happened next, but we are. There's a certain familiarity with this text that breeds content. It reinforces our assumption that God will always be revealed in majestic ways—lights, sound, action. We have larger than life impressions of this text, as if the faces of Mt. Rushmore move to life and start a conversation while hikers on the slopes run for cover. Jesus has been Christ to us for nearly twenty centuries. We assume the names belong together: *Jesus* and *Christ.* We don't feel the sweaty tension of the road to Caesarea Philippi and the questions that pressed and probed at Peter's heart: "Who do you say that I am?" We don't have to follow our merciful questioner with inarticulate longings that we can neither explain nor hide. We know who he is. We know what he means.

Knowing the story gives us the advantage, unlike that trinity of schlemiels, Peter, James and John. The Gospel of Mark narrates their dilemma like a sketch for the Three Stooges. There are pratfalls, stumbles, and slapstick in every scene. Why should they be surprised at his radiant holiness? How could they have missed the signs and miracles? How could they have misinterpreted his penetrating eyes and insights? How could they have failed to see the holy in the human? Like Jesus, we grow impatient and ask, "Do you not understand yet?"

He had taken them up the mountain, the traditional meeting ground for holy-human encounters. There is Moses, the original mountain man, carrying a piece of the Rock of Ages marked with laws. We expect to find Moses on this mountain. We know what Moses means. Of course, if we stopped right now and took a quick quiz on the Ten Commandments and where to find them, we might not be so easy in his presence. An English bishop, John Hooper, made a visitation to his clergy in 1551 and recorded that out of 311 clergy examined, 171 were unable to recite the Ten Commandments, and that 31 who could did not know where to locate them in scripture. Their defense of ignorance was something to the effect that Christ had freed them from the law. But if there's one thing that this mountain atmosphere makes crystal clear, it is the fact that Christ is now the supreme lawgiver. We are not released from the claims of the law of Christ. We are told to listen! What we hear is not comforting: If persons wish to come after me, let them deny themselves and take up their crosses and follow me. That is not news. We've had several hundred centuries to consider the text. Surely we know what it means.

There's a high level conversation going on. Consider the other dialogue partner of Jesus: Elijah, the fiery tongue of God. He had faced the burning issue of his time: idolatry, a nation intent on magic and manipulation instead of prayer and the justice of God. He had blazed against the priests of Baal and was threatened by the consuming hatred of a "might makes right" regime. Elijah had his own mountaintop time (I Kings 19) of wind, earthquake, fire, and then a question more dangerous than all of these: "What are you doing here, Elijah?"

Now, on this mountain centuries later, the answer is easy. Elijah is the messenger of the Messiah. His presence on the mountain is the proof that God had entered the conversation; the Word had become flesh. We know what Elijah means. Yet, who has asked for a double portion of his spirit? Who dares to wear the prophet's mantle in our time? This conversation gets uncomfortable. Perhaps we, like Peter, are tempted to interrupt and offer to put up a plaque and move on. It is hard to do what we're told to do: listen!

Now, the light fades. The disciples look around, and the vision has vanished. They see no one—except Jesus. As they descend, as they return to the level of the expected, Jesus trips them up again. They are to keep quiet until the Son of man rises from the dead. They seize the statement, grateful for something to hang on to. What does rising from the dead mean? It is here, in one verse beyond the lectionary reading, that the weight of the Gospel rests. It is this question that nails this text and our context together.

What does it mean, rising from the dead? Does the answer make a difference in our living, our dying our . . . is it only here that we admit that we are not ready for what happens next? Peter was transfixed by the Transfiguration, but not transformed. That happened on a beach, after breakfast, in between three questions and three answers. James and John were terrified by the encounter with *deus loquens*, the God who speaks, but it is not what happens on this mountain that releases them from silence. They are sent into the streets, proclaiming what they've heard in an empty tomb. What does rising from the dead mean? Why must we catch the light of the gospel of the glory of Christ reflected off a cross? Why must we catch a vision of star and then glimpse that radiance again streaming from an open tomb? What must we see to believe?

It was the strangest Christmas program of my life. I was the volunteer chaplain for the season, and my assignment was a Christmas play in a maximum security prison. Like God, we were limited to what was at hand. Nothing could be carried into the prison, so creativity was a must. The frayed blankets were transformed into realistic shepherds' cloaks. Sheets, a far cry from being radiantly white, draped "angels" and a smooth shaven "Mary." There were some natural advantages to the setting. A prison yard needed no imagination to be mistaken for the barren hills of Bethlehem. There were even "Roman" guards who kept watch over their flocks by day and by night from the tower and the walls.

The only snag was baby Jesus. What could we put in the cardboard box that masqueraded as a manger? A swaddling towel? A handmade doll? I was amazed at the determination that the manger not be empty. They wanted to *see* Jesus. The meaning of seeing and the meaning of believing crossed the beginning of the celebration of light, the center of incarnation. At the end of a year, in a corner of a yard, in the presence of a truly captive audience, a transfiguration occurred. We saw Jesus as he is. As the scraggly shepherds came, wrapped in their ragged reputations; as the kings knelt, crowned with aluminum; as the far from angelic chorus sang, "Mary" lifted the child for all to see: a handmade crucifix for all to see. What did we sing, forgiven sinners all? "Amazing Grace." And what we sang and what we saw, we believed, for there is "[One] who has shone in our hearts to give the light of the knowledge of the glory of God in the face of Christ" (II Cor. 4:6).

Suggestions for Worship

Call to Worship:

Minister: The earth is the Lord's and the fullness thereof,

People: **the world and those who dwell therein;**

Minister: for God has founded it upon the seas,

People: **and established it upon the rivers.**

Minister: Who shall ascend the hill of the Lord?

People: **And who shall stand in God's holy place?**

Minister: Those who have clean hands and pure hearts,

People: **who do not lift up their souls to what is false, and do not swear deceitfully.**

Minister: They will receive blessing from the Lord,

People: **and vindication from the God of their salvation.**

Prayer of Confession: Holy One, in this hour we have dared to ascend your mountain of law, your holy hill of truth. Perhaps we believed that we began the journey alone, but now our eyes have been opened and we see that we have traveled with the one we call "the Way." Perhaps, like Peter, we say the wrong things when we try to pray. Accept our silence and our rash suggestions. Forgive our slowness to understand and our haste to question. We give you thanks for the cloud that obscures all false appearance and your Word, which is too clear to ignore. As we descend to the level of commonplace, may our eyes, which have been opened, retain an image of Christ's face. When we open our eyes and glance at each other, may we be drawn to his light in our eyes.

Continue to shine in our hearts so that neither the shade of doubt nor the shadow of death can blind us to the light and the love that you have placed like a blazing sun in our darkness. We ask this in the name of the one named Jesus, for the sake of the Son called Christ. Amen.

Suggested Hymns: "Immortal, Invisible, God Only Wise"; "We Would See Jesus"; "Be Thou My Vision."

Pastoral Prayer: Holy One, uncreated Creator, Light of light, we, your human creation, praise you. You, who are incomprehensible, have given us a way to know you. You, whose wisdom is beyond speech, have given us the Word made flesh, and we dare to pray in Christ's name. You are the source of life; nurture your life in us. You are the source of light; breathe on our ashes so that our hearts may catch fire again. You are the source of truth; make us hungry for its flavor. You are the source of love; release us from addiction to power, restore our passion for compassion and joy. We ask this in the name of your holy child, Jesus. Amen.

FEBRUARY 17

☐

First Sunday in Lent

Forty days of trial and testing and the ministry of angels are the subjects of the Gospel lesson.

The Sunday Lessons

The Psalm: Psalm 25:1-10.

Genesis 9:8-17: God made a covenant with Noah after the flood. The sign of the covenant was a rainbow. There are no conditions and no requirements. It is God who wants no more destruction.

I Peter 3:18-22: In this baptismal homily, reference is made to a traditional hymn. Another reference is made to Noah's safety in the flood and finally to the waters of baptism "through which you are now brought to safety."

Mark 1:9-15: Verses from this passage were read on the first and third Sundays after Epiphany. The baptism of Jesus and the proclamation of John were the subjects. The temptation of Christ in the wilderness is briefly, though powerfully, stated by Mark: "The Spirit immediately drove him out into the wilderness . . . forty days, tempted by Satan . . . with the wild beasts; and the angels ministered to him" (vv. 12-13). The word *tempted* refers to a time of testing, and not only to enticement.

Interpretation and Imagination

Intertestamental literature includes the Testament of Naphtali. Scholars point to the relationship of Mark's temptation account to Naphtali 8:4: "If you do good, my children, both men and angels shall bless you, the Devil shall flee from you and the wild beasts shall fear you and the Lord shall love you."

The struggle with evil and the threat of wild beasts were not the only things encountered in the wilderness. There were forces of good as well: "The angels ministered to him" (Mark 1:13). The struggle with Satan was not merely human striving in Mark's view. God's power, represented by angels, was present in the conflict.

Countless examples from history reflect God's power to overcome evil. The stories about guardian angels are seldom told in the church. Children's television offers guardians in cartoon caricatures, and movies employ the literary form, but we look for power in politics, money, the military, science, and the like. God's power comes in the form God chooses. Sometimes it is weakness.

Paul Lehman, discussing the temptation, writes:

> The power decision was centered upon a commitment to weakness as against strength, to obedience against domination, to self-giving against self-realization, to responsibility against self-determination. . . . Weakness so chosen is strength, whereas strength so vaunted is weakness. Obedience so chosen is freedom, whereas domination so coveted is bondage. (Dieter T. Hessel, *Social Themes of the Christian Year* [The Geneva Press, 1983])

His discussion of power (pages 124ff.) is worth the price of the commentary.

REMEMBER THE RAINBOW

Genesis 9:8-17

A SERMON BY ROBERT T. BALDRIDGE

Suddenly it started to pour. In the morning the sun was shining. It was a beautiful day. But then came the clouds. The sky got darker and darker, and then came the torrential rain. An hour later it stopped, and the sun reappeared. What was it that everyone expected to find as they searched the sky? We know. We've all looked for the rainbow, haven't we?

Rainbow is defined as "the name for a set of colored arcs seen against the sky whenever falling water droplets are illuminated by a strong light source." Since a rainbow is usually seen against the cloud mass of a retreating thunderstorm, it has become a symbol of a storm that has passed. But remember, in Genesis the rainbow was given a special meaning. God said to Noah: "I set my bow in the cloud, and it shall be a sign of the covenant between me and the earth . . . the waters shall never again become a flood to destroy all flesh" (9:13, 15*b*). God made a promise!

After the flood there was a rainbow, signifying that the storm was over. How many storms have you known? We're talking about more than tornados, earthquakes, and hurricanes. How many storms have you had to endure in your lifetime? How many times have you needed to see a rainbow in the sky? We've all faced crises as dreadful and as devastating as the flood was for Noah. At such times, all we could see were dark clouds no matter where we looked. There might have been a rainbow somewhere, but we couldn't see it. In times of darkness, we tend to see only the darkness, and that immobilizes us. In stormy times we need to remember the rainbow. Noah didn't make the rainbow; God put it in the sky. The ground of our hope is God. Only when we see a rainbow can we, like Noah, have hope for the future.

Hope has been defined as "desire accompanied by expectation." The Apostle Paul listed hope as one of the three basic qualities of the Christian (I Cor. 13:13). He spoke of the hope of salvation as being a helmet (I Thess. 5:8). He said that we are "saved by hope" (Rom. 8:24, 35-39) and described God as the "God of hope" (Rom. 15:13). The song of hope is sung throughout the New Testament. Thomas Hardy, arguing against the church keeping up what he called the farce of hope, asked, "Why not throw in the sponge?" But for us to lose hope and "throw in the sponge" is to surrender the Christian faith.

We remember Pandora because of her intense curiosity. According to Greek mythology, the gods presented her with a box into which each had put something harmful and then told her not to open it. But Pandora just *had* to know what was inside. One day she lifted the lid, and out flew ten thousand woes. But one good thing remained: hope. Hope was the only good the box held along with all that was bad. And that's a parable for us. It is our Christian right to hope.

London's Tate Gallery is home to Frederick Watt's masterpiece called "Hope." Hope is portrayed as a beautiful woman seated upon a globe. What is so striking is that she is blindfolded and holding a lute. Then you notice that only one string of the lute is not broken. The blindfolded girl is bent toward the lute, listening to the sound of that single string. Even with one string, a melody could still be played! That was the way Watt pictured hope, as being not yet done in by sin, sorrow, pain, and disaster.

In the movie *Oh God, Book II*, George Burns explains that every coin must have two sides: up and down, front and back, joy and sorrow, good and evil, laughter and tears, hope and despair. The opposite of hope is despair. Thomas Aquinas called despair the deadliest of all sins because it sinks a life into such a sad dejection of spirit. The despairing person can only see the storm, never the rainbow that is sure to follow. Some people seem to prefer to live that way. They're like that beloved character Joe in the comic strip "Lil' Abner," whose entire life is lived out under a dark cloud of gloom. Wherever he goes, everything goes wrong. He always expects it to be that way—and it is.

Bishop Carl Sanders once told about how the boys down at the country store played a trick on their friend Fred, who had fallen asleep in his favorite chair back by the potbellied stove. One of them got some Limburger cheese and smeared a bit in Fred's mustache. (There's a philosophical question that demands our attention at this point: Why does Swiss cheese have holes, when it's Limburger that needs the ventilation?) After the boys smeared the cheese in Fred's mustache, they all sat back to watch. First his mustache began to twitch. Then he shook his head. Then his eyes shot open, like a window shade flying up when the spring slips. Fred jumped to his feet, looked this way and sniffed, that way and sniffed, and in a loud voice said, "Something stinks!" He stomped to the front of the store, stopped, looked this way and sniffed, that way and sniffed and shouted, "The whole store stinks!" Then he threw open the front door and stomped right out into the middle of Main Street, where he stopped, looked uptown and sniffed, then downtown and sniffed, and then at the top of his lungs screamed, "The whole world stinks!" We all know people who have such a world view. Everything is bad and is only going to get worse. They've never seen a rainbow, only the clouds and the rain.

Halford Luccock told about the little town of Flagstaff, which years ago was flooded as part of a large lake. Long before the dam was completed, all improvements and repairs in town stopped. Why paint a house if it would be torn down in six months? Why repair anything? Week by week, month by month, the town became more and more bedraggled. Someone commented on the situation: "Where there is no faith in the future, there is no power in the present." Since the residents of Flagstaff had no faith in the future, they had no power in the present. The story certainly speaks to our day. We live in a critical time. We don't minimize world, community, or personal problems. But, at the same time, we must never forget the rainbow. We don't know what the future holds, but we do know that God holds the future.

We know that because of Jesus, his life and his message. He knew about storms and rainbows. His baptism was a mountaintop experience. His understanding of who he was, and whose he was, was affirmed at the Jordan River: "Thou art my beloved Son; with thee I am well pleased." (Mark 1:11). Immediately after this high point in his life came his wilderness experience, a dark, foreboding time when he was alone, isolated, separated. Yet, out of this wilderness retreat came dedication to his mission. But first came the storm, a time of testing. Everywhere he looked he saw what might be. Everyone he met was a person of promise. He knew that life wouldn't be all sunshine. He knew that there would come the rainbow. His wilderness experience wasn't easy. Ours isn't either. But he was victorious. Re-creative forces were available to Jesus, and re-creative forces are available to us in our time of struggle.

Emil Brunner once wrote: "What oxygen is for the lungs, such is hope for the meaning of human life . . . the fate of humanity is dependent on its supply of hope." *Hope means the presence of a future. Where there is no faith in the future, there is no power in the present.* Or, as we read in Proverbs 29:18 (KJV): "Where there is no vision, the people perish." Without hope, there can be no openness to a future, only a despair that brings a sense of purposelessness and paralysis. Hope is what gives life its sense of the holy. Hope is what keeps life open to new possibilities. Hope is what helps us to see daffodils and lilies when snow covers the ground.

Blessed are those who remember the rainbow. The rainbow is a gift from God. The rainbow isn't an accident. It's a sign of the covenant. God's eternal goodness will not fail. All things are open to the future, which is God's future. The final transformation is already expected and embodied in the present. In the midst of any crisis, only one thing is certain and beyond all doubt: God is faithful. Remember the rainbow!

> Harms of the world have come unto us,
>   Cups of sorrow we yet shall drain;
> But we have a secret which doth show us
>   Wonderful rainbows in the rain.
> (from "An Old Man's Idyl" by Richard Realf)

Suggestions for Worship

Call to Worship:

> "Rend your hearts and not
>   your garments."
> Return to the Lord, your God,
>   for he is gracious and merciful,
> slow to anger, and abounding in
>   steadfast love,
>   and repents of evil.
> (Joel 2:13)

Prayer of Confession: O God, beneath whose eyes every heart trembles and all consciences are afraid, be merciful to us and heal the wounds of all, that as not one of us is free from fault, so not one may be shut out from pardon, through Jesus Christ, our Lord. Amen.

Suggested Hymns: "Guide Me, O Thou Great Jehovah"; "I Am Thine, O Lord"; "By Thy Birth and by Thy Tears."

Pastoral Prayer: O Lord, our God, gracious and merciful, give us such confidence in your saving grace that we may dare to examine the shadowy side of our lives: our hidden faults, our secret thoughts, our unknown sin. Then let us be quick to ask how we stand before you.

Help us to love what is good and to turn from everything that dishonors your name. Keep us steady in our walk with you, constant in our devotion, and obedient in your service.

You have called us to an inheritance of light in Christ. We pray that your church may be made worthy of this call and be drawn nearer and nearer unto you. Amen.

FEBRUARY 24

□

Second Sunday in Lent

Suffering, humiliation, and death are God's way of achieving final victory. God's way contradicts our ways.

The Sunday Lessons

The Psalm: Psalm 105:1-11.

Genesis 17:1-10, 15-19: God's covenant with Abraham was accompanied with promises—a promised land and a promised son. They were to call the child Isaac, which means "he laughs."

Romans 4:16-25: The promise depends on faith. When hope seemed hopeless, Abraham did not consider his body, weakened by age, or the barrenness of Sarah. This is justification by faith.

Mark 8:31-38: For the first time, Jesus began to teach that he must suffer and die. Peter began to rebuke him. Jesus said to Peter: "Get behind me, Satan! For you are not on the side of God" (v. 33). Final victory is described as "glory of his Father" (v. 38).

Interpretation and Imagination

Where life is cheap, death is careless. Humiliation, pain, and loss are of little importance. Men bleed without looking. Women bury without weeping. Oppressive systems rob the poor, shame the meek, beat the suffering, and let the children die.

No teaching in history has spoken more highly or valued life more sincerely than the teaching of the Bible. No prophet, leader, or teacher has cared more for the individual—though poor, sick, and outcast—than has Jesus Christ. In his final passion and suffering, he dies at the hands of those whom he loves.

Helmut Thielicke, in his book *Living with Death,* reports that Luther said that "only he who inflicts and permits the wound of death can heal it. No one else. Certainly not illusions or silence." The ministry of Christ and his church take death seriously, but not without hope.

Destiny and purpose mark the lessons of this Sunday in Lent. The preacher will, therefore, speak of humiliation, obedience, and cross-bearing not simply in moralistic terms as an appropriate Christian life-style. Certainly, suffering will not be offered as masochistic joy. The suffering of the Christ and cross-bearing followers who take their share of the world's pain is redemptive suffering. It's the shape of hope.

A COVENANT IN BLOOD

Mark 8:31-38

A SERMON BY ROBERT T. BALDRIDGE

Tom Sawyer and Huckleberry Finn were in trouble . . . deep, deep trouble. And the trouble would only get worse if one of them told on the other. Huck said, "Now look-a-here, Tom, less take and swear to one another—that's what we got to do—swear to keep mum." Tom says, "I'm agreed. It's the best thing. Would you just hold hands and swear that we—" Huck interrupted, "O, no, that wouldn't do for this. That's good enough for little rubbishy common things . . . but there orter be writing 'bout a big thing like this. And blood. . . . "

Tom's whole being applauded this idea. It was deep, and dark, and awful; the hour, the circumstances, the surroundings, were in keeping with it. He picked up a clean pine shingle that lay in the moonlight, took a little fragment of "red keel" out of his pocket, got the moon on his work, and painfully scrawled these lines, emphasizing each slow down-stroke by clamping his tongue between his teeth, and letting up the pressure on the up-strokes. Huck Finn and Tom Sawyer swore that they would "keep mum" or drop down dead in their tracks if they ever told.

Then each boy took a pin, pricked his thumb and squeezed out a drop of blood. After a lot of squeezes, each finished signing his name and the oath was complete. "Tom," whispered Huckleberry, "does this keep us from ever telling—always?" And Huck said, "Of course it does. It don't make any difference what happens, we got to keep mum. We'd drop down dead—don't you know that?" Tom and Huck sealed their promise in blood. Theirs was a covenant sealed in blood.

Centuries ago, God made a covenant sealed in blood with Abraham. God's first promise was that Abraham would be the father of a multitude of nations: "I will make you exceedingly fruitful; and I will make nations of you, and kings shall come forth from you" (Gen. 17:6). God's second promise was that the covenant would continue past Abraham's lifetime: "I will establish my covenant between me and you and your descendants after you throughout their generations for an everlasting covenant" (Gen. 17:7). God's third promise concerned a homeland: "And I will give to you, and to your descendants after you, the land of your sojournings, all the land of Canaan, for an everlasting possession; and I will be their God" (Gen. 17:8). And then God promised Abraham an heir: "Sarah your wife shall bear you a son, and you shall call his name Isaac. I will establish my covenant with him as an everlasting covenant for his descendants after him" (Gen. 17:19).

God was the initiator of that covenant, not Abraham. God spoke first. The sign of this covenant relationship for Abraham and his descendants was to be circumcision, a rite that, from that time on, would bind all male Jews together. This, too, like that of Tom and Huck, was a covenant sealed in blood.

Blood is an important word in the Bible. The word *blood* is found 362 times in the Old Testament, and most of the time it has to do with violent death. The ancient Israelites believed that a person's life-force depended on the blood within his or her body. In Leviticus 17:11 we read: "For the life of the flesh is in the blood; and I [God] have given it for you upon the altar to make atonement for your souls; for it is the blood that makes atonement, by reason of the life." When someone's blood flowed out onto the ground, his or her life went with it; the person died (see Gen. 4:10). The same is true for animals.

On Thursday night of Passion week, Jesus shared a meal with his disciples. Matthew describes what happened:

Now as they were eating, Jesus took bread, and blessed, and broke it, and gave it to the disciples and said, "Take, eat; this is my body." And he took a cup, and when he had given thanks he gave it to them, saying, "Drink of it, all of you; for this is my blood of the covenant, which is poured out for many for the forgiveness of sins." (Matt. 26:26-28)

Jesus invited his disciples to enter into a new covenant, one also sealed in blood.

Jesus didn't want people to follow him without knowing the full story of what being a disciple meant. It certainly wouldn't be a picnic. That's why he talked about suffering, the cross, and death. Rather than being the popular Messiah many expected, his way would be that of suffering. Glory and pain would be inseparable. Jesus spoke plainly about how much it would cost those who followed him, but Simon Peter didn't believe what he was hearing and rebuked his Master. He wanted Jesus without the cross. We'd probably prefer that, too. We sing a lot of "crossy" hymns: "Jesus, I my cross have taken"; "In the cross of Christ I glory"; and the like. But we really prefer a happy faith that doesn't cost too much. Ours is a practical world and covenants sealed in blood seem to belong only to international terrorists and hijackers. But we Christians also claim to have undivided loyalty. How did Tom and Huck put it? "Huck Finn and Tom Sawyer swear they will keep mum about this and they wish they may drop down dead in their tracks if they ever tell and rot." Is our commitment to Christ to be any less than that?

This word about self-denial is one of the greatest of Jesus' declarations. During Lent, we might speak of self-denial as abstaining from certain luxuries and delights and thus applaud our own self-control. But true self-denial is a whole lot more. It's the subordination of our ego and its preoccupation with "I, me, and mine" and our insistence on comfort, prestige, power, and control. Jesus' call to deny self also comes to a church. How hard it is for a church to put some larger good ahead of security and prestige. "For whoever would save his life will lose it"—those words were spoken in a day of great persecution. The person who saved his skin by renouncing Christ in this life because he was faithful to Christ would save it in the world of eternity. That was the new covenant that Jesus was talking about. It was a covenant sealed in blood.

As a church, we are a covenant people. We have communion now with all the saints, living and dead, who have been part of the covenant. We don't face the harshness of life alone. We've been given a new name by God. Our name is Christian. We are Christ-bearers. We have taken upon ourselves the name of Christ. We have said that his cross is to be our own. That is the covenant we have made. And ours, too, is a covenant sealed in blood.

Suggestions for Worship

Call to Worship:

Minister: Let us test and examine our ways, and return to the Lord!

People: God has blessed us; let all the ends of the earth fear him!

Minister: Seek the Lord while he may be found, call upon him while he is near; let the wicked forsake his way, and the unrighteous man his thoughts; let him return to the Lord.

People: The sacrifice acceptable to God is a broken spirit; a broken and contrite heart, O God, thou wilt not despise.

Prayer of Confession: Almighty God, who through thy Son dost continually prompt us to conform our wills to thine: Grant that we may love the things that you want for us. Help us to find the commandments dear to the purified wishes of our hearts; through Jesus Christ, our Lord. Amen.

Suggested Hymns: "In the Cross of Christ I Glory"; "Are Ye Able"; "When I Survey the Wondrous Cross."

Pastoral Prayer: "Lord, I know not what I ought to ask of Thee; Thou only knowest what I need; Thou lovest me better than I know how to love myself. O Father! give to Thy child that which he himself knows not how to ask. I dare not ask either for crosses or consolations: I simply present myself before Thee, I open my heart to Thee. Behold my needs which I know not myself; see and do according to Thy tender mercy. Smite, or heal; depress me, or raise me up:

I adore all Thy purposes without knowing them; I am silent; I offer myself in sacrifice: I yield myself to Thee; I would have no other desire than to accomplish Thy will. Teach me to pray. Pray Thyself in me. Amen." (François de la Mothe Fénelon, 1651–1715)

March 3

□

Third Sunday in Lent

The cleansing of the Temple reveals a Christ who is unimpressed by temporal splendor and angered by the priests who profit.

The Sunday Lessons

The Psalm: Psalm 19:7-14.

Exodus 20:1-17: The Ten Commandments were given to Moses on Mount Sinai. Four laws pertain to one's relationship with God. Six prescribe one's relationship with others.

I Corinthians 1:22-25: A crucified god to many is only a dead god. To Greeks it was foolishness. To Jews it was a stumbling block. But to those called, the crucified Christ is "the power of God and the wisdom of God" (v. 24).

John 2:13-22: Jesus drove the Temple profiteers out with a whip. Asked for a sign that gave him authority for such action, Jesus answered, "Destroy this temple, and in three days I will raise it up" (v. 19). John interprets this as reference to Jesus' body as a temple.

Interpretation and Imagination

Deliverance seldom comes easily; it should never be forgotten. That is what the Passover celebration was all about—remembering Israel's deliverance from Egypt. Worshipers came to Jerusalem to make their sacrifices and to pay the annual half-shekel tax for support of the Temple. Stalls were built in the courtyard to provide sheep and oxen for the sacrifices. Exchange tables were set up, where foreign coins could be traded for Tyrian coins, pure enough in silver to be acceptable. Priests and moneychangers made huge profits.

The scene is relived again and again. Fortunes were paid for those wanting to be evacuated from Saigon. In Bombay, India's wealthiest city, water was scarce as residents waited for the monsoons. A water vendor who had just turned away a thirsty beggar was asked how much money he made each day. He answered, "Forty pails, forty rupees." That's a lot of money. The average field hand in India earns about fifteen rupees a day. Deliverance has its price. Doctors and lawyers have their fees. The establishment hardly notices.

Saint Francis, born wealthy, was remembered as the little poor man of Assisi. Francis, like his Lord, became the friend of the poor and the companion of the outcast. He announced that he was taking "Lady Poverty" as his bride. It mattered not if one was poor or a leper or a stranger. He practiced humility and meekness toward all.

A STRANGE PORTRAIT OF JESUS

John 2:13-22

A SERMON BY LUCY ROSE

Lent—a time for examining ourselves and for realigning our lives by our Lord's life. So what do we do with this strange portrait of Jesus? How is he here our model?

The story is a familiar one: Jesus sees the Temple courtyard full of the holiday buying crowd, full of sheep, oxen and doves. He makes a lash of ropes and drives the animals out. He overturns the moneychangers' tables. Then he turns to those selling doves and says, "Take these things away; you shall not make my Father's house a house of trade" (John 2:16). Here the Gospel writer inserts, "His disciples remembered that it was written, 'Zeal for thy house will consume me' " (v. 17). Maybe here is our Lenten clue: Jesus as a model of zeal.

But what does *zeal* mean? Perhaps a more contemporary translation is "jealousy"—not a quality we usually seek after. How are we to be jealous, especially as Jesus was jealous, stirring up such trouble?

Let us go back to the story. Those standing around Jesus are, like us, surprised by his actions. They challenge him, saying, "What sign have you to show us for doing this?" (v. 18). Jesus answers, "Destroy this temple, and in three days I will raise it" (v. 19). Remember, he is standing inside the courtyard of the Temple of Jerusalem. Imagine the puzzled looks on the bystanders' faces as they say, "It has taken forty-six years to build this temple, and you will raise it up in three days?" (v. 20). Neither the bystanders nor the disciples understood Jesus' *spiritual* meaning: He meant the shrine of his body, himself as the dwelling place for God's Spirit. Again the Gospel writer interrupts the narrative, writing that after the resurrection, the disciples remembered this scene and believed the Scripture and Jesus' words. They believed.

Maybe our Lenten clue is to stand not with Jesus but with the disciples. Maybe we can model ourselves after their faith. After the resurrection, certain clues would have helped them to hear the Scripture and Jesus' words differently and to shape their lives by this memory of Jesus. There are perhaps four such clues.

First, after the resurrection they knew that Jesus had been sold by the Jerusalem authorities as a sacrifice, as a bargaining chip with Pilate. In the words of the high priest, one man had to die to save the nation. The house of God was again a house of buying and selling.

Second, the disciples knew after the resurrection that they, too, were houses of God, shrines in which God was dwelling. Jesus had promised his disciples that he and God would come to them and would abide in them through the Spirit. The dwelling place for God's presence was no longer the Temple in Jerusalem but the Christian community and the individual believer.

Third, they knew the precariousness of their own situation; they were in danger of being destroyed, sacrificed for the security of the nation or at the whim of Saul of Tarsus or a deranged Caesar. They, as dwelling places of God's Spirit, were treated as merchandise, as sacrificial animals.

And fourth, the disciples knew Jesus' promise that they, too, would be raised from death to live with him.

So we can imagine their growing conviction that no house of

God, no believer, should be treated as merchandise, no Christian sacrificed for the security, convenience, or aggrandizement of another. In their zeal, during the persecutions, many protected their fellow Christians even at the expense of their own lives. We can imagine their hope that if they or their fellow Christians were destroyed, death was not the final enemy. Rather they steadfastly hoped that Jesus would raise them up to new life. This story would inspire in them both zeal and fearless hope as they believed the Scripture and Jesus' words in the face of uncertain and threatening times.

And what about us in this season of self-examination? How can the disciples' faith reshape our lives?

What would it mean if we believed that all Christians—Methodists, Baptists, charismatics and frozen chosen, liberals, and conservatives—are dwelling places for the Spirit of God? All Christians are shrines in which the presence of the living God abides. All Christians are houses of God.

Are not all people potential shrines for the indwelling Spirit of God? What would it mean for us to catch some of the zeal of the disciples to prevent the sacrifice of human lives, even at the expense of our own lives? Might we then, in our zeal, cry out against exploitation in the name of security, economic development, or corporate gain? Might we then, in our zeal, challenge every institution that sacrifices human lives?

And what if we lost our fear of death? What if we steadfastly believed that were the shrine of our bodies destroyed, Jesus himself would raise us up to live with him? What if during this Lenten season we caught the zeal and fearless faith of the disciples after the resurrection?

This portrait of Jesus, this faith of the disciples, these questions are scary. Yet, by the indwelling power of God in our midst, let us, with the disciples, believe both the Scripture and the words of Jesus. Hear them once again: Do not make the house of God into a house of merchandise; zeal for the house of God consumes me; destroy this shrine and I will raise it up.

By the indwelling power of God, may our apathy be turned to zeal. May our fear of death be transformed into courageous hope. May we model our lives on this strange portrait of a confronting and confident Jesus.

Suggestions for Worship

Call to Worship:

Minister: The earth is the Lord's and everything in it.

People: The world and all who live in it.

Minister: Let us worship.

Prayer of Confession: God, whose ways are most clearly seen in Jesus, our Lord. We confess that we have not loved as he loved, acted as he acted, been willing to die for others as he died. We have set our own agendas, written our own rules, and pattérned our lives on those around us. Forgive us.

In this Lenten season, enable us to reclaim Jesus as our Lord. Enable us to test our lives by his life and to truly repent for our sins and stubborn rebellion. Enable us to allow his Spirit to transform us into faithful disciples.

Suggested Hymns: "Sing Praise to God Who Reigns Above"; "Praise to the Lord, the Almighty"; "All People That on Earth Do Dwell"; "Love Divine, All Loves Excelling"; "Gracious Spirit, Dwell with Me"; "Spirit of God, Descend upon My Heart."

Pastoral Prayer: Loving and ever-present God, we thank you for Jesus Christ, the author and finisher of our faith. We thank you for his life by which we can test and pattern our lives. We thank you for his death through which we have forgiveness from our sins and hope for new life both here and after death. We pray that through our lives the love and trustworthiness of Jesus Christ may be spread so that all the world may one day praise Jesus Christ as Lord and Savior.

We pray for our loved ones and friends, for our nation and its leaders, and for all the nations of this earth. Where there is sickness, grant healing; where there is despair, hope. Where there is oppression, grant freedom; where there is warfare, peace. Where there is ignorance, grant insight; where there is unbelief, saving faith. Hasten the day when the earth shall be filled with your glory as the waters cover the sea.

MARCH 10

□

Fourth Sunday in Lent

Judgment and death are not the last words in these lessons.
They tell of a God, rich in mercy, who wants no one to perish.

The Sunday Lessons

The Psalm: Psalm 137:1-6.

II Chronicles 36:14-23: God's messengers were mocked, his
words despised, his prophets scorned. Jerusalem was conquered. Those who escaped the sword were carried into exile in
Babylon. Then Cyrus, a Persian king, began a new temple.

Ephesians 2:4-10: New life in Christ comes to these dead
through trespasses and sin. God in Christ is the chief actor.
Salvation is God's gift, "not because of works, lest [anyone]
should boast" (v. 9).

John 3:14-21: Moses fashioned a bronze serpent and set it on a
pole. Persons who looked at it were spared the poisonous bite of
fiery serpents (Num. 21:9). John's Gospel refers to Christ as one
lifted up, that all who believe may be saved.

Interpretation and Imagination

"Capability Brown" is the name of a store in New York City that
specializes in repairs and restoration. On seeing the name of this
store, my mind formed the image of an able, old craftsman who
could put broken pieces together and fix just about anything.

Then I learned that "Capability Brown" was a woman who
intended new life for old furniture. "Before you discard
anything, have a chat with Enid Dent," was the first line that
described this restoration business. Ms. Dent named the store
after a famed British landscape gardener.

In times when so many things are considered disposable, it's refreshing to find someone who wants to bring new life to something—even to old furniture. A new temple in a restored Jerusalem, new life for those dead in trespasses, and a loving God who is not willing for any to perish are the themes of these lessons.

New life in Christ—not simply the prolongation of mortal life, not simply time going around in circles like the hands of a clock—new life that is eternal. Such life begins by knowing that God's love is limitless. It embraces the whole world. This life grows through seeing that no sacrifice is too great. This life pulses through every age as love and truth and salvation. Some will question, like Nicodemus, "How can this be?" Others will love their darkness.

GOD SO LOVED. . . .

John 3:14-21

A SERMON BY LUCY ROSE

What familiar words: "God so loved the world that he gave his only Son, that whoever believes in him should not perish but have eternal life" (John 3:16). These words are probably among the most beloved and most memorized in the whole Bible. What does a preacher say about such a well-known verse? Certainly we find ourselves drawn back to the roots of our faith: the love of God, believing in Jesus Christ as Savior. But is there anything *new* to say?

As I studied and meditated on this passage, the first discovery I made was that I really do not think most of us believe the words we find here. We really do not believe that God so loved *the world* or that God continues to love the world. Most of the time, in the normal course of our living, we believe that God loves good people. Why else does the question strike a chord, why do bad things happen to good people? *Good* things are supposed to happen to *good* people to prove God's favor. And *bad* things are suppose to happen to *bad* people to prove God's displeasure with evil.

Some years ago, a young man from my church was in a car accident. He was a popular college student, a regular attender at church, and a caring, gentle person. As a lifeguard one summer, he had saved a woman from drowning. He was a *good* person. And here he was in a coma. I remember his mother saying, "Why my son? There are so many people who are mean and bad. Why him? He's always been so good." And I found my heart resonating with her cry, "Yes, God, why him?"

If bad things happen to good people, and if good things happen to bad people, and if God loves *the world*, then something deep inside us is turned upside down. No, God is supposed to love good people.

There is another facet to our belief that God really loves good people. At times in our lives, we confront the depth of our sinfulness. How often with a sharp word we have hurt those dearest to us or been cruel behind the back of a friend. Sometimes we recognize the violence that lies inside our hearts that usually remains hidden away out of sight. Then we know that God loves good people and the circle of that divine love cuts us out. The light of God's love cannot penetrate the shadows that surround us. Yes, God loves good people, and at times we cannot believe that God loves us.

In those places where most of us live most of our lives, we do not believe that God so loved or loves the world. But what if we set aside our belief that God loves good people and tried to hear what the Gospel of John is trying to say here? What does it mean that "God so loved the world"?

For the beloved disciple who wrote this Gospel, the world was not a safe, benevolent place in which people are kind and gentle and the milk of human kindness flows through most folks's veins. No, for the writer of John, the world is a cruel, violent, scary place. Listen to these words from John 3:19: "The light has come into the world, and [people] loved darkness rather than light, because their deeds were evil." It was the world that hated and killed Jesus. It was the world that hated his followers, threw them out of their religious communities, and persecuted them. For the community gathered around this Gospel, the world is a scary, cruel, violent place. And yet here we find the words preserved, "God so loved the world. . . ."

I suspect that most of us find the world to be a scary, violent place. Wherever we live, we cannot escape the specter of drug and alcohol abuse, child molestation, rape, and murder. Read any newspaper with your heart, and you will be moved to tears and to fear. Daily we continue to strip away the thin protective shield between us and the sun. We fill with filth our streams, lakes, and oceans. Beyond the borders of our nation, we sense the threat to global security from the Middle East, Central America, and South Africa, as well as from the Soviet Union. And our own foreign policies sometimes secure peace and sometimes perpetuate oppression and injustice. The world for most of us is a scary place.

Let us look further at the passage: "God so loved the world that he gave his only Son, that whoever believes in him should not perish but have eternal life. For God sent the Son into the world not to condemn the world, but that the world might be saved through him" (John 3:16-17). The critical key, the turning point, is believing. Whoever believes in him believes not only in Jesus Christ as Savior, but also in Jesus Christ as the expression of God's love for the world. Whoever believes that God loves the world shall live in this world not by fear but by faith and shall have eternal life.

In those moments when we believe not that God loves good people but that God loves the world, then the shadows in our own lives are pierced by the light of God's love. We know that we are never so sinful that God rejects us. Rather, the circle of God's love embraces us, and we know that we are loved by a divine, tenacious love.

In addition, in those moments when we believe that God loves the world, the walls we have built in our gear begin to crumble. The walls between black and white, men and women, Democrat and Republican, victim and murderer, Soviet and American, Contra and Sandinista, Arab and Jew—walls we carefully construct in our fear begin to come down because we recognize God's love for the world, this scary, violent world.

So we find in this passage a challenge to return to the roots of our faith: the love of God and belief in Jesus Christ. Yet, we find also a strange, uncomfortable, new message.

Suggestions for Worship

Call to Worship:

> Minister: God so loved the world that God gave the only Son,

> **People:** **that whoever believes in him should not perish but have eternal life.**

> Minister: Let us worship God.

Prayer of Confession: Eternal God, who in your love sent your only Son that all the world might be saved, we confess that we have ignored your love and lived self-centered, self-interested lives. We have sought our own happiness and security and built walls to protect ourselves from the pain and threat of the world around us. Forgive us.

We have been reluctant to speak of our faith in your Son and hindered your saving work in our interactions with family and neighbors, friends and colleagues at work, and strangers we meet along life's way. Forgive us.

Call us to claim anew the depth of your love for us and for all people. Embolden us to be instruments of your saving power.

Suggested Hymns: "Joyful, Joyful, We Adore Thee"; "The King of Love My Shepherd Is"; "There's a Wideness in God's Mercy"; "Draw Thou My Soul, O Christ"; "Christ for the World We Sing."

Pastoral Prayer: Loving God, whom we know most surely in Jesus Christ, your only Son, we thank you for his saving presence in our lives—comforting, challenging, refreshing, and calling us to new and deeper commitments.

In this season of Lent, when we test our lives by the light of his life and claim afresh your forgiving and transforming power, free us from the fears that hinder your love at work in us and through us. Free us from fear to be instruments of your love in the world.

We pray for those whose lives are overwhelmed by sickness and pain, by the fear of death and crippling anxiety, by fearful memories and uncertain tomorrows. We pray for those who, in their doubt and unbelief, cannot pray for themselves. Hear their cries; turn their cries into prayers; and in your love comfort them with your peace-filled love.

We pray for the church as it seeks to be faithful in a confusing age. Guard it from self-preservation when our Savior has warned us about saving our own lives. Help the church instead to be a bold, evangelistic, prophetic presence in a timid and fear-filled world.

We pray for all peoples of the world in places of violence and chaos. We pray for victims of oppression and natural disaster. On this fragile earth, where plowshares are beaten into swords and the food of the hungry given to cattle to feed the overweight, we pray that your kingdom may come and your will be done. Give us a vision of that day when every knee shall bow and every tongue confess Jesus Christ as Lord and when everyone shall sit securely and contentedly beneath a vine and fig tree.

For such a time of faith and peace, we pray in Jesus' name. Amen.

MARCH 17

□

Fifth Sunday in Lent

"Hallowed be thy name," we pray. Christ prayed, "Glorify thy name," and lived the prayer by doing God's will. "I have glorified it!" declared heaven's voice.

The Sunday Lessons

The Psalm: Psalm 51:10-17.

Jeremiah 31:31-34: The prophet tells of a new covenant not like the covenant made in Egypt. The new law would be written on their hearts.

Hebrews 5:7-10: Christ, the great high priest, was made perfect through suffering. He became "the source of eternal salvation to all who obey him" (v. 9).

John 12:20-33: Greeks came saying, "Sir, we wish to see Jesus" (v. 21). The passage that follows speaks of the Son of man being glorified. Troubled by the prospect of death, Christ prays, "Father, save me from this hour" (v. 27), and then, "Father, glorify thy name" (v. 28). A voice from heaven—some said thunder, others an angel—declared, "I have glorified it" (v. 28).

Interpretation and Imagination

They had prayer together. They served in God's name together. They studied together, dreamed together, laughed together, wept together. They had sinned together. They plotted and schemed for their own satisfaction and personal agenda, but with little or no concern for the welfare of others or for the highest and best they had come to know through Christian teaching.

Now, one of them, repentant, turned to the other saying,

78

"Will you be my priest—will you hear my confession; intercede for me, declare my forgiveness?" "I cannot," the other answered, "I share the guilt."

It means nothing at all when one who doesn't care—one who respects neither God nor the rights of others—says, "It's okay. Don't worry about it. Don't feel guilty." On the other hand, if there is one who has not been compromised by self-interest, he or she will both know and reflect the blessing of God and the peace of God.

Hebrews 5:7-10 speaks of the obedience of Christ that set him apart as high priest. John's Gospel tells of a soul struggle, like the Gethsemane experience recorded in the synoptics, and speaks of Jesus' subjection to the glory of God as saving power.

LET GOODS AND KINDRED GO

John 12:20-33

A SERMON BY LUCY ROSE

We are at the end of a long journey—a Lenten journey of self-denial, self-examination, and penitence. We are at the end of a journey with Jesus as he moves toward the hour of his death and glorification. In today's lesson, several Greeks, representatives of the non-Jewish world, wish to see Jesus. And Jesus knows that his mission is ended. He must die for his Spirit to be let loose in all the world. He must die so that all peoples might, by faith, see him as Savior, King, Lord, Teacher, Son of God. He must die because his life has meaning only as part of God's mission in the world. His death is near. He is troubled; yet, he is confident, saying, "for this purpose I have come to this hour" (John 12:27).

Once more Jesus is our model—a disturbing, challenging model. He says, "He who loves his life loses it, and he who hates his life in this world will keep it for eternal life. If any one serves me, he must follow me" (John 12:25-26).

Who are those hating their lives in this world? Psychotics, those on the verge of suicide, those haunted by despair, and meaninglessness?

Who are those hating their lives in this world? Susan Potrosyan was trapped with her four-year-old daughter under concrete and rubble in the 1988 earthquake in Armenia. "Mommy, I need to drink," sobbed her daughter, "Please give me something." Mrs. Potrosyan recalled, "I thought my child was going to die of thirst. I had not water, no fruit juice, no liquids. It was then I remembered that I had my own blood." She groped in the darkness, found some shattered glass, sliced open her index finger, and gave it to her daughter. "Please Mommy, some more. Cut another finger," came the desperate cry. She cut more fingers and squeezed them to bring more blood. "I knew I was going to die," she said. "But I wanted my daughter to live" (John-Thor Dahlburg, "Buried Alive," *The Richmond News Leader* [Dec. 29, 1988]: 1). She was troubled, perhaps, yet confident, for her life was caught up in a larger purpose.

Who are those hating their lives in this world? Martin Luther King, Jr., in his final speech in Memphis on the night before his assassination, said:

> I don't know what will happen now. We've got some difficult days ahead. But it really doesn't matter with me now. Because I've been to the mountaintop. Like anybody I would like to live a long life. Longevity has its place. But I'm not concerned about that now. I just want to do God's will. And He's allowed me to go up to the mountain. And I've looked over. And I've *seen* the Promised Land. And I may not get there with you. But I want you to know tonight that we as a people *will* get to the Promised Land. So I'm happy tonight. I'm not worried about *any*thing. I'm not fearing *any* man. Mine eyes have seen the glory of the coming of the Lord. (Stephen B. Oates, *Let the Trumpet Sound: The Life of Martin Luther King, Jr.* [New York: Mentor, 1982], p. 467.)

He was troubled, perhaps, yet confident, for his life was caught up in a larger purpose.

Who are those hating their lives in this world? Allan Boesak is a black church leader, active in the struggle against apartheid in his country, South Africa. He writes:

> I was in a plane somewhere between Nairobi and Johannesburg when I opened a newspaper and came across the account of the trial of the two Afrikaner Resistance Movement men in which,

among other things, details of the plans to assassinate Bishop Desmond Tutu and myself were revealed. I shall not try to tell you how I felt when our seven-year-old daughter came home from school in tears and said: "Daddy, the children at school say that the white people are going to kill you."

. . . I would like nothing better than to live with my family without fear . . . experience the joys and pains of any normal father and husband. But not if that means I cannot do God's bidding in this struggle for justice and human dignity in this country. To struggle against apartheid is not simply to struggle *against* injustice and inhumanity. It is also to struggle *for* the integrity of the Gospel of Jesus Christ. When I think of this, and when I think of the needless suffering of millions, caused by greed, political domination and racialism, I really have no choice . . . and we must all remember that there are some things so dear, some things so precious, some things so eternally true that they are worth dying for.

. . . I have a strange joy this morning, because I have discovered that I am no longer afraid, my life is in the hands of the God who is the Living One. I do not claim to understand everything that is happening to us, but I do know I want to do God's will. (Quoted in *Light in the Darkness: Peacemaking in the Gospel of John* [Presbyterian Peacemaking Program, Presbyterian Church (USA)].)

He is troubled, perhaps, yet confident, for his life is caught up in a larger purpose. Who hates their lives in this world? Those who sing with Martin Luther

> Let goods and kindred go,
> This mortal life also;
> The body they may kill:
> God's truth abideth still;
> his kingdom is forever.

Where are you, where am I in obeying Jesus' final call to follow him? Where are we in our struggle against greed and false security, racism and fear of death?

Jesus, by his Spirit let loose in the world, calls us to continue his mission to bring God's will to rule here on earth. Jesus, by his death, frees us to "let goods and kindred go, this mortal life also," for the kingdom of God is forever. And "there are some things so dear, some things so precious, some things so eternally true that they are worth dying for."

Suggestions for Worship

Call to Worship:

Minister: Do you believe in the Son of humanity?

People: **Who is he?**

Minister: Jesus said, "You have now seen him; in fact, he is the one speaking with you."

People: **Lord, we believe.**

Minister: And they worshiped him.

Prayer of Confession: O God, whose forgiveness is assured in the death of Jesus Christ, we are bold to come before you as sinners. We confess our pride and greed, our love of those like us and our fear of strangers; our clinging to life as it is with its securities and benefits, and our reluctance to allow you to transform our lives.

Free us from love of our possessions, from fear that holds too tightly to this world, from faith that falters, from hearts that fail to risk.

Free us to serve and follow Jesus Christ as Savior and Lord.

Suggested Hymns: "A Mighty Fortress Is Our God"; "Take My Life and Let It Be"; "Saviour! Thy Dying Love"; "Take Thou Our Minds, Dear Lord."

Pastoral Prayer: Eternal God, in Jesus Christ you demonstrated your love for all the world and entrusted the church with the mission to spread the message of that love. Give us our tasks in that worldwide mission. Inspire us to speak of Jesus Christ in our homes and work places, schools and places of leisure. Inspire us to oppose injustice and oppression and to work for peace and liberation for the oppressed and oppressors. Inspire us to pray for and hope for the day of your kingdom on earth.

Hear our prayers for those in need. We place in your loving care the sick and the dying, the hungry and the homeless, the victims of violence and the imprisoned. May your will be accomplished in their lives.

Hear our prayers for our president and all world leaders. May your will be accomplished in their lives.

Hear our prayers for ourselves and this church. May your will be accomplished in our lives. Amen.

MARCH 24

□

Passion/Palm Sunday

Peace and freedom are hallmarks of the messianic kingdom. Humility and submission are the ways of this king.

The Sunday Lessons

The Psalm: Psalm 31:9-16.

Isaiah 50:4-9a: This lesson is traditionally read on the sixth Sunday of Lent. The obedient and suffering servant will not be put to shame. "He who vindicates me is near" (v. 8).

Philippians 2:5-11: Paul encourages the church at Philippi to practice the humility and obedience of Christ. Though Christ was in the form of God, he did not seek equality with God.

Mark 11:1-11: Mark's record of Jesus' entry into Jerusalem suggests a demonstration of messianic rule. Riding on a borrowed donkey ("the Lord had need of him"), he is greeted by the crowds. "Hosanna! Blessed is he who comes in the name of the Lord!" (v. 9).

Interpretation and Imagination

Divine power chose a lowly path that day. It did not have to be like that. Mark shows clearly that Jesus had the knowledge of where to find a colt and told them what to say. It happened just as he said it would.

Divine power was deaf to praise that day. The shouts were not faint nor the homage poor. The people carpeted the roads with their coats and stripped the trees to get their fronds. Anyone who hears the hosannas knows that this crowd is ready to receive a king and recognize a new kingdom.

Divine power chose a way of peace that day. The donkey was

the parable. Jewish pilgrims knew the prophet's words: "The war horse from Jerusalem . . . shall be cut off" (Zech. 9:10). If a war horse had served as Jesus' mount for the ride into Jerusalem, the city would expect a militant policy to follow. This king offered the rule of grace, not military might.

Divine power was quiet and submissive that day. The style of this prince of peace had taught a policy of patience and humility. On the first Palm Sunday, his coronation day, he lived it out.

But the city failed to recognize those things that belonged to its peace. And so today, on another Palm Sunday, in another battle-scarred and angry age, a new king comes with a kingdom still untried. Divine power chooses a lowly path today.

HAIL, KING JESUS

John 12:12-16

A SERMON BY LUCY ROSE

It is Palm Sunday, and we welcome Jesus into the city with hallelujahs. Rejoice, Jesus is King. So we sing; so we believe. And what do we mean? That Jesus has power and is in control today? How is Jesus King? Maybe our answer is in a story.

Christina sat on the side of the bed in the dark. The bright red numbers on the clock showed 4:36. She had been tossing and turning for two hours. She turned on the light and reached for a tattered orange notebook and a pen. She wrote, "Palm Sunday, day before yesterday, enjoyed the sermon on the triumphal entry. How is Jesus King? Is he the one in control?"

A light tap on the door startled her. "Christina?" came a woman's voice. "Are you awake?"

"Yes, Marie, come in."

"I saw your light on as I was coming down the hall. Can't sleep?"

"No, I've been awake since 2:30. What about you?"

Marie chuckled. "I drank too much ginger ale with Tom last night. Had to get up. But I'm not sleepy. You said your day was pretty awful. Want to talk about it a few minutes?"

"Yeah, thanks." The words tumbled out of Christina's mouth.

"Registration at the university is a zoo, Marie, a zoo! You'd think they'd have a better system than hassled administrators sitting at desks pulling cards and stamping forms. It's the twentieth century, not the fourteenth.

"Professor Bianci had to sign my registration card, and he didn't come in until 11:30. While I was waiting for him, I checked by Dr. White's office to see if I could get her course. It's the only one I really wanted. She said it wasn't closed, though more students wanted in than she'd hoped for. I had lunch with Dr. Pepperell and went to the gym to register about 2:00. You stand in line at table 1 to pick up card A. You stand in line at table 2 to pick up course cards. Table 3 told me I had to go to table 4. Table 4 sent me back to table 3. Table 3 said curtly, 'Course 756 is closed.'

" 'Course 756,' I thought. 'Oh, no! That's Dr. White's course.' I felt sick.

"To see if I could get in over the limit, the table 3 woman sent me to some professor in the physics building. He said he was the wrong person and sent me to Dr. White. Dr. White was in a meeting that could last all afternoon. I really wanted in her course! I waited outside her office about an hour and a half. I even prayed. I reminded God how much I wanted this course, but I said, 'God, may your will be done.' Registration would close at 4:30, and at 4:20 her meeting was over. I thought, 'Oh, good. God's heard my prayer.'

"Would Dr. White let me overload? 'Well,' she hesitated, 'I can't remember what limit I set. If there are 12 in the class, you may be number 13. But if there are 15, that's too many.' She signed the overload slip.

"I rushed back to the gym and stood in line again. How many have registered for 756?" I held my breath.

" 'The limit was 15, and I've given out 15 cards.' The woman's words felt cold. My weariness suddenly caught up with me.

"Then register me for 801," I mumbled. "I had to go to five more tables before I was through. I was so tired I went to the wrong places twice. On the way home I wanted a nap so bad, but I was out of gas. While I was pumping gas, the pump shut off. Like a zombie I walked back to the pay station. 'Our fault,' the boy shouted. 'Shut it off and turn it back on.'

"I finally got here about 5:45. It was one of those days when nothing goes right and you know your whole future's been screwed up. You know those days?"

Marie nodded knowingly. Christina plunged on, "I walked in the door and Betty Sue said, 'That teenager from down the street, the boy you talk to sometimes? He came by, said he needs to see you. He got suspended again or something. Said he'll be back about 6:00.'

"Marie, it was more than I could handle. I didn't even have the energy to answer Betty Sue. I came in here and slammed the door. I think I hurt Betty Sue's feelings and apologized to her later. Now I've had two hours of sleep. My brain's in a knot. I can't feel anything; I can't even think. Maybe I'll quit school."

Marie looked at her slippers and said quietly, "I've had days like that, and they're awful."

"You know what I wonder, Marie? Last Sunday was Palm Sunday. I wonder, how is Jesus King? He doesn't seem very much in control sometimes."

Marie bit gently on a finger nail. "Christina, I don't know anything about religion."

The two sat for a while without talking. Christina broke the silence. "It's ten after five, Marie. Thanks for being with me. I think I'll try to go to sleep. Thanks a lot."

"Sure," Marie answered. "Hope you can sleep." Christina lay back down and turned off the light.

Talking had helped loosen the knot of her brain. Dream shapes floated through her mind. She began carrying on a conversation with a fourteenth-century monk—something about an illumination he was gilding of the triumphal entry. Suddenly—scratch, scratch. Scriptorium and monk disappeared. Wide awake again, Christina listened to the sounds in the walls. "Squirrels," she whispered. "I thought the landlord blocked up all their holes months ago." She didn't want to pound on the walls, afraid she'd wake Marie and Betty Sue. After a few minutes the noise stopped and she closed her eyes. She was still fairly relaxed. Sleep wasn't far away, when—scratch, scratch, scratch. Her eyes popped open. She was sure the squirrels were *in* the room. The rattling was up near the ceiling over her bed. She looked at the clock—6:02. "Two hours of sleep this whole night," she sighed. "Maybe I'll read the passage on the triumphal entry from church last Sunday. It was in John somewhere. Maybe I'll skim all of

John. I can read pretty fast, and I already know the plot." She put on her robe and curled up in a chair. At 7:30 she reached chapter 21, verse 25: The End. She put the Bible down. The room was quiet.

"Maybe I can rest 'til 8:30," she thought. "Three hours of sleep are better than two."

The bed felt cozy; the silence was peaceful. She smiled, "An hour of rest would be wonderful."

Scratch, scratch, scratch—this time from under the desk across the room. Christina let out a long sigh. "Forget it. I'll just get up."

On the way down the hall to wash her face, she passed Betty Sue. Betty Sue stared at her with a kind, honest look of concern.

"Christina, you look awful," she blurted out.

"I know, only two hours of beauty rest." Then Christina brightened. "Betty Sue, let me ask you something. You go to church. How is Jesus King? He doesn't seem very much in control of things sometimes. I told you about yesterday; it was an awful day. A king's supposed to have power to make things work right. I prayed. I mean, maybe Jesus doesn't want me in Dr. White's course. I don't know, but it didn't have to be such an awful day. And did Jesus send the squirrels to keep me awake three times this morning? How is Jesus King in a chaotic world like this? And I'm not the only one with problems. Marie has bad days; her mom's dying of cancer. The world's polluting itself, and folks are bombing each other all over the world. You hear me, Betty Sue? How is Jesus King?"

Christina didn't usually ask Betty Sue very many questions. She thought Betty Sue was a little simple, and too religious. But she waited in the cold hallway for her answer. Betty Sue looked shy, especially in her pair of old pajamas and a patched robe.

"Christina," she began softly. "You've had a pretty good life. Things usually seem to work for you, always have. When I was growing up, nothing worked well. Papa would get drunk, and Mama couldn't make much money. Jesus wasn't so much the Super Being in control as . . . as," she stumbled for words, "as a comforting, encouraging, suffering Presence with us in the chaos. I never expected life to be all together. Still don't. Jesus for me is King, but not like . . . " she paused again. "Jesus' power is not like that guy's, what's his name, Rambo."

That was all Betty Sue had to say. She never said much. Quietly she walked down the hall toward her room. Christina turned right into the kitchen, not left into the bathroom. Washing her face could wait. She sat down in the rocking chair in the semidarkness and began to think.

Betty Sue was right. She wanted Jesus to be in control, to make things work for her. She expected life to fit together, and when it did, she assumed Jesus was being a proper king. "But maybe," she thought, "maybe Jesus isn't that kind of king. What did he say to Pilate, 'My kingdom is not of this world.' And I expect him to be king *here, in this world*, with power to rule so that my life feels in control. Maybe Jesus isn't that kind of king."

She thought of the speeches Jesus made early in John's Gospel about bread. He meant spiritual bread, but the people thought he meant physical bread. He spoke of water and meant living water bubbling up in the human soul, but the Samaritan woman thought he meant the physical water at the bottom of Jacob's well. Christina thought, "Jesus is King, and I think he means a king with power like Rambo's, to make sure no matter what happens he gets his way, but he means a king who rides humbly into Jerusalem on a donkey. And," Christina caught her breath, "he means a king who stoops to wash feet, to kneel before people like me and Betty Sue and wash away the filth from our feet. Not a king like Rambo. Not a king with super power, interested only in making everything right, but a king who recognizes the pain and frustration, the fragmentation and chaos of life."

The movie *Ordinary People* popped into her mind. Conrad had tried to commit suicide and was in counseling with Dr. Berger. He told Dr. Berger he wanted to be more in control of his life, and Dr. Berger replied, "Okay, but I want you to know something. I'm not big on control." Suddenly it was as if Jesus were saying to her, "Christina, I know you like to feel in control, but I want you to know something, I'm not big on control."

Christina thought, "In John's Gospel there's a king named Caesar, or Rambo, if you like, and there's a king named Jesus—who trots into the city on a donkey and washes feet. Maybe before Marie's mom dies of cancer, I can talk to her about Jesus, about *that* kind of king. Maybe days like yesterday happen and people get cancer and bombs explode and innocent folks are killed and who knows why—and Jesus still comes riding up on a donkey with a towel and a basin, ready to wash away the filth and the tears and to pass the towel and basin on to us. Maybe that's how Jesus is king."

It is Palm Sunday, and we welcome Jesus into the city with hallelujahs. Rejoice, Jesus is King—and he comes today carrying once again a towel and a basin.

Suggestions for Worship

Call to Worship:

Minister: Hosanna!

People: Blessed is the King of Israel who comes in the name of the Lord.

Minister: Let us worship God.

Suggested Hymns: "Rejoice, the Lord Is King"; "All Glory, Laud, and Honor"; "Tell Me the Stories of Jesus"; "Seal Us, O Holy Spirit"; "Come, Christians, Join to Sing."

Pastoral Prayer: Loving God, your love in Jesus Christ stretches from time's distant beginning to the final day when the universe disappears. Your love in Jesus Christ encompasses the entire creation and cares for the sparrow and for our every need. We lift our prayers of thanksgiving for our faith, however weak, in such divine love. We thank you for every good gift from your hand—human love, shelter, food, health, work, hope. Grant that our lives may more and more be lived under the kingship of Jesus Christ, who lived not to secure his own life, but to willingly lay down his life for his friends. Teach us to live by faith that we may share your good gifts with others.

We lift also our prayers of intercession. We pray for the sick, the suffering, and the dying. Grant them the assurance that your Spirit sustains them both in life and in death. Comfort them, strengthen them, and keep them faithful to the end of their days.

We pray for the hungry, the homeless, the jobless, the hopeless. Help us to find ways to restructure our society, our economy, and our world so that they, too, may enjoy your good gifts intended for all.

We pray for our president and for all world leaders. Replace fear with visions of your coming kingdom, that the nations of this world may cease their warring and live in peace, sharing your good gifts.

May your church keep alive these visions of your kingdom, which is here now, struggling to be born in our lives, and which is coming in its fullness at the end of time. Amen.

MARCH 31

□

Easter Sunday

Jesus' followers could not find his body. Instead they found a living Christ.

The Sunday Lessons

The Psalm: Psalm 118:14-24.

Acts 10:34-43: At Caesarea, Peter preached to Cornelius and his friends, saying "God shows no partiality" (v. 34). Christ appeared to a few who were chosen to be witnesses to all nations. Peter's message centered on Christ's death and resurrection. Peter speaks as one who "ate and drank with him after he rose from the dead" (v. 41).

I Corinthians 15:1-11: The resurrection is Paul's primary message. He lists Christ's appearances to Peter, to the disciples, to five hundred, to James, to the apostles, and "last of all, as to one untimely born, he appeared also to me" (v. 8).

John 20:1-18: Mary Magdalene, Simon Peter, and another disciple found the garden tomb empty—the stone rolled away, grave clothes lying there, and a rolled-up napkin. Later, Jesus appeared to Mary saying, "Woman, why are you weeping? Whom do you seek?" (v. 15). She clung to the risen Christ until he told her, "Do not hold me . . . go to my brethren and say to them, I am ascending to my Father and your Father, to my God and your God" (v. 17).

Interpretation and Imagination

Vacher Burch, a biblical scholar, believed that the original Aramaic draft of John's Gospel ended with the passage that includes Christ's dying words, "It is finished" (John 19:28-35).

"The end" are words often used in literature. They suggest two things: that the work is complete and the story has ended.

Easter day, the empty tomb, the risen Christ, and the witness of Mary and Peter and the church join to say that it is not finished. Death on the cross was not the final verdict. The grave could not hold him. Death is not the last word for us either.

Mary Magdalene came to the garden tomb with expectations that were as mortal as they were modest. She only wanted to preserve a dead body. She was met with surprises—an empty tomb, a risen Lord. The stuff of life is always like that—more wonder than form. But still we come to Easter wanting to preserve rather than discover. We come as keepers of truth more than finders of truth.

Ancient Greeks (Empedocles, for example) were convinced that four natural elements could be seen in a burning log—fire, air (smoke), water (from the end of the log) and earth (ashes). A fifth, "quintessence," was thought to be the "stuff of life."

Impressive schemes were developed to interpret life. Although wrong, these ideas survived until the Renaissance— almost 2,000 years. We still use "ashes to ashes" in the burial of the dead and muddle through concepts of body and soul.

Empedocles and his followers wanted to preserve their ideas more than they wanted to discover new truth. In their train, the church wanted to preserve its doctrine more than it wanted to be intellectually vital. But "as our island of knowledge grows, our shoreline of wonder should expand" (Richard Bergland, *The Fabric of the Mind* [New York: Penguin Books, 1985]).

Today, scientists suggest that forces, not matter, are nature's building blocks. They identify four—electromagnetism, the strong, the weak, and gravity. They seek a fifth—a unifying force that defies reduction.

A SONG OF VICTORY

Psalm 118:14-24

A SERMON BY BISHOP ERNEST A. FITZGERALD

There is an old story about a man and his wife who lived in a remote section of southern Appalachia. One day the woman found at their door a little leaflet left there by a traveling evangelist. In the leaflet there was a prediction about the end of the world. Greatly disturbed, the woman said to her husband, "John, it says here that God's going to destroy the world." "So, what," drawled her husband. "It's his'n, ain't it?"

There is something about this man's calm and placid spirit that is attractive to us. Louis Valbrecht once wrote a book entitled *Survival in the Rat Race.* That title speaks to us. The bewildering pace and calamitous events of our times make us wonder whether we will survive. We who have an abiding faith in God feel that we have a better chance than other people at handling what H. L. Mencken called the "dizzy flywheel." We have discovered a unique sturdiness among the people of faith.

In the book of Psalms, there is a marvelous sound of praise and thanksgiving. Here the author gives a joyful affirmation that he has come through impossible times. His song reflects some very primitive notions about God, but when you read his testimony carefully, you discover that some of his ideas are worthy of thought.

For one thing, the psalmist was grateful for adequate resources. Listen to the psalmist, "The Lord is on my side . . . The Lord is my strength." People who believe that are always people of courage. Do you remember that the disciples fled in despair after the crucifixion? For three years they had listened to the promises of Jesus. They had believed what he said. Then came that terrible afternoon at Golgotha. When Jesus died, the hopes of the disciples died with him. The resurrection, however, gave the disciples the assurance that Jesus was still alive. With renewed courage they traveled the ancient world declaring, "Jesus Christ is Lord!"

Never underestimate the strength God's presence can bring to one's life. Remember that beautiful story about a man whose hobby was growing roses. When he worked in his rose garden, he always whistled, often, it seemed, louder than needed. One day a new neighbor asked him why he always whistled. The man took the neighbor into his home to meet his wife. The woman was not only a near invalid, but she was also totally blind. The man was whistling for her benefit. He wanted her to know he was nearby, and she was not alone.

That story is a splendid commentary on the significance of

Easter. The affirmation "He is risen" suggests that God is near. It reminds us that there is something stable and permanent in creation that does not yield to our evil designs. God stands behind the moral order, ready to back anything that is harmonized with its purposes. The psalmist must have had this in mind when he said, "The gates of the Lord are opened for the righteous."

Second, the courage of the psalmist was related to the life-giving strength of hope. "I shall not die, but live, and declare the works of the Lord" (v. 17 KJV): These are the words of a person with optimism and hope. There is power in hope. Several years ago some students at Johns Hopkins placed some mice in a maze that had no outlet. With no hope of escape, the mice quickly gave up and succumbed. Other mice, not given such hopeless limitations, did not surrender, but kept working until they were free. The lesson here is clear: Life loses its meaning when all hope is eliminated.

It is precisely to this circumstance that the resurrection speaks. Life is not limited to the narrow confines of one little world. We have been freed from the frustration of annihilation. Death is not the master of life, but merely a servant that God uses on our behalf. In this faith, the people of God live and work and are not afraid.

Third, the psalmist was certain that the ultimate victory was in God's hands. The Battle of New Orleans during the War of 1812 holds a unique place in the annals of military warfare: The battle was fought after the war was over. The agreement to end the conflict had been reached, but word had not been delivered to the front. Thus a useless battle was waged.

Some things have been decided no matter how the battle goes. Is that not the promise Jesus made to his followers? "My kingdom is forever, and nothing, not even the gates of hell, can prevail against it."

Ian McPherson, the great Scottish preacher, once wrote a sermon entitled "What Jesus Made of the Cross." In that sermon there is this striking sentence: "Jesus made the cross a throne from which he rules the ages." Little did those soldiers know as they hammered the cross together that they were building a throne for a king.

Long ago the psalmist declared: "I called upon the Lord in

distress; the Lord answered me, and set me in a large place" (v. 5). Centuries later, Jesus made a similar affirmation: "Be of good cheer; I have overcome the world" (John 16:33 KJV). I take this to mean that the final word of history is in God's hands. If we ever really hear the words "He is risen," we have no reason to despair. Charles Wesley gave voice to our faith:

> His kingdom cannot fail;
> He rules o'er earth and heaven;
> The keys of death and hell
> Are to our Jesus given.

That is what we believe—we who truly celebrate Easter day. Amen.

Suggestions for Worship

Call to Worship:

Minister: Lift up your head and shout, O Zion.

People: Christ is Risen.

Minister: Let the people proclaim his matchless power.

People: He is risen, indeed.

Prayer of Confession: Holy Spirit, Truth Divine, we come remembering our need to sense anew the gladness of this Easter day. Lift from our eyes the shadows of this earth that we may see the light that is eternal. Forgive us all that prevents us from an awareness of your presence. Make us ever grateful for your gift of love. Give us a heart and voice to proclaim the good news to people everywhere. Through the victorious name of Jesus, amen.

Suggested Hymns: "Christ the Lord Is Risen Today"; "I Know That My Redeemer Lives."

Pastoral Prayer: In the certain faith that Christ is not dead, but alive, let us pray: Eternal God, the incredible majesty of this glorious day causes us to lift our voices in triumphant praise. The night of death has been turned into the morning, the narrow confines of this world have been opened into everlasting life. We hear the thrilling news that life cannot be buried and truth cannot be entombed. Christ is risen!

Teach us that we need no longer walk in darkness, confused about life's meaning. The last enemy has been conquered, and death is swallowed up in victory. Through the resurrection, Jesus Christ has freed us from the bondage of sin. He has established a kingdom for us that knows no end.

We pray that in this place the message of Easter may be made to live again. Then let us go forth with tidings of release for your children everywhere. Be present with each person who has a claim on our prayers. Make us responsive to their needs. Praise be to thee, O Lord Most High. Amen.

APRIL 7

□

Second Sunday of Easter

We, like the first readers and Thomas, were not there to see. John's Gospel is for all of us; that we may have faith and life.

The Sunday Lessons

The Psalm: Psalm 133.

Acts 4:32-35: The community of believers "were of one heart and soul." Possessions were held in common. Distribution was based on need. "With great power the apostles gave their testimony to the resurrection of the Lord Jesus" (v. 33). New Testament Christians shared a common belief, a common life, and a common mission.

I John 1:1–2:2: Toward the end of the first century John writes of that "which we have seen with our eyes" (v. 1) to those without benefit of experience. His purpose is that they might be part of Christ's church and have fellowship with the apostles.

John 20:19-31: On the evening of the day of resurrection, Jesus appeared to his disciples. Thomas was absent and did not believe until he was confronted by the risen Christ eight days later. How blessed are those who have not seen and yet believe.

Interpretation and Imagination

Numerous happenings affect us without our ever experiencing them. Most of us have not been in a battle, endured famine, or suffered torture. None of us have known death firsthand. Yet, words have conveyed the reality of such things in compelling ways that influence our hopes and fears. The witness of others has shaped our beliefs.

Thomas had not seen the empty tomb. He wasn't in the room with the risen Christ. He was skeptical and wanted to do more than see. He wanted to press his finger into the nail prints. The Gospel story makes this point: Many are blessed without firsthand experience. They are made part of the community of believers through the witness of others.

Some communities, like some clubs, tend to be exclusive. Only those who have climbed the mountain or played with the varsity or achieved a certain standard of excellence can become part of the group. Such groups, never communities by Christian standards, seek to defend status, protect private interests, and promote the superiority of a few.

Suppose that Peter and the other disciples had decided that a personal visit from the risen Christ was the only credential that could open the doors of the church. Suppose that second generation Christians excluded themselves because they had not seen. There would be no church; no community of faith.

An elitist heresy threatened the early church. Some persons claimed special knowledge and private experience. The First Epistle of John seeks to correct this. Fellowship with the apostles was possible for all who devoted themselves to their teaching. Fellowship with the risen Christ is offered to all who "walk in the light."

THE AGE OF THE QUESTION MARK

John 20:19-31

A SERMON BY BISHOP ERNEST A. FITZGERALD

Several years ago, a widely known minister spoke at a national conference on evangelism. He concluded his sermon with an interesting sentence: "If you were considering being a Christian, would there be enough evidence to convince you?" People who study such things tell us that all across the country there is a resurgence of interest in religion. We are said to be toying with a variety of faiths, only one of which is Christianity. Oriental religions are attracting followers, especially in large metropolitan areas. This faith quest has taken on supermarket dimensions where many options are displayed. A lot of people are trying to make up their minds about what they believe. It is a valid question, therefore, to ask about the evidence necessary to convince us.

In the New Testament, there is a story about a man who has difficulty believing the stories about the resurrection. Said Thomas to his friends, "Unless I can see Jesus himself, I will not believe." A few days later, Thomas did see Jesus, and his faith was confirmed. Thomas has often been censured for his callous disbelief, but his doubts are often akin to our own. We, too, find it difficult to believe.

We must admit from the beginning that much of what Christians believe is open to question. Bishop Robert Goodrich, in *Dear God, Where Are You?*, observed:

> Most of the creeds and many of our hymns include some variation of the words, "I believe in God the Father Almighty . . . How Great Thou Art." It is a big, brave, grand, majestic affirmation, and often in public worship we join our voices in some such expression, some of us honestly, some of us wistfully, some of us hopefully and some of us with our fingers crossed—saying the words but inwardly thinking, "I want to believe and try, but, Dear God, where are you?"

Most thoughtful Christians identify with that circumstance. Ours is the age of the question mark. We have trouble believing what cannot be proved in the laboratory. Our faith contains many ideas that lie beyond such proof. The agnostic's position is not totally untenable. It is even possible to construct a logical position for the nonexistence of God.

The credibility of the Christian faith is even more questionable in its claim about the nature of God. If we do admit that creation requires a Creator, to suggest that this Creator cares for us is open to serious debate. Not in all the long history of Christian thought have we been able to square the compassion of God with the cruelty of nature. Pain, suffering, accident, disease, and death often raise unanswered questions about the goodness of God. We understand Thomas's concern for better evidence.

We must say, however, that what Christians believe is not just fantasy and dreams. Jesus reminded Thomas that there are people who find it easy to believe. Long ago someone referred to the Christian faith as the "grand *surmise* of the soul." The suggestion is that a Christian surveys the evidence and then makes a leap of faith. We do this in other areas of human knowledge. An astronomer, for instance, often discovers a planet or star, not by seeing the planet or star itself, but by the behavior of other known heavenly bodies. A lot of what we know in astronomy is based on surmises.

John Wesley declared that the Christian's "knowledge" should be subjected to the test of "Scripture, tradition, experience and reason." Through this process we assemble the evidence. For instance, we may not be able to demonstrate the resurrection in the laboratory, but what we do know leads us to the firm conviction that there is a "living Christ." Our faith may be described as full of guesses, but they are not random guesses. They are conclusions reached by following where the evidence points.

How then do we become convinced that our guesses are true? There is a story from the life of philosopher Blaise Pascal. Pascal had lost a beloved daughter in death. A friend came by to visit and observed the great French scholar's quiet trust and confidence. "I wish I had your creed; then I could live your life," said the visitor. Pascal replied, "Live my life, and you will soon have my creed."

That thought is worth pondering. We not only "believe our way into acting," but we also "act our way into believing." Indeed, it was this latter process that made Thomas a believer.

This means that faith is not always instantly achieved. Near my office in downtown Atlanta a new office building is being erected. I have watched the workers put in place the steel girders. These skilled construction people often walk those tiny ribbons of steel. I have wondered how they learn to move so confidently on a six-inch catwalk, thirty stories above the street. I am sure of this: You do not do it overnight. You come at it a little at a time, achieving balance, sure-footedness, and adjustment to height. Little by little you learn to move with agility and ease.

The confidence of a Christian is gained in a similar way. You test God's promises a little at a time until you can say "I believe." It is a bit like getting to know a friend. The better you know the friend, the higher the level of trust. People who set out to know God as a friend finally come to know him, and when they know him, they trust him. That is the best evidence one can find that the Christian faith is true.

Suggestions for Worship

Call to Worship:

> **All:** This is the message we have heard and proclaim to you. God is light and in him is no darkness at all. If we walk in the light as he is in the light, we have fellowship with one another and with him. Come let us worship together.

Prayer of Confession: Give ear, O God, unto our prayers and harken to the voice of our supplications. We wait at the altar to seek forgiveness for our sins. Our faith often falters, and our trust is not always in you. We ask now for a love that refines all human frailties and makes us fully whole. Amen.

Suggested Hymns: "Open My Eyes, That I May See"; "O For a Faith That Will Not Shrink."

Pastoral Prayer: Eternal God, we assemble in this place seeking the light of hope and the assurance of your love. We are grateful for your promised presence among us. We ask forgiveness for the waywardness of our minds and for the faintness of our hearts. Amen.

APRIL 14

□

Third Sunday of Easter

These lessons give the resurrection a "this world" context.

The Sunday Lessons

The Psalm: Psalm 4.

Acts 3:12-19: Following the healing of a lame man, Peter ascribes such power to God. He reminds his hearers that Pilate had offered to release Jesus, but that they had asked for a murderer's release. They had acted in ignorance. Now they are called to repentance.

I John 3:1-7: Being like God is the theme of this passage. Christ provides the model. Made in the image of God, we will grow into God's likeness. Christ is the norm.

Luke 24:35-48: Jesus appeared to the disciples gathered in Jerusalem. Luke emphasizes a bodily resurrection and records the words of Christ. Christ ate with them. His commission follows with the instruction, "Stay in the city, until you are clothed with power from on high" (v. 49).

Interpretation and Imagination

Resurrection power means little unless it is as real as human life and as current as today's newspaper. And the risen Christ does confront us in present historical situations. The resurrection is not for some other place and some later time.

In local churches, in hometown places, in family, in work, in government we are confronted by the risen Christ. We are not called away from life on this earth. Instead, we are sent into the world in a wholly new way and with new power.

Bonhoeffer played down the traditional idea of repentance as a religious act, concerned only with separating from the world. He emphasized the power of "allowing oneself to be caught up into the way of Jesus Christ." He spoke of worldliness and of living unreservedly in life's duties, problems, successes, and failures.

Both the church and the Christian exist not for themselves but for others. The risen Christ does not simply provide an escape from distress and fear, from sin and death, and promise a better place beyond the grave. Instead, we are commissioned to live his life in the world, confronted with flesh and blood needs and assured of power from on high.

WHO IS JESUS?

Luke 24:35-48

A SERMON BY KENNETH L. CARDER

The August 18, 1988, issue of *Time* carried on its cover the question "Who Was Jesus?" It was the sixteenth time that Jesus had appeared on the cover of *Time* magazine.

The picture on the cover was striking. The portrait of Jesus was a composite portrait made up of various artists' images of Jesus, ranging from a sixth century painting to a stained-glass portrayal dating to the reign of Charlemagne to that of a twentieth-century artist. The art director of *Time* had taken segments of each portrayal and formed them into an image of Jesus. The result was a grotesque and confusing Jesus.

The composite picture on the magazine cover isn't unlike what we have done to Jesus. We have tended to make Jesus a reflection of our own likeness and a champion of our narrow prejudices and cultural biases. He has been distorted beyond recognition.

Jesus had been dressed in white sheets and had his name invoked as a divine blessing upon racial hatred and violence. The Nazi holocaust took place under the sign of a cross; the swastika is a Greek rending of a cross.

Every age, every generation, and almost every group has a tendency to make Jesus over into its own likeness. That is a backhanded compliment. Everybody wants Jesus on his or her side.

A billboard outside a neighboring city several years ago consisted of a picture of Solman's "Head of Christ." Beside it were the words "If he were alive today he would be a right wing extremist."

A couple of decades ago a column by the popular psychologist and writer Dr. George Crane appeared in my local newspaper. It had the title "Jesus as a Capitalist." In the article, Dr. Crane affirmed that the parable of the talents proves that "Jesus was a capitalist."

If the parable of the talents proves that Jesus was a capitalist, then what does Jesus' advice to the rich young ruler prove about Jesus? "Go, sell all that you have and give to the poor."

See what we can do with Jesus? We can make him a champion of our causes, a projection of our own image, the embodiment of our culture's values. Nations dress him in the uniform of their military and march him off under their flag to do battle with other nations who have put their uniform on him as well.

The question has to be raised, seriously raised: Who is this Jesus whom everyone wants as an ally? It is a question behind the writing of the Synoptic Gospels. It is the unwritten inquiry beneath every story, every narrative.

Soon after the crucifixion, the issue of Jesus' identity took on added importance. Numerous stories circulated about him. Many of them contradicted what the early church had known about the Christ. How were the people to know the real Christ? What criteria should be used to evaluate the various portrayals of the risen One?

Those questions lurk behind the scene of Luke's account of the disciples on the Emmaus Road and the risen Christ's subsequent appearance to the disciples. Close attention to the story has the potential of helping us answer the question of who Jesus is. Getting inside the story might, in fact, help us really know who Jesus is.

Luke knew that it isn't sufficient to be "committed to Jesus." That can even be dangerously demonic. One must be committed to the real Jesus, the Jesus of the Galilean and Emmaus Roads. Below are some ways we can discern, even meet, the real Jesus, according to Luke.

First, be sure the Jesus you are committed to is compatible with the Jesus of scripture. Is your concept of Jesus formulated out of your exposure to the scriptures, or are the scriptures used to support your predetermined view of Jesus? Do you go to the Gospels to learn who Jesus is, or do you arrive at your notion of Jesus from our culture's bias? Jesus must be met in the scriptures, or we will have created a false Jesus.

It was in the opening of the scriptures that the disciples recognized the risen Christ. On the Emmaus Road, the disciples remembered how their hearts burned within them as Jesus interpreted the scriptures. When the risen One appeared to the disciples, "he opened their minds to understand the scriptures." He even helped them to see the continuity between what was written in the law of Moses, the prophets, and the psalms and his own life, death, and resurrection. When they understood the scriptures, they knew Jesus.

If those earliest disciples recognized the real Jesus through a confrontation with scripture, how much more important the scriptures are to us in our quest for the real Jesus! As we bathe our minds with his teachings, put ourselves in his stories, seek to obey his commands, and travel with him to Calvary, he comes walking out of the pages of the ancient past and into our lives.

Further, according to Luke, we don't know the real Jesus apart from his humanity. The temptation in the early church was to make Jesus "spirit," to divorce him from his humanness, to make him another god.

When Jesus appears to the disciples in Luke's narrative, he says, "See my hands and my feet . . . handle me, and see; for a spirit has not flesh and bones as you see that I have" (24:39). Then he asked for something to eat, "and he took it and ate before them" (24:43). This was no ghost. Jesus is no extraterrestrial visitor. He is flesh of our flesh and bone of our bone.

The point is that the real Jesus cannot be separated from the flesh and blood struggle of the human lot. Any concept of Jesus that removes him from human anguish and pain and the struggle for justice and wholeness is a distortion. It is a heretical Jesus.

John tells the story of Thomas and his struggle to know the real Jesus following the crucifixion. His problem was not really an intellectual doubting. No, Thomas wanted to be sure that the risen Christ was the same as the crucified Christ. Was the victorious Christ a wounded Christ? You see, only a wounded Jesus who is victorious can really save us from our own mortal wounds.

The real Jesus is the one who says hold me, touch me, feel me, put your hands in my wounds. The real Jesus is no spiritual phantom, removed from the nitty gritty of everyday life. The real Jesus is known in the real world of birth and death, laughter and tears, pleasure and pain, the flesh and blood of authentic life.

Finally, Luke affirms that the real Jesus is known in a community without barriers. The Emmaus disciples recognized Jesus when they invited a stranger into their home for the breaking of bread. When Jesus appeared to the disciples, he reminded them "that repentance and forgiveness of sins should be preached in his name to all nations" (24:47).

Luke, more than Matthew and Mark, makes much to do about table fellowship. Remember, in the ancient world of Jesus, sharing meals with other persons was a sign of friendship, acceptance, and love. Inviting someone to dinner was an expression of honor. When Jesus ate with sinners, respectable people got upset. Eating with sinners was a sign of friendship and forgiveness and affirmation.

The most serious question facing the modern church may be that of whom to invite to dinner. Who is included within the circle of fellowship and care? Jesus ate with tax collectors and sinners, the poor and the outcast. We aren't likely to know who Jesus is unless our fellowship is inclusive. I'm sure that any Jesus who sanctions racism, classism, sexism, and elitism is a false Jesus. A Jesus that allows persons to be excluded from the table on the basis of their color or income or nationality or education or social standing is an impostor. The real Jesus will allow no barriers!

Albert Schweitzer set out to do what many scholars were attempting around the turn of the century: He wanted to discover the historical Jesus. He concluded that the "lives of Jesus" were basically reflections of the authors' own cultural and religious biases. Schweitzer immersed himself in the question of who Jesus is. He studied the Gospels in Greek and German and read the writings of other scholars. His book *The Quest for the Historical Jesus* is the product of his research. In it he says:

> [Jesus] comes to us as One unknown, without a name, as of old, by the lake-side, He came to those men who knew Him not. He speaks to us the same word: "Follow thou me!" and sets us to the

tasks which He has to fulfill for our time. He commands. And to those who obey Him, whether they be wise or simple, He will reveal Himself in the toils, the conflicts, the sufferings which they shall pass through in His fellowship, and, as an ineffable mystery, they shall learn in their own experience Who He is.

May that experience be ours! As we search the scriptures for him, in the human struggle for justice and wholeness, and open our fellowship to "the least of these," we will come to know Christ and be transformed by Christ.

Suggestions for Worship

Call to Worship:

Minister: Since then we have a great priest who has passed through the heavens, Jesus the Son of God.

People: Let us with confidence draw near to the throne of grace, that we may receive mercy and find grace to help in time of need.

Prayer of Confession: Almighty God, who through the resurrection put your seal of approval on all that Jesus was and all that he did, we confess our own failure to faithfully follow the risen Christ. Rather than being transformed into Christ's image, we fashion a Christ who confirms our prejudices, supports our idolatry, and caters to our selfishness. Even our adoration of the Christ often becomes a means by which we remove him from the world of human anguish and social justice. Forgive us, O God, for failing to live in the radiance of your victory in Jesus Christ, in whose name we pray. Amen.

Suggested Hymns: "All Hail the Power of Jesus' Name"; "Fairest Lord Jesus"; "O Young and Fearless Prophet."

Pastoral Prayer: Eternal God, whose beauty bursts forth in the splendor of a new springtime, whose power holds the planets in their orbits, whose truth challenges the best of human thought, whose goodness judges the purest human endeavors, and whose love binds all things together: We are grateful for a universe that shows forth your beauty and power, for the human mind that seeks after truth, for a conscience that both condemns our sinfulness and challenges our complacency, for relationships in which we know the depth and breadth of love.

Most of all, we are grateful for Jesus Christ, the crucified and risen Lord, for the challenge of his life, the insight of his teaching, the redemption wrought through his death, the victory won in the resurrection. For these and all other benefits of Christ's life, death, and resurrection, we give you thanks, O God.

Free us, O God, from distorting the meaning of Christ's life and teachings by making him the champion of causes and values that thwart your purposes. Deliver us from the temptation to create an exclusive Christ who caters to our prejudices, our nationalistic self-interest, and our personal success and advantage.

Help us to follow the risen Christ revealed in scripture, experienced in human anguish and struggle, and known in a community that knows no barriers of race or class or nation; through the same Jesus Christ, our Lord. Amen.

APRIL 21

□

Fourth Sunday of Easter

These lessons tell of Christ's death and rejection, but lift him up as a saving power.

The Sunday Lessons

The Psalm: Psalm 23.

Acts 4:8-12: After healing the lame man, Peter is questioned by the high priestly family. "By what power or by what name did you do that?" they wanted to know. Naming the name of Jesus Christ, Peter charges, "Whom you crucified, whom God raised" (v. 10). A rejected stone has become the main stone. "There is no other name . . . by which we must be saved" (v. 12).

I John 3:18-24: Love is the chief test by which "we know that we have passed out of death into life" (v. 14). Such love is marked by deeds and confirmed by hearts that do not condemn us. "This is his commandment, that we should believe in the name of his Son Jesus Christ and love one another" (v. 23).

John 10:11-18: Contrasting a true shepherd with hirelings, Christ teaches that true shepherds do not flee death in order to save themselves. They know their own and are known by them; they bring the entire flock together. "For this reason the Father loves me, because I lay down my life, that I may take it again" (v. 17).

Interpretation and Imagination

Christ did not die because he was weak before the power of his enemies. Rather he chose to be vulnerable. "No one takes my life. I lay it down." By making himself weak, Christ makes himself inescapable.

They rejected him, misunderstood him, maligned him, but

they could not drive him away. They did not get rid of him. The true shepherd will never go away.

Sometimes, we wish that Christ would. It would be simpler if we could make up our minds decisively and then, if we chose to reject Christ, even kill the Chosen One, we would be through. But Christ cannot be set aside. Our indifference will not be a final answer any more than the cross ended his claim in the first century. He chose to lay down his life, and he can choose to take it again.

Christian youth were holding a rally in East Germany. Their meeting was held in the town hall, which was dominated by two large pictures—one of Lenin, the other of Stalin. These could not be removed, so the youths hung their banner with the words, "The earth is the Lord's and the fulness thereof" (Ps. 24:1) beneath the pictures. Suddenly, they saw how compelling the word of God became in the context of weakness.

We, like sheep, are scattered and threatened by powers of evil and death that are greater than our power to resist. But our God is never more strong, more inescapable, more compelling than when God is weak.

THE GOOD SHEPHERD

John 10:11-18

A SERMON BY CHAPLAIN MILFORD OXENDINE, JR., LCDR, CHC, USN

I am the good shepherd: the good shepherd lays down his life for the sheep. (John 10:11 NIV)

Sheep have a long and very prominent place in the Bible. The earliest mention of sheep in the Bible is in Genesis 4:2, where it is stated that Abel was a keeper of sheep. Figures of speech concerning shepherding were used repeatedly as God warned Israel of its shortcomings. The reason why so much attention is given to sheep in the Bible must stem from the fact that they were used for centuries as sacrifices. Offerings consisted of lambs, ewes, and rams in sacrificial services and rituals in the Temple and in other places.

Sheep are dumb animals that always stand in the need of a shepherd to tend, guard, guide, and feed them. A good shepherd always leads his sheep. He knows them by name, and they know his voice. At night, he always sees that they are safe in the field.

How fitting it is, then, that in the fullness of time God looked down upon humanity and saw us as sheep without a shepherd. God sent his only Son to become our good shepherd. His arrival was announced by shepherds, who were keeping watch over their flocks by night out on the Judean hills. How glad we should be that he came to find the lost sheep and to return them to the fold, in which they could become recipients of the good shepherd's loving care, provision, protection, and guidance.

Why is Christ the good shepherd? He is the good shepherd because he laid down his life for the sheep. The whole life of the good shepherd must be completely sacrificed to meet the needs of the dependent, needy, hungry, foolish creatures who have been put under his care. In contrast, the hireling will do something for the sheep, but he will not risk himself to save the sheep. The good shepherd, on the other hand, sets himself between the flock of sheep and whatever endangers them. If it is necessary, he will die—he will give his life to save the sheep. Evil, harm, and doom can reach the sheep only over the good shepherd's dead body. Isn't this what Jesus, the good shepherd, did for us?

A minister went to spend a brief vacation with a Scottish shepherd. The Scottish shepherd met the visiting minister at the station, and on their way back to the ranch, the shepherd talked very little. He seemed to have a very heavily burned heart. The minister finally asked him what was wrong. The old shepherd began to cry as he replied between sobs: "I lost sixty-five of my best lambs last night. The wolves got in." The minister expressed his sorrow and asked: "How many sheep did the wolves kill besides the lambs?" The shepherd looked surprised and replied, "Don't you know that a wolf will never take an old sheep as long as he can get a lamb?"

Sometimes, we, the people of his pasture and the sheep of his flock, don't really know who we are. We are such wandering, erring, and erratic sheep; we are so often missing or straying from the flock until we wonder whether we really belong. The good shepherd, however, says: I am the good shepherd and know my sheep. Isn't that what really matters after all—that he knows those who are his? In addition, we know we are his and that his watchful, unselfish care surrounds us always. We are never left alone, because he is ever with us, and when we wander from the fold, he seeks us out. No wonder one hymn writer wrote:

> Jesus sought me when a stranger,
> Wandering from the fold of God;
> He, to rescue me from danger,
> Interposed his precious blood.

I am the good shepherd: the good shepherd lays down his life for the sheep. This is one of the most staggering metaphors in all literature. It points out that there is such a close and intimate relationship between Christ and his sheep that he dares to compare that relationship to that which exists between God and himself. Jesus, knowing us so thoroughly, sees how helpless we are without him. Therefore, he devotes his whole life to us and eventually throws it away in one supreme act of self-sacrifice to save us from our sins.

> But none of the ransomed ever knew
> How deep were the waters crossed;
> Nor how dark the night that the Lord
>   passed through
> Ere He found His sheep that was lost.

No picture was more dear to the early church than that of Jesus, the good shepherd. He came as a personification of the shepherd who is portrayed in Psalm 23 and in Isaiah 40:11, which says: "He shall feed his flock like a shepherd: he shall gather the lambs with his arm, and carry them in his bosom, and shall gently lead those that are with young" (KJV). As set forth so beautifully in Luke 15, the good shepherd is never content with just a favorable percentage of the flock. He is not even content with ninety-nine. No, his entire concern at the moment seems to be for the one who is lost, strayed and out of place. Computers want to reduce us to numbers; some factions look at people as so many herds or numbers; wars refer to casualties lost, but Jesus, the good shepherd, sees the worth of one human being—an eternal soul. In the parable of the lost sheep, Jesus, the good shepherd, is saying that all heaven's angels are turned out to find one lost person.

You see, the good shepherd gives his life for the sheep: "He is brought as a lamb to the slaughter, and as a sheep before her shearers is dumb, so he openeth not his mouth" (Isa. 53:7*b* KJV); "He hath poured out his soul unto death: and he was numbered with the transgressors; and he bare the sin of many, and made intercession for the transgressors" (Isa. 53:12 KJV). That is why he is called the good shepherd. When Abraham said to Israel: "My son, God will provide himself a lamb for a burnt offering" (Gen. 22:8 KJV), he foreshadowed the time when God's spotless lamb, the good shepherd, would become the one and only, final sacrifice for all people.

Suggestions for Worship

Call to Worship: "I am the good shepherd: the good shepherd lays down his life for the sheep" (John 10:11 NIV).

Prayer of Invocation: Our Father, we have come to your holy temple to affirm, to proclaim, and to celebrate life. We believe! Help our unbelief! Amen!

Prayer of Confession: O Lord, we have been shown that you are through loving persons who affirm the faith. Forgive us for failing to show and to give our love in return. You are known to us through trusting acts that proclaim the truth. Forgive us for not trusting you. You are known to us through the joyous story of Christmas, the good news of your resurrection, which allows us to celebrate life through your Son, Jesus Christ. Forgive us for not sharing your Son, the good shepherd, with others. Amen.

Suggested Hymns: "Stand Up and Bless the Lord"; "He Leadeth Me: O Blessed Thought"; "In Heavenly Love Abiding."

Pastoral Prayer: Our Father, we are thankful for your abiding presence in every time of human need. Even though we dwell temporarily in life's valleys amid shadows, we know that our journey does not end in a darkened valley. Through your steadying power, we are able to pass through life's depths and emerge victorious on the other side. Just as it always takes light to make a shadow, so also we are confident that beyond hardship, disappointment, tragedy, and even death, there lie the light and reality of eternity. For the vision of a clear dawn and the assurance of a brighter tomorrow, we give you thanks.

We are grateful for your presence with us not only in times of crisis but also in times when we experience joy and when our cup overflows and we partake of life in all of its fullness. For your indwelling Spirit, at the time of our rebirth and entrance into salvation, we give thanks. For the continuous witness of your Spirit, which causes us to experience gladness and to approach each new day with expectancy, happiness, and love, we give thanks. Amen.

APRIL 28

□

Fifth Sunday of Easter

Keeping close to the presence and power of the risen Christ is essential for both individuals and the church.

The Sunday Lessons

The Psalm: Psalm 22:25-31.

Acts 8:26-40: An Ethiopian eunuch, in the service of his queen, had been to Jerusalem to worship. Prompted by the Holy Spirit, Philip gently confronted the man, interpreted the scriptures, and shared the gospel. The Ethiopian was converted and baptized. Philip asked, "Do you understand what you are reading?" (v. 30). And the man answered, "How can I, unless someone guides me?" (v. 31).

I John 4:7-12: Love is the goal of the Christian life. It begins with God, who is the very essence of love. "Love is of God . . . God is love" (vv. 7-8). The manifestation of God's love is "that God sent his only Son into the world, so that we might live through him" (v. 9). Love is the test for determining one's knowledge of God. "He who does not love does not know God" (v. 8).

John 15:1-8: The vine, the branches, the vine dresser, and fruit bearing are the images John employs to emphasize the necessity of remaining in a close relationship with the risen Christ. "As the branch cannot bear fruit by itself, unless it abides in the vine, neither can you, unless you abide in me" (v. 4). The fruit of abiding discipleship is love. This passage is a part of Jesus' farewell discourses.

Interpretation and Imagination

"Let's stay in touch," she said, and both of them knew the way to do it. There would be phone calls, letters, and remembrances on special days, sharing the joys and sorrows of life in small things

115

as well as great. Meetings would be arranged whenever possible. Lunches would last more than an hour. Every separation would know the promise of being together again.

Yet, keeping close is not an ordinary development in most relationships. Children grow up and move away. Friendships are displaced by other friendships. Changes cause us to be different persons. Demanding responsibilities limit the time we can be together. We move to new positions, new churches, new communities. Staying in touch requires a special grace and a compelling desire.

The image of the vine and the branches speaks plainly concerning the importance of staying in contact, "abiding." The life of the branch and the fruit of it depend absolutely on the vine. The way of abiding, or staying in touch with the life-giving power of Christ, is not as obvious.

The text provides no practical guidelines, such as quiet solitude, meditation, spiritual guides, support groups, word and sacrament, shared mission, or public acknowledgment of rituals. It speaks, rather, of deeply felt need and full satisfaction as the motivating influences that cause us to want to be one with the risen Christ. Reminded of our need, warned of dire consequence, and assured of life in Christ, we are left with the promise: "If you abide in me, and my words abide in you, ask whatever you will, and it shall be done for you" (John 15:7).

NOT BY YOURSELF, YOU CAN'T

John 15:1-8

A SERMON BY R. CARL FRAZIER, JR.

On the back door of our house hangs a grapevine wreath. You know the type: a wreath made from the intertwining and encircling of branches from a grapevine. My family is very fond of it, and we decorate it with all types of accessories. At Christmas it is festooned with red ribbon and bows; in the spring and summer, fresh greenery is added; during autumn months it is adorned with autumn colors. In many respects, the wreath has become an important addition to the household, for it helps us mark the comings and goings of the seasons.

Yet, there is something about that wreath that bothers me—something I can't quite put my finger on. Maybe it is the memory of Uncle Waylon's scuppernong vine.

As a child, I had the normal childlike resistance to visiting great-aunts and great-uncles who smelled heavily of perfume and after-shave and who wanted, it seemed, to do nothing but hug you and comment on how big you'd grown since the last visit. But going to Uncle Waylon's was a little bit different. We had to suffer through our aunt's interminable hugs, to be sure, but we would soon be set free to head for the scuppernongs. There we would play and hide and, occasionally, be so bold as to sneak a few as compensation for having to visit relatives. However, we knew to be careful, for the scuppernong vines were Uncle Waylon's pride and joy. Of all the plants in his garden, the scuppernong vine was accorded special honor. It was the scuppernong vine that was pruned and trimmed with special care. It was the scuppernongs that Uncle Waylon offered his first morning greeting in his gravelly voice (much, it seemed to my child's mind, as God must have greeted the Garden of Eden). It was the scuppernongs that were planted so that they could be seen from his chair in the den. And it was the scuppernongs that have ever since shaped my image of what a grapevine is: green, full, and fruitful.

Perhaps that is what bothers me about the grapevine wreath on our back door. Compared to my uncle's scuppernong vine, that wreath looks dead. It does not seem to matter how much we dress it up—how many ribbons or bows or boughs are added. It is dead, lifeless, barren. Grapevines are meant to bear grapes, not hang on doors.

Jesus must have known something of grapevines and the difference between one that pleases and one that has lost its vitality. He invites those who would follow him, those who would be his disciples, to consider the image.

> Abide in me, and I in you. As the branch cannot bear fruit by itself, unless it abides in the vine, neither can you, unless you abide in me. I am the vine, you are the branches. He who abides in me, and I in him, he it is that bears much fruit, for apart from me you can do nothing. (John 15:4-5)

Apart from me you can do nothing. The words echo as a reminder that life off the branch becomes death. They signal an invitation—an invitation to depend on Christ for life and grace and to accept the fact that, away from Christ, we are incapable of being the church.

Dependency is an uncomfortable state for us to be in. We are not, as a general rule, a people who enjoy dependency. We'd much rather do things for ourselves. Watch a child trying to master a jungle gym for the first time. Watch a teenager driving a car with no one else for the first time. Watch a surgical resident perform surgery for the first time. On each face, one can witness pride, a growing sense of maturity, and independence. Offers for help may well be rejected. Yet, if you are the baby-sitter, you hope someone has taught the child about safety and caution. If you are a driver coming from the opposite direction, you hope someone has taught the teenager traffic rules. And if you are the patient, you hope and pray someone has taught the resident how to operate. We enjoy our independence, but we devoutly hope that others are dependent.

So, in spite of declarations of independence, we do need others. How much more, then, do we need an Other in the life of faith? The truth of the gospel is that in the face of our do-it-yourself lives, we are called to an abide-in-me faith. Beneath our bold assertions that "I can do it!" we hear the whisper of "not by yourself, you can't." We may believe that we are autonomous, but Christ calls us to live in relationship with him—or not to live at all. Jesus' last word to the disciples is a reminder that fundamental to the life of faith is life in him, connected to him as a branch to a vine and drawing from him nurture, sustenance, and strength. Jesus' word of good-bye contains a caution that the church that seeks to exist apart from him will find itself without voice, without message, without power. It will be barren, little more than an adornment eventually to be cast aside and abandoned.

Yet, the last word is not without hope, for Jesus' farewell instructions also remind us that the people who find their lives in his life will be people with voice, with message, with power. Those who seek to live with him will bear fruit and will prove to be his disciples.

The invitation of the gospel is to abide and to recognize that faith comes as a gift, not as that which we can do by ourselves.

The call is to live in relationship with Christ—a relationship made possible by the power of his resurrection and the abiding presence of his Spirit. The summons is to a daily and constant devotion, to attend to the means of grace as signs of that relationship—to prayer, to sacrament, and to service.

The promise is that if we accept the invitation, we will find life; that if we will abide in him, we will find that we are empowered to be the people of God in the world and will bear fruit that befit the kingdom; that when we bear in our lives the mark of Christ's life—his cross, his suffering, his resurrection—God will be glorified, which is, after all, our chief end. The promise, if we will claim it, is that our lives will grow from his—as a vine does from a branch.

A congregation is like a branch of a grapevine—either like the one at my house or like the one at my Uncle Waylon's. The difference is that one just decorates a door, while the other one bears grapes.

Suggestions for Worship

Call to Worship:

> All the ends of the earth shall
>   remember
> and turn to the Lord;
> and all the families of the nations
>   shall worship before him.
> For dominion belongs to the
>   Lord,
>   and God rules over the nations.
> (Ps. 22:27-28)

Prayer of Confession: Gracious God, you have planted us as a vineyard on a fertile hill and have cleared from before us stones and weeds, all that would hamper our growth. Yet, our lives have borne wild grapes, and we have done that which is not pleasing in your sight. Prune from our hearts, we pray, all envy, malice, jealousy, and fear. Graft in their place the love of your name and the faith of true religion. This we ask in the name and Spirit of our Lord Jesus Christ. Amen.

Suggested Hymns: "All Praise to Thee, for Thou, O King Divine"; "I Need Thee Every Hour"; "Blest Be the Tie That Binds."

Pastoral Prayer: Holy God, as a branch withers and dies apart from the vine, so do we wither and die apart from your presence. As the branch finds life and sustenance in the vine, so do we find our lives and sustenance in you. We pray that you would remind us this day of our connectedness.

Remind us that we are joined with you through the gift of Jesus Christ and the abiding presence of your Holy Spirit. Remind us that it is from that covenantal relationship that we find the power, the strength, and the grace to do your holy will and to be your holy people in the world.

Remind us that through Christ we are bound to our brothers and sisters in the Christian community. Grant that your church, in this place and throughout the world, may find in its life those expressions of unity which reflect the unity within you.

Remind us of our solidarity with your whole creation: those who hurt, those who are lonely, those who are oppressed, those who are poor, those who are sick. Grant that our lives, rooted in your life, may bear the fruits of solace, companionship, freedom, charity, and grace, which are reflective of your kingdom.

This we pray in the name of Christ, the true vine, who brings life to those who abide in him. Amen.

MAY 5

□

Sixth Sunday of Easter

Love and obedience are brought together in these lessons, which speak of slaves and friends.

The Sunday Lessons

The Psalm: Psalm 98.

Acts 10:44-48: Following Peter's sermon in the house of Cornelius, the "Holy Spirit fell on all who heard the word" (v. 44). Jewish Christians were amazed that Gentiles could experience such an outpouring. The pouring of the waters of baptism followed. "Can any one forbid water for baptizing these people who have received the Holy Spirit just as we have?" (v. 47).

I John 5:1-6: John's favorite themes crowd into this passage: one who believes, one who loves, one who obeys, one born of God, one who overcomes the world. "And this is the victory that overcomes the world, our faith" (v. 4). We may know that we are numbered among God's faithful children through the tests of love and obedience. "His commandments are not burdensome" (v. 3).

John 15:9-17: The new commandment to love one another (13:34) is considered again following Christ's promise of "my love" and "my joy." The measure of our love for others is "as I have loved you" (v. 12). Friends are contrasted with servants: "The servant does not know what his master is doing" (v. 15). The initiative remains with God. Obedience, love, and joy begin with God and are given to the world through Christ. "All that I have heard from my Father I have made known to you" (v. 15).

Interpretation and Imagination

"Stop your grieving," we say. "Don't cry anymore. Be happy!" Yet, even as we say it we don't expect emotions to obey orders.

121

Hard pressed to remain in command of our own seething passions, we don't set out to command the emotions of others.

"Stop your fighting," the preacher says. "Don't hate anymore. Love one another!" And the preacher has a text for the message: "This is my commandment, that you love one another." Commandments, however, are more often disregarded than they are obeyed. Paul testified to that fact. Can one command love?

We may say it gently, "You ought to love your neighbor"; or scream it selfishly, "You don't love me!" implying that you should. Demand love and justice in the streets, the schools, the courts, the church—but the command to love needs something more.

That's what makes Jesus' reference to servants and friends so important in relation to his new commandment. Servants are required to obey. Friends are offered privilege and invitation. They aren't given orders. Yet, to be one with Christ, friend of Christ, is to be like him, and he has chosen to be a servant (see John 13).

He has called us to be friends and then servants: "I chose you and appointed you." In Christ the two opposites, love and obedience, come together, and their test is one—that you love one another. His command sets me free even as it binds.

READING THE FINE PRINT

John 15:9-17

A SERMON BY R. CARL FRAZIER, JR.

The offers seem to come daily in the mail: "You may have already won a *free* car (or a cruise or a television or a boat or whatever)," they say. It is exciting—getting something free. Exciting, that is, until you read the fine print: "You may have already won a free car *if* you will only come tour our resort (only one car to be given away; everyone else will receive a complimentary travel clock)." And excitement wanes into disappointment or cynicism.

It is different in church, however. Here we come and expect to find something offered for free. Grace distributed at no cost. The love of God doled out unconditionally to everyone passing by. If this is so, why is the Gospel lesson for today so full of conditions?

If you keep my commandments, you will abide in my
love. . . . You are my friends if you do what I command
you. . . . This I command you, to love one another. (John 15:10,
14, 17)

Just what is happening here? Jesus seems to be placing
conditions on grace. It certainly appears from a quick glance at
the text that a relationship with Christ and the gift of his love are
predicated on obedience. Yet, we object in our best theological
voices, the love of God does not depend on human obedience;
the offer of grace is free. Our relationship with God is initiated
out of God's love for us, not from our desire to save ourselves.

Yes, but. . . . The conditional phrase is present in the
beginning, the middle, and the end of the text. Yes,
but. . . . The text makes it clear that something is expected.
Yes, but. . . . There always seems to be a yes, but. . . . Even
here we need to read the fine print.

Maybe the conditions are so unsettling because we have failed
in the past to read the fine print in the life of faith. Every
covenant has them. Maybe "Christian" has become too much
like a label worn like a badge of honor, rather than a style of life.
For many, faith has cost little, particularly when placed next to
the blessing to those who "lay down their lives." Few of us go so
far or pay so much. Unfortunately, the truth is that what costs us
nothing is of little value to us. We value those things in life that
are expensive.

Who among us buys an expensive pet for companionship and
refuses to feed it? Who buys a new house and neglects its care
and upkeep? What loving parents have a child and fail to provide
him or her with nurture and care? In the same way, then,
discipleship has a price tag if it is valued. And the price is an
abiding relationship; the cost is that we receive the gift—and
honor the giver.

Christ asks for a mutuality of love from those who would bear
his name. Love is both the invitation for keeping the
commandments ("if you love me") and the essence of them ("love
one another"). It is because we love Christ that we obey
him—and what he commands that we do is love.

This begs the question of whether love can be commanded. It
would seem not—at least not love as the stuff of romance novels

and happy-ever-after endings, or as a warm feeling of affection for someone or something, or even as the love spoken of when a child is commanded to "eat all your peas and love it" or to "go hug Aunt Agatha and tell her that you love her." One simply cannot command that kind of affection and feeling.

The Gospel commands that we love, however, and implies that such a love can be willed. Our problem may be one of language; we have one word to express that for which the Greeks had three. The love that is commanded here is more than feeling or emotion or affection. It is a love that is active, one that can be willed, for it transcends the level of feeling and occupies the place of doing. It is the love seen in the faces of hospice volunteers, in the eyes of tutors helping children learn to read, and in the hands of those who work in soup kitchens and clothing closets. It is the love that takes a meal to a bereaved family weeks after the funeral and stays to listen to their hurt. It is a love that embodies the heart of God "who so loved the world that he gave . . . " Such a love can be commanded, and such a command can be obeyed.

There is more to the fine print, though. The command and the promise are not for just anyone. Christ abides with those who abide with him, with those who possess the spirit and love that God commands. The gift is evidenced in those who received it—and are willing to bear its price. Those who are his friends are those who are the world's servants—the ones who see God's love and reflect it. Only they can truly sing:

> Love so amazing, so divine,
> Demands my soul, my life, my all.

Augustine once wrote that it is "love that separates the saints from the world." So it is. That's the fine print of the Gospel; that's the price.

Suggestions for Worship

Call to Worship:

> Make a joyful noise to the Lord, all
>   the earth;
>   break forth into joyous song and
>   sing praises!
> (Ps. 98:4)

Prayer of Confession: Most merciful God, you call us to love you with all that we are and all that we have and to love our neighbors as well. We confess before you our failure to devote our lives to you and our reluctance to love our neighbor. Create in us new and loving hearts, that all we say and do may be pleasing in your sight, and express the love of your Son, our Savior, Jesus Christ, in whose name we pray. Amen.

Suggested Hymns: "Come, We That Love the Lord"; "Lord Jesus, I Love Thee"; "Trust and Obey."

Pastoral Prayer: Loving God, we live in a world marked, it seems, by an absence of love. Where there should be concord, there is strife; where there should be harmony, there is dissension; where there should be love, there is hatred. Voices of calm and peace are drowned among the shouts of chaos and confusion. Even the church bears on this life the marks of dissidence and discord. In the face of such tumult, we turn to you, who offers us life and grace.

As Christ has loved us and laid down his life for us, so enable us to love others. Fill our lives with the Spirit that empowered him, that we may share in his ministry of reconciliation in the world. Open our eyes, that we may look upon the world with Christ's vision and see the needs of our sisters and brothers. Open our ears, that we may hear with Christ's ears their cries of pain and hurt. Open our hearts and hands, that we may respond with Christlike compassion and bring your love to bear in a hurting, confused world.

By the power of your love at work in the world, bring to pass the day so long awaited, when all people will live in harmony and the human family will be united under your sovereign rule. And grant that we, who would be a society of your friends, may answer your high calling to serve toward that end. Amen.

MAY 12

□

Seventh Sunday of Easter

Sent forth into the world, Christians are called to be centered in Christ, one with him and one with the Father.

The Sunday Lessons

The Psalm: Psalm 1.

Acts 1:15-17, 21-26: Peter proposed that the eleven remaining disciples choose someone who had been with them the whole time to replace Judas. They prayed, cast lots, and the lot fell to Matthias.

I John 5:9-13: We accept humanity's testimony, but God's testimony is greater. God's testimony was made known through his Son. Being united with Christ through belief in him, we have eternal life. "He who has the Son has life" (v. 12).

John 17:11b-19: Jesus' farewell discourses were directed to the disciples. In these verses, he addresses God. Christ's prayer for those who will remain in the world, hated by the world, is that they may be kept from evil and sanctified (reserved for sacred uses). Christ's mission in the world depends on the faithfulness and purity of his follower's witness.

Interpretational and Imagination

"Surely, when the Master prayed, he met somebody," wrote Fosdick in his great book *The Morning of Prayer*. "He met a Presence that disturbed him with the joy of elevated thoughts."

We readily assume that the disciples were with Jesus in the upper room, with him in an intimate and meaningful way as they shared the last supper together. Jesus spoke of his departure. There is another relationship also evident in the upper room.

126

It is deeper, stronger, better, and more lasting than Jesus' relationship with the disciples who will so soon betray and deny him and run away. This is Jesus' relationship—oneness is a better word—with the Holy Father. After telling the disciples that he will soon be gone from them, the Master prays for those he will leave.

A relatively young mother who knew she was dying said to her pastor, "I'm so afraid. Not for myself. Nor do I fear death. I'm afraid for my children. I hate to leave them alone in this world." Then she prayed for them.

How should one pray for those left in an evil, hostile world? That they grow wise and strong? That they gain many friends and become powerful and wealthy? Should one pray that they be spared suffering, sickness, failure, and conflict? Should one pray that they become well married and well employed?

Christ's prayer for his disciples is that they may be purified, reserved for sacred use, and made one with the Father even as he is one. The best gift of prayer is not that we receive great power and wonderful gifts, but rather that "we establish ourselves in a sense of God's presence" (Brother Lawrence).

Fosdick writes, "Prayer is neither chiefly begging for things, nor is it merely self-communion; it is the loftiest experience within the reach of any soul, communion with God."

CALLED AND CONSECRATED

John 17:11b-19

A SERMON BY KENNETH L. CARDER

Ernest Becker, an anthropologist and psychologist, writes in *The Escape from Evil:*

> I think that today Christianity is in trouble not because its myths are dead, but because it does not offer its ideal of heroic sainthood as an immediate personal one to be lived by believers. In a perverse way, the churches have turned their backs both on the miraculousness of creation and on the need to do something heroic in the world!

Personal sainthood and doing something heroic in the world have given way in this generation to other goals. Psychiatrist Aaron Stern, in his book *Me: The Narcissistic American,* and social critic Christopher Lasch, in *The Culture of Narcissism,* contend that such goals have been replaced with more narcissistic preoccupations. Personal gratification has become a more powerful motivator than the desire for moral and ethical excellence. Getting all we can from the world seems to occupy our attention more than contributing to the world.

What is it that motivates us and gives our lives a motivating center? We seem to lack a motivating center other than self-fulfillment. We have no master capable of moving us toward moral excellence and social responsibility.

Jesus' disciples were facing a transition. Their lives had been held together and given meaning by their commitment to and relationship with Jesus. Now he was facing execution. He would no longer be present as a human companion, encouraging them, teaching them, chiding them, supporting them, holding them together. They were losing their Master. Would they revert back to their fragmented lives? Would they lose their sense of identity as the community of Christ?

According to the Gospel of John, Jesus prayed for his disciples prior to his arrest, trial, and crucifixion. That prayer contains a much needed petition for a generation that is no longer held together by the pursuit of personal sainthood and the desire to do something heroic in the world.

In Jesus' prayer, the disciples, both ancient and contemporary, are reminded that *they have been called and consecrated.* It is really a prayer of consecration of the disciples, a confirmation of their calling as citizens of a new world.

The conviction that one has been called and consecrated, set apart for the fulfillment of a transcendent purpose, has been a driving force for the people of God throughout the ages. The Hebrew people were originated in the call of God to Abraham. Abraham left the security of his homeland and went out in search of "a city not made with human hands." The Hebrews were called and consecrated to be the people of God. They were to be revealers of the divine nature, vehicles of the divine activity. That sense of being called and consecrated, set apart, enabled them to move through the wilderness and toward the Promised

Land. During the Exile, the prophets reminded the people of their calling and consecration; they have been able to survive throughout history partly as a result of that conviction.

Some have interpreted the call as a privilege. The prophets, who themselves felt called and consecrated, reminded the people that the call was to responsibility, not a privilege. It was a call to be a light to all nations, to serve the world and its people.

What kept the early church alive during horrible persecution was their calling and consecration. They were called and set apart to be an outpost of the kingdom of God. Living out that calling was the central focus of the church's existence. Persecution only intensified their conviction that they had been set apart to be agents of God's reconciling, redeeming love in the world.

That, too, is our task. We have not been called as the church to receive special favors from God, even special eternal protection. We have been called to be agents of justice, righteousness, and moral and ethical excellence. The awareness of that calling can enable us to emerge from the moral muddle and narcissism of our day.

John Wesley lived in an age of rampant self-indulgence and moral decay. His ministry greatly influenced the course of British history, and we are the beneficiaries of his committed, disciplined life. John Wesley's experience at Aldersgate Street, when he felt his "heart strangely warmed," was a pivotal event in his life. However, his experience at the age of five may have been an even more determinative one. The rectory in which his family lived caught fire, and little John was rescued from the burning flames. Upon his rescue, his mother exclaimed, "You are a brand plucked from the burning."

Susannah Wesley was convinced that her son John had been spared for a purpose. Wesley was reminded throughout his formative years that God had set him apart for a purpose. That sense of being called and consecrated became the haunting, driving force of his life.

John Wesley first asked the following question at the conference in 1763: "What may we reasonably believe to be God's design in raising up the preachers called Methodists? A. Not to form any new sect, but to reform the nation, particularly the Church, and to spread spiritual holiness over the land"

(*Minutes*, 1789, Q. 3). That is no less our calling today: To reform the nation, particularly the church, and to spread scriptural holiness throughout the land. We've been called, consecrated by our baptism, to be the people of God.

The sense of calling and consecration leads to several consequences. For one thing, it reminds us that we are accountable to God for what we do with this gift called life.

I grew up in a religious climate of fear and judgment. Obedience to God was motivated by fear of God's wrath and judgment. I bear some scars of such a graceless emphasis. I would not for a moment want to recover that climate.

However, I am concerned that in reacting against obedience motivated by fear we may have eliminated the need to be obedient. We really are accountable to God. We have been called to be the people of God who act like the children of God that we have been consecrated to be.

Recently in our soup kitchen I had a conversation with "Captain," one of our regular participants. I asked him, "Captain, is there something more we as a church can do to improve life for these persons? We surely can do more than provide a meal." Captain's answer was rather startling. He said, "There really ain't much religion can do anymore. You see, religion has lost its control on folks. What I mean is, it no longer controls people from inside their hearts, then we're going be controlled by something outside us." Then he asked this profound question: "If we don't feel responsible to God, then who are we responsible to? And not many of us folks on the street have much to do with God." He then added, "And I doubt many of your church people do either."

Well, he may be right. We need to remember that the great high priest, before his crucifixion, consecrated us in truth. We are accountable to him!

Also, the sense that we have been called and consecrated makes us change agents in the world. Jesus prayed that we would not be taken out of the world but that we would remain in the world, protected from the evil one. Our mission is this world, but our citizenship is in God's world. Paul reflected the spirit of Jesus' prayer. He said to the church at Rome, "Do not be conformed to this world but be transformed by the renewal of your mind" (Rom. 12:2).

We are citizens of another world, God's world, a new heaven and a new earth. God is forever calling us to live for that world within this world. We are called to live now as if God's future has come.

Furthermore, the sense of being called and consecrated brings hope. The message is that God's new world will come! God will triumph! We can stake our lives on it! The One who proclaimed that the disciples would remain in the world has overcome the world. The One who called and consecrated us for a new world has not, and will not, be defeated. The future belongs to the Christ whom the powers of death and sin cannot contain.

We can face the future hopefully and confidently because it belongs to the One who calls and consecrates us. Our destiny is, after all, not the most crucial reality. God's kingdom is what matters most—and that kingdom will come. The triumph of God's kingdom has been sealed. Though the foundations of our lives may crumble, nevertheless the foundation of God's kingdom stands sure. That victory was won in the cross of Christ. The resurrection affirms God's eternal triumph over all evil and death. The One through whom God's victory has been won has claimed and consecrated us as citizens of that new world. Let us live triumphantly toward that world!

Suggestions for Worship

Call to Worship:

> Minister: Come, walk in the way of the Lord with songs of gladness and joy.

> **People:** **Christ is the way, the truth, and the life, both now and for evermore.**

Prayer of Confession: O God, who through Jesus Christ has called and consecrated us as citizens of your new world: We confess our failure to fulfill our calling. You call us toward a world of justice and peace, service and compassion, integrity and faithfulness, joy and hope. Yet, we remain captive to injustice and violence, self-seeking and hatred, expediency and deceit, discouragement and despair. Forgive our wavering trust in and

131

weak commitment to your victory in Jesus Christ. Through your grace, consecrate us anew for the fulfillment of your purposes; through Jesus Christ our Lord. Amen.

Suggested Hymns: "Jesus Shall Reign"; "Love Divine, All Loves Excelling"; "Make Me a Captive, Lord"; "Draw Then My Soul, O Christ."

Pastoral Prayer: Almighty God, who in your infinite confession made us in your own image and ever redeems us as your children, we praise you for creating us with the potential to live as citizens of a new heaven and a new earth, where justice conquers violence, love triumphs over hate, hope drives out despair, and greatness is achieved through humble service.

You have called and consecrated us to be agents of reconciliation in a fragmented world, to be channels of love in a world of hatred and violence, to be persons of integrity and goodness in a world that is entertained by betrayal and seduced by expediency. Through your mercy, forgive our failure to live out our calling; and in your grace, consecrate us anew as children of your kingdom.

Free us, O God, from all that prevents this world from becoming the kingdom of our Lord and your Christ. Shatter our idols, purify our motives, shape our values, mold our relationships, liberate our minds so that our ordered lives will confess the beauty of your peace; through Jesus Christ, in whom we have been called and consecrated as a community of grace and goodness. Amen.

MAY 19

□

Pentecost Sunday

There are many themes in the Pentecost lessons. All of them refer to the Holy Spirit, and they promise freedom, unity, and power.

The Sunday Lessons

The Psalm: Psalm 104:24-34.

Acts 2:1-21: A sound like the rush of a mighty wind, fire touching each of them, and the understanding of foreign tongues were manifestations of the gift of the Spirit. Some mocked ("They are filled with new wine" v. 13), but Peter proclaimed, "This is what was spoken by the prophet Joel . . . I will pour out my Spirit on all flesh . . . I will show wonders in the heaven above and signs on the earth beneath" (vv. 16, 17, 19).

I Corinthians 12:4-13: "For by one Spirit we were all baptized into one body" (v. 13). The Corinthian church was divided by differing views on the gifts of the Spirit. Addressing that confusion, Paul says, "There are varieties of gifts, but the same Spirit" (v. 4). He appeals for unity in diversity.

John 16:5-15: "When the Spirit of truth comes, he will guide you into all truth" (v. 13). Jesus tells his disciples that he is "going to him who sent me" (v. 5). In response to their sorrow, he promises them "the Counselor." When he comes, "He will convince the world concerning sin and righteousness and judgment" (v. 8).

Interpretation and Imagination

The sights and sounds of Pentecost are many and varied. There is the sound of wind—*ruach* is the word in Hebrew. The same word is used for wind and spirit. Sometimes it means the

133

breath of life. Sometimes it refers to a raging desert storm that changes everything when it blows. Sometimes it is the gentle murmur that caused Elijah to cover his face when the Lord God passed by. When Nicodemus wondered about new birth, Jesus said, "Listen to the wind."

There is the appearance of fire. The fire burned, but the bush remained when Moses stood on holy ground. Fire by night led God's children through the wilderness. Fire fell on Mount Sinai when the law was given. It consumed Elijah's altar and sacrifice. And fire came again on Pentecost. Wesley spoke of "painted fire" that appeared as fire but had neither warmth or light.

There is the sound of many tongues. Confusion reigned at the tower of Babel. There was the babble of many languages, and division followed. At Pentecost there were many tongues, but a common understanding. When confusion threatened the church at Corinth, Paul spoke of this remarkable unity once again.

There is the word of truth. Challenges to every teaching and to its witnesses always abound. The need for an authentic word and a final authority is always present. John's Gospel proclaims that the truth of God revealed by Christ is convincingly supported by the Spirit.

There is the evidence of power. Recently, I watched a young stallion run bold and free across a broad pasture. Every step exploded with grace and power. An old ranger remarked, "Sure wish I had some of his fire."

The disciples, once timid and confused, the apostles, so often doubtful and hesitant, received power on Pentecost, and the church, bold and free, was born.

LET THE SPIRIT LOOSE

Acts 2:1-21

A SERMON BY JAMES C. CAMMACK

On the day of Pentecost, the Holy Spirit came as a strong wind and as a flame, and each one present understood the gospel in his or her own language. They asked in amazement, "What does this mean?"

To the Jew, Pentecost was the celebration of the Feast of Harvest, which came seven weeks—or fifty days—after Passover. It was a celebration of the end of the barley harvest and the beginning of the wheat harvest. Later, Pentecost became a celebration of the giving of the law to Moses at Sinai. At this Harvest Festival, the Jews gave a peace offering of two yearling rams.

To the Christian church, however, Pentecost had an entirely different meaning. Pentecost was the fiftieth day after the resurrection of Jesus—the exciting day when the Holy Spirit was poured out on the people and his presence was made manifest by wind and fire. In the later history of the Christian church, Pentecost became "Whit Sunday," a season of rejoicing because of the risen Lord and the outpouring of his Spirit.

"When the day of Pentecost had come, they were all together" (Acts 2:1). This statement should still have meaning for the Christian church. All believers were together in one place. At the beach? On the golf course? Trying out a new boat? No! The church was all together in eager, expectant prayerful fellowship, waiting to see what God would say to them. They had gathered because they needed one another. They drew strength from one another. They had gathered because they had expected God to pour out his power on them.

Churches do not have spiritual power just because they are full of people. But no church can be powerful that is empty! One of the strongest assurances of God's presence is the togetherness of believers. Outsiders will never become indifferent to the church until the church becomes indifferent to itself. A half-empty church on the Lord's Day is a blatant denial of God's power to draw his people together.

On my way to church one morning, I passed another church that had an outdoor sign that read: "Visitors Welcome—Members Expected!" That is putting it bluntly, but the motivation for church attendance is not from the outside. It is from the inside. Until Christians feel compelled to be together out of need and love for one another, no force on earth can compel them to attend church—not even a "Members Expected" sign on the church lawn.

Notice also that believers were present. What draws unbelievers to church? Chandeliers? Comfortable pews? Lovely flowers? Compatible friends? No! Unbelievers are present in our churches today because we bring them. Very few people drift into church. Most are brought by someone who cares about their spiritual need.

Recapture the picture of the first Pentecost. There was a noise like the sound of rushing wind. Tongues of fire settled on each believer present, and "they were all filled with the Holy Spirit" (Acts 2:4). The miracle of Pentecost was more than the presence of God. God is always present where believers gather. The miracle of Pentecost was the visible expression of his presence. They were all excited because each of them heard the good news of the gospel in his or her own language. These people were from every section of the Mediterranean area, from Cappadocia, from Mesopotamia, from Asia, from Africa, even from Rome. There were Jews from Crete and proselytes from Arabia. They came from everywhere, and the miracle was that each heard the gospel in his or her own language.

This miracle of Pentecost needs repeating. The church needs to speak the gospel in a language that the world will understand. The cynic needs to hear the story of faith and childlikeness. The rebel must come to terms with God and know the joy of victory through surrender. The outcast must be spoken to in the language of love. The lame, the blind, the halt must be offered the healing presence of Christ. Nothing less than the Spirit of God can make this possible, and nothing less than Spirit-filled Christians can witness good news like this to an alienated world.

The task of the church is to let the Spirit loose in the world. The world is full of hungry-hearted persons who are tired of our clichés and are turned off by our apologetic approach. If the Spirit is to be let loose on the world, the Spirit must speak with authority through our lips, must work with power through our weakness, must do the miraculous in the lives of ordinary persons who have an extraordinary commitment to Jesus Christ.

What has the Spirit to say to our age of technology? The Spirit is saying, "You have achieved mightily. Has it brought you peace? God has revealed to you the secret of the atom, and you have made a bomb. God has opened for you the exploration of space, and one noisy atheist has browbeaten the American public into embarrassed retreat. God may not be "out there," but the awesomeness of God's creation gave the astronauts a new dimension of wonder.

During the rebellious 1960s, we went through an age of cynicism. "Bring down the curtain! The farce is done!" the cynic of another day once said. The mood of this past decade makes the language of that generation almost current. The sixties were a decade of frustration. "We are living in a post-Christian era," we were told. The sixties were a decade of rebellion. "God is dead," our youth cried, and with this puny announcement they felt they had done away with the Almighty. The decade of the sixties was a time of disbelief and desecration. "Down with the establishment" was the battle cry of those who burned libraries and defied laws and traditions. Nothing was sacred to them. They chanted, "Don't believe in a God over thirty." One bumper sticker read, "God Is a Tired Old Man," as though God could be thus summarily dismissed. Paul's word to the sophisticated Corinthians strikes at the heart of our problem today: "My message and my preaching were not with wise and persuasive words, but with a demonstration of the Spirit's power, so that your faith might not rest on men's wisdom, but on God's power" (I Cor. 2:4-5 NIV). From the rebellious sixties, through the brazen and blasphemous seventies, we have emerged into an age of technology that seems to have need of no god.

But with all our learning, we are still needy. We still have broken hearts. Heart transplants cannot eradicate that problem. We are still in bondage to habits, ignorance, and sin. Science has not solved those problems.

My brothers and sisters, our healing and enlightenment can be done only in the power of the Spirit! "Not by might, nor by power, but by my spirit, saith the Lord" (Zech. 4:6 KJV). If the Spirit is being bound up by our timidity or our ignorance, we must let the Spirit loose!

Late one night, our phone roused us from sleep. I recognized the voice of a young woman whom I had baptized as a child. "Toby" had been given the advantages of wealth and education. Now married, with three small children, she had suffered a heart attack at the age of thirty-four. For twelve years, she and her husband had had marital difficulty. Her father had died. Her mother was seriously ill. Always an active person, she was now confined to bed for a year. Life had fallen apart for her.

"William," her husband, bathed the children and brought them each night to their mother's bedside to say their prayers.

One night "Melinda," the five-year-old "daddy's girl," looked up at her father and asked, "Why doesn't Daddy have to kneel?" Without a word, William fell on his knees. "Why doesn't Daddy have to say his prayers?" Melinda persisted. That night, they heard him pray for the first time. Toby concluded our phone call by saying, "I guess some good has come out of my illness. What I've been trying to do for twelve years, Melinda did in one night!" Not by might nor by power, but through the lips of a little child, the Spirit was let loose in that family.

When the Holy Spirit came into the life of James Hervey, John Wesley's friend at Oxford, he described the new power in his life as the difference between an arrow and a bullet. All the speed and force of the arrow depended on the strength of his arm as he bent the bow. The new power in his life was like the firing of a rifle: The power was within the bullet and needed only his finger-touch to release it.

So it is with the Spirit in each of us. God is pleading for a new Pentecost in our lives, a plea to let the Spirit loose so that the world around us may hear the good news in the language of its own need.

Suggestions for Worship

Call to Worship:

> Minister: You shall receive power when the Holy Spirit has come upon you; and you shall be my witnesses,

> **People: In Jerusalem and in all Judea and Samaria and to the end of the earth.**

> Minister: And they were all filled with the Holy Spirit

> **People: And spoke the word of God with boldness.**

Prayer of Confession: Grant, we beseech you, merciful God, that your church, being gathered together in unity by the Holy Spirit, may manifest your power among all peoples, to the glory of your name; through Jesus Christ, our Lord, who lives and reigns with you, and the same Spirit, one God, world without end. Amen.

Pastoral Prayer: Good Father of us all, you know the things we need more than we know them ourselves. And you have better gifts to give than we have will or wisdom to receive. You are the creator and sustainer of our whole life. Hear us as we ask again for the gift of days; for seed time and harvest; for blessed sun and blessed rain; for the good earth and daily bread. Care for us who need your care, good Father.

Saving Christ, you know who we are. You have lived among us in our own flesh. You have taught and healed. You have rebuked darkness. You have brought us light. You are for us the way and the truth. You have died our death and broken out the end of every tomb. Forgive our sins, we pray.

Holy Spirit, you are near to us—nearer than our breathing, closer than our hands and feet. You are the source of joy for the whole church. You make us shout and sing. You are the fire that refines and purifies our souls. You are the inspiration of dreams and the reach of visions. You make us one.

Father, Son, and Holy Spirit, blessed Trinity. Amen.

MAY 26

□

Trinity Sunday

We believe in one God (three persons/one nature), whose purpose is always to save.

The Sunday Lessons

The Psalm: Psalm 29.

Isaiah 6:1-8: Isaiah's vision was of God the King holding court in heaven. Made aware of his sinfulness and that his sin was forgiven, he overheard the Lord asking, "Whom shall I send?" (v. 8). The young Isaiah answered, "Here am I! Send me" (v. 8).

Romans 8:12-17: New life in the Spirit stems from a presence that Paul describes as "the Spirit of God [dwelling] in you" (v. 9). Faith is the evidence of this inner presence.

John 3:1-17: Nicodemus, a teacher whose faith was based on signs, asked Jesus, "How can a man be born when he is old?" (v. 4). The birth from above is associated with baptism and the indwelling of the Spirit. It is like the wind: unseen and unpredictable, but you know when it's been there. God's sovereignty surrounds the work of Christ and the power of the Spirit.

Interpretation and Imagination

Josephus, in describing King Herod, called attention to "the diversity of Herod's nature and purposes." When the benefits which he brought to all humankind are considered:

> There is no possibility for even those who had the least respect for him to deny, or not openly confess, that he had a nature vastly beneficent. However, when one remembers Herod's cruel punishment, his ruthless slavery and the death and injury he

brought even to near relatives, one sees his severe and unrelenting disposition, and will be forced to allow that he was brutish, and a stranger to all humanity. (Josephus, *Antiquities of the Jews*)

W. E. Sangster told of a man who was described as being "always the same." It did not mean that the man was uninvolved or uninteresting. Rather it meant that he had a steady and dependable character that was not swayed by every changing breeze. The great Methodist clergyman spoke of our God in like terms, saying, "He's always the same."

There are great differences in the expressions of God's power and love in these lessons for Trinity Sunday. They reveal a God whose majesty fills heaven and earth. They reveal God incarnate, born of flesh, teaching new birth from above. They reveal God as spirit, dwelling in our innermost being. In every case God's purposes are the same—not to condemn, but to save.

OUR THREE-IN-ONE GOD

Romans 5:1-5

A SERMON BY JOHN K. BERGLAND

Some things are compelling and urgent. Some things are seemingly unimportant. There had been a minor accident. It was thirty minutes past midnight, and every house on the street was without a light. Folks were asleep, but that did not deter the young woman who had been driving. She kept the horn blaring until a light appeared. Then she rushed to the house saying, "I'm sorry to wake you, but this is important."

The doctrine of the Trinity, one God in three persons, is important enough to command a special day in the church. Today is that day—Trinity Sunday. Regardless of the great doctrine and the special day, it is safe to assume that most, if not all, of us did not wake up this morning with a compelling interest in the doctrine of the Trinity.

To be sure, there are many interesting ways in which this teaching of the nature of God is expressed. A shamrock with three leaves and one stem is shown to children as a symbol of the three-in-one God. A preschool teacher held up an apple, asking

"How many apples do I have?" "One," the children answered. Then she cut it in two and pointed out three parts, the apple skin, the apple fruit, and the apple seeds. Each was different. Each was the same. Each had a different usefulness.

When the church fathers considered the nature of God, they were confronted with the question of whether there is only one God. Their answer was yes. Is Jesus Christ also divine? Yes, and also different. Is the Holy Spirit divine? Yes, and a very different Presence from the Creator and the Savior. "Then you have three Gods," detractors argued. "No, only one!" professed the fathers—three persons, blessed Trinity. Each is much more than a person and not one bit less than personal.

The church fathers employed the word *ousia* to speak of the shared nature of the Trinity. One might translate the word in a homely way and call it "stuff." The Three are of the same "stuff." Consider the wood stuff of this pulpit, and of that pew, and of that door. All are the same; yet, all are different.

At a baptism, the Trinity is named: "I baptize thee in the name of God the Father, the Son, and the Holy Spirit." The marriage service includes a ring vow and the giving and receiving of rings that symbolize to all a union made before God. The vows are sealed in "the name of God, the Father, the Son, and the Holy Spirit." The historic creed familiar to the entire church unites us in saying: "I believe in God the Father, maker of heaven and earth . . . I believe in Jesus Christ his only Son, our Lord . . . I believe in the Holy Spirit."

Yet, one thing continues to haunt me. The whole concept of the Trinity is confusing enough to provide an interesting puzzle but not important enough to be compelling. "So what?" we ask. "Is it important?" Yes!

After forty years in the ministry, I have learned that persons who lose hope die. Sometimes it is said that as long as there is life there is hope. Turn it around and the statement is surely true: "As long as there is hope there is life." Have you ever known a man with all hope gone out of him? He's dead when he's still alive. Hope is often born of adversity: "Suffering produces perseverance; perseverance, character; and character, hope. And hope does not disappoint us, because God has poured out his love into our hearts by the Holy Spirit, whom he has given us" (Rom. 5:3-5 NIV).

What, then, is the shape of this hope that does not disappoint? It is to know God and the love of God. Hope is not simply knowing about God. It is knowing Father, Son, and Holy Spirit in a very personal way.

Sometimes I think I know the Atlantic Ocean. I've crossed it several times. I've stood on many of its beaches. Ocean Isle beach in North Carolina is a favorite. I've also seen the Atlantic at Virginia Beach and at Myrtle Beach in South Carolina. I've stood on Atlantic shores in Boston, New York, and Miami. Yet, in every place I have not seen the Atlantic except for a few hundred feet of shoreline and a few miles distant from my little site. I've stood on the near edge of a great ocean. I've been at the near edge of God, too. Have you?

It's almost summertime, and the sea is calling to me again. I'll find my way down to its shores and stand at the edge once again. But the great Atlantic will remain a mystery, too broad and wide to know the whole of it; too awesome and deep to reach the depths of it. So let me always know, let us all know again, that we can no more grasp the reality of an infinite God in these finite minds of ours than we can get the whole sea in a two-gallon bucket.

Still, the mysteries beckon. There are three: the mystery of creation, the mystery of love, and the mystery of communion. There is a reality always just beyond our reach, just beyond our vision, just beyond our understanding that keeps calling us. These are the mysteries that limit our knowledge of God.

Little children ask the questions: Who made me? Who made the world? Who made the sky? Who made God? Why did God make snakes and mosquitoes? Why does everything that lives, die? We may become wonderfully knowledgeable about the created order of God's world; yet, our theories of the beginning and our knowledge of the end are forever shrouded in mystery. The mystery is addressed in our belief in God and so we say, "I believe in God the Father Almighty, maker of heaven and earth." The mystery of creation suggests the first person of the Trinity.

A second mystery that grips me is the mystery of love. Song writers and poets make it the theme of their creations. Storytellers and screen writers offer it as the most frequent plot of the novels and movies that entertain us. Love so ordinary, yet so mysterious—who knows from whence it comes and where it goes? What makes it start? What makes it end? The truest reality in all of life is surely love. It's the best way of all. Love is revealed, lived out, and shown as victory over sin and death in the life, death, and resurrection of Jesus Christ. And so we say, "I believe in Jesus Christ, his only Son, our Lord."

The third mystery that is compelling in its call and claim on human personality is communion. Intimacy and deep knowing are the hunger of our hearts. We long for peace, joy, patience, kindness, goodness—all fruits of the Spirit in every relationship. Yet, how feeble is our own effort to establish peace or to gain patience. The wonderful harmony that results from a unity with God's power and Christ's love is the gift of the Holy Spirit, and so we say, "I believe in the Holy Spirit."

We are nearsighted and unheeding children of God. We are slow to respond to his sovereignty, his love, and his pleading. So, we will always be feeling a bit like orphans in the universe, unloved, unwanted, and unheard.

To know God is to know the shape of hope. Thanks be to God for the mighty revelations that have the church singing today, "Holy, holy, holy. Lord God of hosts. . . . God in three persons, blessed Trinity."

Suggestions for Worship

Call to Worship:

Minister: Since we have been justified through faith, we have peace with God through our Lord Jesus Christ.

People: **Through him we have gained access by faith into this grace in which we now stand.**

Minister: And we rejoice in the hope of the glory of God.

People: **And such hope does not disappoint us, because God has poured out his love into our hearts by the Holy Spirit.**

Prayer of Confession: Father, Son, and Holy Spirit, more than we can know, more than we can conceive, more than we can utter, you are our peace, the source of all our life and love. Come to us in your grace and power today and tune us to join all angels, all saints, all creatures, and all creation in songs of blessing and honor, thanksgiving and praise. Amen.

Suggested Hymns: "Holy, Holy, Holy! Lord God Almighty"; "Jesu, Thy Boundless Love to Me"; "Love Divine, All Loves Excelling."

Pastoral Prayer: Come, Holy Spirit, power divine, with your gifts of freedom. Set us free from sin and guilt. Break the chains of prejudice and tradition. Let us not be slaves to any created thing or bond servants of any fear. Set us free, O Holy Spirit.

Come, Holy Spirit, one and only one. Unite us in your own unity. Cause us to be of one heart and mind. Center us in the common cause of Christ. Quiet the confusion of our clamoring cries. Unite our tongues with those in every age and nation who praise the risen Christ.

Come, Holy Spirit, with your gift of power. Give power to every man and woman who is a witness for the risen Christ. Cause an increase of faith and love. Inspire vision and hope. Heal our sickness. Forgive our sins. Deliver us from evil, for yours is the power. Amen.

JUNE 2

□

Second Sunday After Pentecost

The criteria for leadership and the standards of faithfulness and success are not necessarily measured by appearance, success, and status quo.

The Sunday Lessons

The Psalm: Psalm 20.

I Samuel 16:1-13: The prophet Samuel was commissioned to anoint a new king to succeed Saul. Seven of Jesse's sons were rejected. "Man looks on the outward appearance, but the Lord looks on the heart." David, the youngest, was called from sheepherding to be anointed and "The Spirit of the Lord came mightily upon him."

II Corinthians 4:6-11: Paul's ministry was marked by persecution, hardship, and suffering. There were not many places to celebrate victories. Was his ministry invalidated by a painful career? No! His "being given up to death" enabled the life of Jesus to be manifest through weakness. The treasure is carried in earthen vessels.

Mark 2:23–3:6: Human need overrides sabbath requirements. The disciples picked grain, and Christ healed a man with a withered hand on the day for rest. Pharisees accused Christ of disregarding sabbath laws. "The sabbath was made for man, not man for the sabbath" (2:27).

Interpretation and Imagination

In an age when we choose leaders in ways that are complex and manipulative, can the story of the anointing of King David provide helpful insights? Carefully programmed candidates and

146

big budget media blitzes shape our elections. Legislated quotas for minority and ethnic representations influence our appointments. Standards for excellence are often based on short-term profit and growth. *How shall we surface leadership today?*

George Washington was unanimously elected as the first president of the United States. His character was the singular quality that endeared him to all. Even his enemies admired the sterling character of this great leader. King David's actions were flawed. Almost every heinous sin can be found in his story. Was it not his fear of God and his relationship to God that made him Israel's greatest king? People look on the outward appearances. The Lord looks on the heart.

The lesson from Paul's letter to the Corinthians causes one to reflect on criteria we use to measure success. *How shall we measure our victories?* Paul's life was marked with so much conflict, rejection, suffering, and discouragement that his detractors used his life as evidence that he was not one of God's chosen. Surely God would bless the labors and the life of one anointed. Paul offered up his suffering as a gift of obedience to Christ and service to the gospel. Paul is a wonderful example to persons who find few places to celebrate victories. The standards by which we measure achievement—wealth, comfort, places of honor, and power—are not necessarily standards by which we should measure success. They do not necessarily reflect integrity. They cannot measure faithfulness.

Commitment to status quo may be as limiting to our services in the world as are unworthy standards for leadership and success. Tradition has its blessings. Tradition may also become a burden. Sabbath laws, which required more from life than they could ever return, were subjected to a higher allegiance to life and well being. The sabbath was made for us, we were not made for the sabbath.

DAVID—DARKNESS AND LIGHT

I Samuel 16:1-13

A SERMON BY H. PAT ALBRIGHT

Today we are beginning the story of David, King David, King of Israel. Why go back to the story of David in 1991? That is a fair question, and I shall try to answer it before we begin the story. Granted that the story of David is one of the best stories ever written and in prose that has never been surpassed in any language by any writer, this morning's service is not a class in literature. David is certainly no model of a man, no fit subject for an ethical study. Many of you may have seen Richard Gere in the movie *King David,* with his mighty portrayal of sin and sorrow. There is no gospel in David—David antedates the gospel by over nine hundred years—no story of God's grace, no cross, no sacrifice, no salvation. And above all, David lived a long time ago, in an obscure corner of the world. There is no material in his story for political analysts or commentators as they try to apply their minds to the urgencies and issues of our times. Why, then, present David? Why all the extended references in I and II Samuel as well as in many other books? I will tell you why.

From time to time there appears on the horizon of human events a person who gathers to a focus all the energies and issues of the age as a piece of curved glass gathers to a blazing focus the rays of the sun. Such a man was David. The drama, therefore, of David's life is the drama of life itself—intensified, amplified, glorified to be sure, but the drama of all our lives nevertheless. If we are honest, we can see the reflected image of ourselves, the passions, lusts, ambitions, destiny, all the things that make us good and bad, reflected on the still water of that deep well of life. Behind the drama of David is the figure of the divine dramatist, for this story is set as a crowning jewel in the story of God. Beyond the drama is the figure of the One who fulfilled the story of redemption, who was called the son of David. In this atmosphere and with these overtones, we turn to the colossal figure of King David as the springboard of our thinking and meditating.

Almost with a sense of clairvoyance, Samuel recognized the genius of this once and future king. Abiathur, the author of this amazing story, witnessed the power and glory. Undoubtedly some editing took place, but he wrote the original narrative. He would become part of David's administration in those wonderful years, for he knew David intimately. A summary statement characterizes the rise from shepherd to king with these words: "And the God blessed his servant David."

And then an amazing thing happened in the story. In the time before critical historical writing, kings were thought to be divine. They were treated as gods. This was a time when people believed that human events, and especially the lives of kings, were controlled by supernatural powers in the heavens. Each king had his own star. Out of that time, this story came to us. It came as revelation and redemption because it proclaimed that not only are kings human, but also that this king, King David, the superstar king, was a sinful human just like the rest of us. This history was not fabricated to suit the purposes of the king; it was written to record the errors of the king. We learn that individual persons, not the stars in their courses are in control of their lives.

Our story today is cast in the larger context of I Samuel. Novelist Jerome Charyn, in the recent book *Congregation*, speaks of the book of Samuel as the recording of the history of a tribe that has become tone-deaf. The Hebrews have forgotten how to listen. The Lord is absent from their lives. They lose the Ark to the Philistines. Enter Samuel. He grows into prophet, priest, and judge of Israel. He hears the voice. Samuel becomes the nation. In his old age, he is pressed into anointing the first king of Israel: Saul. After Saul's failure, the Lord has Samuel anoint David, a young, ruddy shepherd boy and singer of songs.

But God looks not on outward appearance. Enter Goliath. The giant of Gath challenges the entire Hebrew nation. Saul shivers along with the rest of the Hebrews when Goliath stands in his armor "with greaves of bronze upon his legs, and a javelin of bronze slung between his shoulders" and says "I defy the ranks of Israel this day; give me a man, that we may fight together" (I Sam. 17:6, 10). And this "child" accepts the challenge of Goliath. This miraculous shepherd-musician, with God on his side, "prevailed over the Philistine with a sling and with a stone, and struck the Philistine, and killed him; there was no sword in the hand of David" (17:50).

The Hebrews have a new champion, and that champion is neither Samuel nor Saul. The new hero is David. The folk authenticate the choice that God makes through his servant Samuel. The people feel adulation for this youth who nicely uses his wits and not his weight. The story reminds us of many "heroes with a thousand faces" who won their victories in life not with bulk, but with brains. Consider all the folk who continue to struggle against great odds and learn that victory comes by faith over fear.

pride in freedom and invent new slaveries. We ask you to help us as we strive for light. We beseech you to shine mercifully in our hearts, that the night and darkness of sin and the mists of error on every side may be driven away, and that all our life long we may walk without stumbling as children of the light and the day. Amen.

Suggested Hymns: "How Firm a Foundation"; "Be Thou My Vision"; "God Is My Strong Salvation."

Pastoral Prayer: Holy God, you have created us with potentials to develop, interests to pursue, dreams to follow, discoveries to make. Forgive us when we allow ourselves to become defeated by discouragements, fenced in by fears, paralyzed by problems. Through worship we pray for wings of hope to make us soar, for vitality to make us come alive again, for power to rise up and walk by faith.

Hear us as we ask to be moved out from the overcast, the fog, the dripping skies of self-pity and self-blame, out into the sunlight of your love. We have roads to walk and hills to climb, songs to sing, love to be shared, days and nights of glory ahead. Glory be to you, O God.

If you will help us, we can make it through Jesus Christ, our Lord. Amen.

JUNE 9

□

Third Sunday After Pentecost

"There is no privilege which you cannot turn into a curse" (Phillips Brooks).

The Sunday Lessons

The Psalm: Psalm 57.

I Samuel 16:14-23: For the next twelve Sundays, the Old Testament readings will come from the story of David in I and II Samuel. Young David's introduction into King Saul's house came when "the Spirit of the Lord departed from Saul" (v. 14). The puzzling words are "an evil spirit from God is tormenting you" (v. 15).

II Corinthians 4:13–5:1: After confessing that he has been afflicted, perplexed, and struck down, Paul shares the source of his strength. The foundation of the apostle's faith is that the god who raised Christ from the dead will raise those who have faith.

Mark 3:20-35: Great crowds followed Jesus, but his family feared he was insane. The parables of 'the house divided' and 'a strong man's house' are followed by the teaching, "whoever blasphemes against the Holy Spirit never has forgiveness, but is guilty of an eternal sin" (v. 29).

Interpretation and Imagination

Throughout Israel's long history of broken promises and unfaithfulness, the prophets spoke of God's steadfast mercy. The story of Saul suggests that such patience should never be taken for granted. "The Spirit of the Lord departed from Saul."

The very thought of it chills one's soul and, like the mention of the unpardonable sin, makes one want to quickly turn the page and put the idea aside. One thing is certain: Saul, who stood head and shoulders above all others at the outset of his reign, became a tragic figure before he finally begged a stranger to kill him.

We may note that the Hebrews tended to ascribe everything that happened, whether good or bad, to God and thus saw God as being responsible for Saul's insanity. We may reason that God allows what God may not approve. Thus we absolve God of responsibility for our ills. (Saul simply reaped what he sowed.) But the sobering idea of being forsaken by God still confronts us.

Phillips Brooks, preaching this text from Samuel, said, "There is no privilege which you cannot turn into a curse. God does love you, and will never cease to love you . . . but His love shall be to you either a spirit of help or a spirit of harm." Brooks saw this to be a doctrine of strength, important to men and women who face "the reality and the solemnity of life." He concludes "I beg you to take this truth. It is not hard and cruel. Let it fill your life. Let it make you serious, brave, thoughtful, hopeful and fearful both . . . feeling already in your obedient souls the power of His everlasting life" (*Visions and Tasks*, Sermon XVII [E. P. Dutton, 1886]).

DANGEROUS LIAISONS

I Samuel 16:14-23

A SERMON BY H. PAT ALBRIGHT

There is no king like King David. The prototype for the kings of Israel, all must stand in his shadow. The Messiah would be like King David, so the prophets said. And to this day most Jewish scholars say that David ranks among the greatest of all Jews.

He was popular and handsome, irresistibly attractive, fatally so to some. But that is another part of this powerful drama. This extraordinary man became famous overnight. One day he was an unknown shepherd boy. The next he killed Goliath and became the hero of Israel. His name was on everybody's lips. His career was skyrocketing.

Sometimes we envy such a person, those of us who have to take the plodding way, and we look upon people like David with secret jealousy. I think we might better pity him. This is a difficult position for a young person to be in, to be taken out of obscurity and set upon the pinnacle of fame. Not many can handle themselves well in such a situation. Our text this morning finds him in that precarious position.

What was the secret of David's success? Was it his ability to kill a giant? It was not altogether that, but something far more subtle. His secret lay in the fact that he captivated everybody by his *charm*. Charm is one of those undefinable, yet unmistakable, things—delicate, subtle, yet always recognizable when you meet it. David could kill a giant, but he could also kill with kindness.

Look at how he caught people in the net of his charm, beginning with no less a person than the king himself. King Saul was one of those unfortunate, complicated human beings who was subject, as he grew older, to moods of melancholy. His cycles of depression became so profound that his friends despaired of him and searched for ways to relieve him. Enter David, a singer of songs.

Imagine the experience for that young man to be taken out of his rather simple environment and thrust into a tent where the king lay on the floor, a psychopathic case of melancholia. David took up his harp and began to sing songs about the heroes of the old days, battle songs, love songs. David played and sang, but nothing seemed to stir Saul; nothing relieved the dreariness of his mood. Then, let us imagine, David in one last, brave effort, abandoned all the songs he had learned and created a new one from the depths of his own heart. We heard him there in Saul's large tent as he began to sing: "The Lord is my shepherd; I shall not want. He maketh me to lie down in green pastures: he leadeth me beside the still waters" (Ps.23:1-2 KJV). The song grew and swelled until it attained a great climax of confidence: "Surely . . . I will dwell in the house of the Lord for ever" (Ps. 23:6 KJV). The king began to stir, to come to himself. He emerged from darkness into light. No wonder Saul loved David.

Yes, David was a charmer. Remember the beautiful story of Jonathan, the king's son who was himself a great hero, fearless in battle. Jonathan loved David with a love that remains a picture of perfect friendship. And Michal, Saul's beautiful daughter, was literally swept off her feet by David's charm and became his wife. Our handsome hero was soon praised in a taunting tune: "Saul has slain his thousands, and David his ten thousands" (I Sam. 18:7). The story says that all Israel and Judah loved David. David's star was definitely ascending.

To his everlasting credit, he behaved well through all this. He was an idol; yet, up until this point, he acted wisely. But David's success was as short as it was sweet. Skyrockets that go up with such splendor always come down, and David's descent was as rapid as his ascent. Saul turned against David, which leads us to a most interesting facet of human nature: Why did Saul, who loved David so much, turn against him?

The reason was simple, Saul was afraid of David. That old demon insecurity prevailed. Saul, you remember, had not been born to the throne. He was chosen because of his prowess, and the throne was often uncomfortable for him. Samuel made Saul even more insecure when he denounced him. Saul's depression frightened him. How long could he endure these mood swings? The war with the Philistines frightened him. Could he bring certain victory? Then along came David, a hero of the people, popular beyond belief, too popular to tolerate in the end. Saul could not allow this free, uninhibited person to rise like the morning sun, an idol of the multitudes. And, most important, Saul was *afraid* of David.

There is a less obvious reason for Saul's fear of David, and knowing human nature as we do, we can see it beneath the surface of Saul's consciousness. Saul feared David because he was the kind of person Saul wanted to be. Saul would have liked to have had the freedom, the flexibility, and the spontaneity of David, but he just did not. People admired Saul, but they loved David. Saul desperately wanted to be loved, and not just admired for his abilities. How tempting it is for us to despise the person we would like to be.

Thus we see one of the most amazing contradictions in life. If we could understand it, we would penetrate a profound mystery of human nature. Saul hated the person he loved. Some call this behavior ambivalence, an evil emotional conflict. We see it between husbands and wives: They love each other, and yet in that love there is a hatred that makes one person want to destroy the other one. We see it in relationships between people of all ages, a fear growing out of insecurity. So Saul "sought to smite David even to the wall with the javelin" (I Sam. 19:10 KJV). This was the ultimate tragedy—love turned inward, destroying not creating, its sweetness turned utterly bitter.

Saul could not be blamed for being what he was, neither can

we blame David for having an extraordinary gift of charm. These qualities are beyond the realm of conscious choice. David, the giant killer, was helpless against this intangible enemy whose name is evil. Evil was what Paul had in mind when he wrote: "For we wrestle not against flesh and blood, but against principalities, against powers, against the rulers of the darkness of this world" (Eph. 6:12 KJV). This is an evil that is deep and irrational. (If you wish to understand this complexity, read best-selling author M. Scott Peck's *People of the Lie,* a scientific view of the demonic.) An enemy much more terrifying than Goliath, this evil is all the more difficult to handle because it is mixed with love.

These battles come to life over and over again, and even though you may not recognize it, there are conflicts like that right here among those who worship here—evil that is too deep for analysis; evil that is too subtle to be comprehended; evil that is dark, irrational, mysterious; a giant that we cannot kill alone.

The story of David is a drama with many acts, a number of them exhilarating. This episode brings us face-to-face with the real dangers of life, dangers of self-deception, dangers that involve the human predicament and powers of darkness that threaten us every minute of our lives. This is grim but true.

As we see the tragic figures of Saul and David opposed in a life and death conflict, our attention is pointed beyond ourselves to the son of David who is the Savior of the world and who alone can come to our rescue in the dark moments of life.

Robert Browning brings to us words of hope through Christ. In his poem "Saul," he portrays David's futile attempts to bring comfort to the king. May his closing lines bring to you a message of love that transcends all evil and infirmities.

> Tis the weakness in strength that I cry for!
>   my flesh that I seek
> In the Godhead! I seek and I find it. O Saul,
>   it shall be
> A Face like my face that receives thee; a Man
>   like to me,
> Thou shalt love and be loved by, forever; a
>   Hand like his hand
> Shall throw open the gates of new life to thee!
>   See the Christ stand!

Suggestions for Worship

Call to Worship:

Minister: Friends, we have come to celebrate!

People: **Worship is the celebration of life. Worship is an expression of that which gives life and holds off death.**

Minister: Our celebration is focused on an event in the world.

People: **For us that one event is that in which God made himself known to his people Israel, in Jesus, and in his church.**

Minister: What joy has come!

People: **Thanks be to God forever.**

Prayer of Confession:

Minister: For lack of hope; for our yielding to despair; for our complacency and fear of change; for being satisfied with the way things are; for the trust we put in war and violence; for the trust we put in wealth and property; for our failure to see signs of hope—

People: **Lord, have mercy upon us. Forgive our sins of omission and commission.**

Suggested Hymns: "O Worship the King"; "The Lord's My Shepherd, I'll Not Want"; "Lead On, O King Eternal."

Pastoral Prayer: Eternal and almighty God, today is the very stuff of life. On this day of worship we see that every single day is a precious gift—every minute is fragile, every hour can be holy. We know that you do see us, all busy with life, running after happiness, running after success, running after gain, pursuing positions, striving, breathless, panting.

Help us in this hour of worship to pause, to slow our pace, to step back from the routine, to take a new look at Jesus Christ, at the cross, at our priorities, our ideals, and our values.

We pray that we will see you in our moments and our days, our sins and our defeats, our hope and our despair, our families and loved ones, our friends and fellow worshipers.

O God, give us the courage to cut out of the lives and liaisons that threaten our spirits, any indulgence that saps our strength of purpose, any doubt that leads us to disobey you. Restore us to health of body, mind, and spirit in the matchless name of the good shepherd. Amen.

JUNE 16

☐

Fourth Sunday After Pentecost

When the old has passed, do not look back with bitterness or regret. Honor the new beginning and keep looking forward.

The Sunday Lessons

The Psalm: Psalm 46.

II Samuel 1:1, 17-27: Both king and prince had fallen. Saul and Jonathan were dead. David laments their passing, but without bitterness or regret. As he honors all that was worthy in the fallen king, he asks that none rejoice in his death.

II Corinthians 5:6-10, 14-17: The apostle, well aware of the life-threatening conflict in which he is engaged, writes: "We are always of good courage" (v. 6). Paul had already experienced life that never ends, and so he was at ease about leaving his body to be "at home with the Lord." The epistle sums up the theme of these lessons: "The old has passed away, behold, the new has come" (v. 17).

Mark 4:26-34: These two parables about the kingdom center on seeds. The first tells of seeds growing secretly. The second refers to the mustard seed, the smallest seed and the greatest tree. Both teach that the new kingdom has begun. It carries its own life force and grows whether we pay attention or not. Though the beginning is small and unimpressive, the end will be glorious.

Interpretation and Imagination

God Knows, a novel by Joseph Heller, is the story of King David told from his perspective. Heller has the warrior, lover, poet king tell all, including what David might really have been thinking and feeling behind the Old Testament events and psalms.

David recalls the death of Saul and his three sons in the battle of Gilboa and tells of the comfort he found in writing the famous elegy found in II Samuel 1:17-27. Then David says: "My term of mourning ending . . . I took stock like an able realist, and discovered myself relieved in some ways that Saul was gone. I could now surge ahead to whatever fate the future held for me."

Andrew Blackwood referred to the same scripture passage when preaching "a wise leader's attitude toward the past." He made the point that David, the new king, kept looking forward. "Then he encouraged the people to forget the failures, the heartaches and the bitterness of the days bygone."

David's lament is a rite of passage. The old is gone, the new has come. Mature Christians don't find fallen leadership an occasion for joy. Life's changes are ruthless. Fruit-bearing years are few at best. When an old apple tree is cut down, appreciation is an appropriate mood even as a new sapling is put in its place.

A tragic auto accident claimed the lives of three distinguished ministers. All were pastors of large churches in the same annual conference. Their successors would need to be appointed. A district superintendent observed sardonically, "I suppose some misguided young preachers will view our loss as their opportunity. Sure hope they don't think it's God's way of moving them up."

Christ wept over Jerusalem and at the same time taught that a new age had come. Sure hope that some misguided folk don't seek the fall of oppressive regimes for personal or political advantage.

GOD IS AT WORK

Mark 4:26-29

SERMON BY J. DANIEL BAUMAN

Arrogance is a popular sin among Christians. We parade our accomplishments, we brag about our churches, and we generally commend ourselves for the slightest acts of normal Christian behavior. We have these "love affairs with ourselves" in public. It is not a pretty sight.

The problem has been around for a long time. Jesus once told a parable that was intended to put kingdom truth into proper perspective and, in the process, ground the pompous and puncture the dirigible of the proud.

The story is quite simple. Jesus likens the kingdom of God to the process begun when we plant seeds. We plant the seed, and then the growth begins, slowly, almost by itself, until the proper time when the crop is harvested.

Two truths are clear. First, growth is beyond our comprehension. Jesus said, "The seed sprouts and grows, though he does not knows how" (Mark 4:27 NIV). The mystery of life is all around us in the garden. One need not understand what is going on in order for the crop to proceed toward harvest. It is both difficult and unnecessary to completely understand growth in the natural realm.

When I was a junior boy in Sunday school, my teacher asked the question, "How is it that a black cow eats green grass, produces white milk that makes yellow butter, which grows brown hair on the head of a blue-eyed girl?" I didn't know then, and I don't know now. And what difference does it make anyhow? The process does not depend on the understanding of the observers.

Even further beyond our comprehension is the miracle that occurs in the life of an individual touched by God. We marvel at the transformation of Saul who became Paul. It is a tribute to the mysterious working of God when a hateful zealot like Saul becomes the tenderhearted evangelist Paul. It is both miracle and mystery. God is still at work, doing things we do not completely understand. Who can comprehend the miracle of God touched, changed lives?

Second, growth is outside of our control. Jesus went on to say: "All by itself the soil produces grain—first the stalk, then the head, then the full kernel in the head" (Mark 4:28 NIV). This parable exposes our tendency toward narcissism. At the same time that we applaud the exploits of Augustine, Luther, Calvin, or Wesley, a contemporary church growth theorist informs us that the pastor is the key to all significant growth in the local church. The result of this is that we develop pedestals for our champions. We all know what happens—ecclesiastical leaders develop messianic complexes and begin to take themselves much too seriously. They become self-congratulatory.

The truth of the matter is that God does what God chooses to do. If God wants to raise up people who call him Father, he will do so. Consider the church in China. Years ago, at the time of the Cultural Revolution, the missionaries fled, leaving behind one million professing Chinese believers. Today, there are perhaps fifty million Christians in China. What a witness to the work of God. He did it. We weren't even around!

God also works when he chooses to work. He does not march to the tune of our tightly orchestrated schedules. God works the way a seed processes. You cannot rush what God wants to do. The conversion of the thief on the cross appears as a spur-of-the-moment decision just prior to his death on Good Friday afternoon. More than likely, he had wondered about Jesus for weeks. Who is he? What can he do? Could he make a difference in my life? George Muller, through an incredible faith in God, regularly placed food on the table at his orphanage in Bristol, England. He witnessed this activity of God, without a missed meal, for over two score years. On the other hand, he prayed for fifty years before he witnessed the conversion of a dear friend. God's timing may not be ours, but he is working.

In Paul's letter to the church at Philippi, he brings together two truths that must always be kept in dynamic tension, for both are true. First, "Continue to work out your salvation with fear and trembling" (Phil. 2:12 NIV)—that is, human endeavor—and second, "For it is God who works in you to will and to act according to his good purpose" (Phil. 2:13 NIV)—that is, the activity of God.

I see two challenges for us that arise out of this potent little parable. First, let us continue to be faithful. This text does not discount the role of human endeavor. Planting (Mark 4:26) and harvesting (v. 29), to say nothing of cultivating, are clearly the works of people. To be sure, the searchlight of scripture fixes upon God, who alone is capable of producing growth. But nothing grows that was not first planted, and nothing is really enjoyed that is not eventually harvested.

Some years ago churches, in close proximity to a major American metropolitan area adopted diverse philosophies. The first congregation decided to stop "pushing" programs. If something is true and necessary, God will keep it alive, they decided. They argued that human endeavor is carnal, whereas

God's work is both spiritual and lasting. The second congregation imbibed heavily of the Protestant work ethic as it applied to their church campus. Pastors and people alike encouraged and stimulated one another and their programs. The results are not surprising. The first congregation has essentially died. It had taken a half-truth and made it the whole truth. The second congregation is thriving. They recalled the word of Paul: "Those who have been given a trust must prove faithful" (I Cor. 4:2 NIV).

The New Testament is generously sprinkled with action verbs—*yield, commit, obey, fight, follow, serve,* and so on. There is no biblical support for Christians who choose to be spectators rather than participants. When the Master returned to his people, he raised the question "What have you done with the opportunity I gave you?" (see Matt. 25). Faithfulness is never to be treated as an abnormality—it is the norm! Vance Havner, the old-time evangelist, frequently intoned, "The church is so subnormal that if it became normal the world would think it was abnormal."

Second, let us celebrate God's faithfulness. Growth is what God does. The early church was a vital organism—it preached the apostolic message, the people lovingly supported one another, praised God and prayed with a room-shaking kind of faith. And we do well to note that "the Lord added to their number daily those who were being saved" (Acts 2:47 NIV). We need to give credit where credit is due.

Suggestions for Worship

Call to Worship:

> God is our refuge and strength,
> an ever-present help in trouble. . . .
> The Lord Almighty is with us;
> the God of Jacob is our fortress. . . .
> "Be still, and know that I am God. . . ."
> The Lord Almighty is with us;
> the God of Jacob is our fortress.
> (Ps. 46:1, 7, 10a, 11 NIV)

Prayer of Confession: Eternal God, forgive us for our frequent fits of pride.

We act so often in complete independence of you. We give the impression that your kingdom is great because we are good. We congratulate ourselves for that which you have done. We fail to see ourselves in the light of Calvary necessity. Thanks, heavenly Father, for your patience with us.

We are unworthy, and you continue to shower your grace upon us. Help us to see ourselves today as you see us: needy and candidates for a fresh touch of your cleansing and restoration. Thanks, O Lord! We need you!

Suggested Hymns: "Doxology"; "We Sing the Greatness of Our God"; "How Great Thou Art"; "To God Be the Glory"; "Let's Just Praise the Lord."

Pastoral Prayer:
Heavenly Father, we praise You!
We praise You for Your acts of power.
We praise You for Your surpassing greatness.
We praise You for what You do and for who You are.
Strong Son of God, we love You!
We love You because You went to Mount Calvary for us.
We love You for providing eternal salvation.
We love You—not because we are naturally lovers—but, because You first loved us and have enabled us to reflect Your love.
Spirit of God, we need You!
We need You to empower our witness.
We need You to enable us to walk righteously.
We need You to direct us into paths that are good, acceptable and perfect.
Lord, there are so many needs among us—
Guide those who are facing mysterious intersections.
Forgive those who carry the heavy burden of guilt.
Comfort those who grieve.
Strengthen those who are weak.
Heal those who hurt.
Hear these our prayers—we offer them in confidence because of who You are.
We pray, in the Strong Name of Jesus Christ,
Amen.

JUNE 23

□

Fifth Sunday After Pentecost

The fact of God's omnipotence does not mean that we have no freedom to choose. It does mean that God will be fully divine and finally in control.

The Sunday Lessons

The Psalm: Psalm 48.

II Samuel 5:1-12: Representatives of the northern tribes came to Hebron and anointed David king. They reminded him of God's promise: "You shall be shepherd of my people Israel" (v. 2). He reigned for forty years.

II Corinthians 5:18–6:2: Reconciliation is the controlling idea. We are reconciled to God (all anxiety and fear are set aside by peace and goodwill) and given the ministry of reconciliation.

Mark 4:35-41: The stilling of the storm is the first of four miracle stories that proclaim Jesus' authority over natural disasters, the demonic, disease, and death. Jesus commands wind and waves, saying, "Peace! Be Still!" (v. 39). After the storm, the disciples were filled with awe, terribly afraid. It was not the storm they feared, but evidence of God acting in their midst: "Who then is this?" (v. 41).

Interpretation and Imagination

"The House of Representatives shall be composed of members chosen every second year by the people of the several states." These words (Article 1, Section 2, Paragraph 1 of the Constitution of the United States) ensure that we will have a major election every two years. They get us into the habit of choosing our leaders and voting for those who will have authority over us.

Old Testament prophets had a different view of government and a way to choose a king. They wanted a theocracy, a political organization in which God is the supreme ruler. Earthly kings could only receive authority from God. For example, the prophet Samuel had been directed by God to choose and anoint David. The people knew it. They reminded David of God's promise as they sought his leadership.

Oliver Cromwell wanted a theocracy for England. John Calvin sought it in Geneva. John Wesley did not think it wise to give authority to the common people. But we believe in democracy—government of the people, by the people, for the people. The idea that all power belongs to God and that God gives some to prophets and a little to kings is foreign to us.

The fact remains, however, that presidents, no matter how popular and powerful, cannot command wind and waves. There is a creative authority that is also the final authority. It belongs only to God. That reality makes one who tries to choose his or her God foolish indeed. Authority that cannot be understood or reduced in any way can only be revered. To be reconciled to such sovereignty and sovereign grace is a nation's highest calling.

THE STORMS OF LIFE

Mark 4:35-41

A SERMON BY J. DANIEL BAUMAN

Dad was driving, and I was praying. Never in all our lives had we seen a storm of this magnitude on Green Bay in Northern Wisconsin. The little twenty-foot cabin boat we were aboard was like a cork on a turbulent river. If Dad drove too fast, we would top the next wave and plunge headlong into the watery trough ahead of us, whereas, if he slowed up, the twenty-five foot wave behind us would flood us with tons of water. Finally, Dad steered us safely into the L-shaped harbor. What a relief! It had been as fearful an experience as either one of us had ever had. If I never again face a storm at sea, I will be a happy man. Storms at sea are harrowing, to say the least.

The disciples knew all about storms. Today's text recounts one of those days on the Sea of Galilee when it was necessary to be rescued by Jesus.

Basically, there are two types of storms in the human experience: those we bring on ourselves and those that come for no apparent reason.

Storms we bring on ourselves are the result of stupidity, foolishness, or outright sin. Jonah the prophet of Jehovah had been called to declare the message of God. Specifically, he was commissioned to go to Nineveh and preach repentance. It was more than the prophet could take. Weren't the Jews God's chosen people? Why offer grace to the Gentiles? In his bigotry he went west when he had been called to go east. He boarded a ship at Joppa and headed for Tarshish. The Lord was not pleased and "sent a great wind on the sea, and such a violent storm arose that the ship threatened to break up" (Jon. 1:4 NIV). Jonah is thrown overboard and spends three days in the tummy of a big fish. He repents and is vomited up on the beach and is recommissioned.

Jonah earned his punishment. He paid the price for his willful disobedience. Paul put it succinctly: "Do not be deceived: God cannot be mocked. A man reaps what he sows" (Gal. 6:7 NIV). Fast, reckless drivers invite traffic accidents. Smokers invite lung cancer. Overeaters invite heart attacks. And sinners invite grave consequences.

Many of life's storms should not surprise us. They come by invitation. It is built into the fabric of life. God doesn't need to send them; we bring them on ourselves.

Some storms come for no apparent reason. Jesus was weary from a long day of teaching. It was time for him and the disciples to get away and find rest. As they traveled by boat a terrible storm broke loose and their boat nearly capsized. The geographical location of the small Sea of Galilee (eight miles long and five miles wide) made sudden, violent storms a rather common occurrence, for it is situated in a basin surrounded by mountains. Storms at night, such as this one, were especially treacherous.

Three principles emerge as this nature miracle unfolds in Mark 4: (1) life is a storm (vv. 35-37); (2) we are not alone in the storms (vv. 38-39); and (3) storms can be times of growth.

Life is a storm. The Galileans were well aware of the situation. Many a fisherman had been plying his trade when the winds suddenly began to whip and the water began to churn. Mark writes:

"A furious squall came up, and the waves broke over the boat, so that it was nearly swamped" (4:37 NIV). There is no apparent cause for this sudden storm in this account. The disciples were not being punished by a troubled God nor had they acted foolishly and brought the storm on themselves. It just came.

This is mysterious business. Wonderful Christian people are not immune from storm. Why does cancer come and pluck a thirty-two year old mother of four out of her home? Why are good people victimized by speeding drunks? Why is a child born with cerebral palsy, blindness, or a faulty heart? Why do tornadoes ravage homes and leave people crippled in their wake? Why? Why? Why? Life has some huge imponderables. We concur with Paul, who said: "Now we see but a poor reflection. . . . Now I know in part" (I Cor. 13:12 NIV).

We are not alone in the storms. The disciples were frightened by the storm. They needed help. Much to their chagrin, "Jesus was in the stern, sleeping on a cushion." (Mark 4:38 NIV). They woke him and asked, "Teacher, don't you care if we drown?" (v. 38). We may assume the answer: "Of course, I care!"

Regardless of the intensity of life's storms, Jesus will be in the boat with us. "Surely I am with you always, to the very end of the age" (Matt. 28:20 NIV). In Psalm 23:4 (NIV), which has parallels to John 10, we read:

> Even though I walk
>   through the valley of the shadow of
>   death,
> I will fear no evil,
>   for you are with me.

Count on it! Our faith may fail, but he will never fail. He is the ever faithful one. We are not alone.

Storms can be times of growth. Jesus addressed the wind and the waves, "Quiet! Be still!" And it was so. Mark adds, "It was completely calm" (4:39) How unique. It usually takes time for calm to return. The difference here? Jesus was the Master!

Jesus now uses the situation to teach a lesson. "Why are you so afraid? Do you still have no faith?" (v. 40 NIV). Storms can become the occasion for God to do a fresh thing in our lives. We need to trust him. The choice is ours.

Some of our Lord's choicest people have struggled with storms. Paul had "a thorn in the flesh" (II Cor. 12:7). The Lord did not answer his prayer for healing, but told his troubled servant, "My grace is sufficient for you" (II Cor. 12:9 NIV). Who can read the story of Helen Keller without knowing something of the power of faith in the midst of life's storms?

When our daughter was five months old, she contracted spinal meningitis. It was a dark time for her and extremely difficult for us. For six weeks, we watched her body respond to heavy doses of medication, daily brain taps, and finally brain surgery. We prayed with a fervor we had never known. What had we done to deserve this?

One day we turned it all over to God. We prayed, "Lord, she is yours. Take her to heal her; we rest in you." The struggle was over. Our daughter is now in her twenties, struggling with the typical limitations of brain damage. All of us made a difficult discovery: God can be trusted in the midst of life's storm. It was hard, but *now* we thank God!

Life is not an extended pleasure trip on a luxury liner that is sailing across calm seas. Life is a journey in a storm-buffeted boat. Storms may come because we were foolish or sinful. For these, there is no excuse. It is the storms that come in the midst of our best Christian intentions that challenge us. Shall we choose to shake our fists in the face of God as we turn bitter? Or shall we put our hand in the hand of the Master and walk through the storm together?

Suggestions for Worship

Call to Worship:

> Great is the Lord, and most worthy of
>   praise.
> Within your temple, O God,
>   we meditate on your unfailing love.
> Like your name, O God,
>   your praise reaches to the end of
>   the earth;
>   your right hand is filled with
>   righteousness.
> For this God is our God for ever and
>   ever;
>   he will be our guide even to the end.
> (Ps. 48:1, 9, 10, 14 NIV)

Prayer of Confession:
Father, we come before you like Isaiah of old—
   In so doing, we discover again Your character—
   You are holy, holy, holy.
As we kneel in Your presence we are struck by our
   unworthiness
      our hands are unclean
      our feet have strayed
      our motives are mixed
      our thoughts have been ungodly
Be pleased, Oh God, to touch our lips, to cleanse our
   hearts, to restore to us the "joy of our salvation."
This we pray for Your glory for our good.
   In the name which is above every name, Jesus the Lord,
Amen.

Suggested Hymns: "Holy, Holy, Holy! Lord God Almighty";
"Hiding in Thee"; "All Hail the Power of Jesus' Name"; "Jesus
Calls Us"; "Alleluia."

Pastoral Prayer:
Our kind Heavenly Father,
   It is good to come apart from all the distractions of
      life.
   It is good to know that You have invited us to come
      boldly with confidence.
   It is good to realize that You know us completely and
      still love us.
Receive our praise this morning
   You are worthy God
   And we adore You!
This has been a difficult week for some.
   Our lives have been buffeted by the storms of
      temptation, financial unrest, emotional upheaval,
      social frustrations and physical sickness.
   We have felt the arrows of attack from the
      world, the flesh and the devil.
   Be pleased to minister Your healing, O great Physician.
We praise You that Your grace is sufficient.
   We have not faced anything that is greater than Your
      provision.

For "greater is he that is us, than he that is in the world."

May we, like the psalmist, discover the privilege of trusting in You, delighting in You, committing our way to You and then finally being at rest in You.

We delight to call You our Father,
Through the merits of Christ,
Amen.

JUNE 30

□

Sixth Sunday After Pentecost

The nature of our God determines the spirit of our worship.

The Sunday Lessons

The Psalm: Psalm 24.

II Samuel 6:1-15: The ark of the covenant was a visible symbol of God's presence. David ordered that it be brought to Jerusalem. On the way, a man named Uzzah reached out to steady it. Having touched the ark, he immediately fell dead. "And David was afraid of the Lord that day" (v. 9). Psalm 24 was part of the ritual used to celebrate the arrival of the ark. The king "danced before the Lord with all his might" (v. 14).

II Corinthians 8:7-15: The Macedonians gave generously to the offering for Christians in Jerusalem, and Paul urged the Corinthians, who excelled in everything, to excel in this gracious work also. Christ is offered as an example. "You know the grace of our Lord Jesus Christ, that though he was rich, yet for your sake he became poor" (v. 9). Reference is made to the manna in the wilderness—nothing left over, but never a lack.

Mark 5:21-43: Mark combines two miracle stories—the healing of the woman who touched the hem of his garment and the raising of a little girl who died before Jesus reached her. A common theme is present in both: all hope was gone. The woman had sought treatment for twelve years without relief. The girl was dead. The response to Jesus' authority over sin and death was fear and trembling: "[She] fell down before him" (v. 33); "They were immediately overcome with amazement" (v. 42).

Interpretation and Imagination

Three texts suggest three different ways by which the power and presence of God were visible among his people. Varying insights produced varied responses—fear and joy, reverence and awe, faith and generosity.

In the Old Testament story of the ark of the covenant, a symbol of God's presence and a source of divine blessing was being brought to Jerusalem. It was untouchable, and the man who unwisely reached out to steady it fell dead. David was afraid of his God that day. Ceremony, ritual, and celebration accompanied the ark to the Holy City.

Touching the untouchable is also evident in the New Testament miracle stories. The woman suffering from an issue of blood was considered unclean. She knew better, but she reached out and touched Jesus. She was healed. A corpse was untouchable, but Jesus took the dead girl's hand and said, "Little girl, arise." Majesty and power are evident in these stories, but their manifestations are more tender, more human, more available.

The Macedonians' gift to poor Christians in Jerusalem also symbolizes the presence and power of Christ in the community of faith. It is not as dramatic and awesome as the ark and the miracles, but it is nearer to our daily life and work. A church that responds to human need in Macedonian terms, "first they gave themselves," demonstrates faith in Christ and a love that is genuine.

HOW TO GET THINGS DONE

Mark 5:21-43

A SERMON BY C. THOMAS HILTON

In a play by Elie Wiesel, Berish, the innkeeper, and his daughter, who has been emotionally damaged by the slaughter of her friends and family, are speaking in the inn. Berish has just come in, and he yells at Maria, "Don't tell me what to do. You're getting on my nerves. The whole world is getting on my nerves."

She responds, "Then you better get yourselves another trade, Mister. Better yet, get yourself another world."

Sometimes I feel like that. Most of the news items are depressing. Nobody seems to want to print any good news anymore. A plane crash here, a nation starving there, a hurricane here, a flood there, an earthquake here, a war there, and on, and on, and on. It's not a very pretty picture, our world in 1991.

Twelve hundred years ago, the conquering Muslim majority allowed a small group of Christians to remain in Spain. The Mozarabs, as they were called, became the object of many cruel acts and blatant discrimination, even persecution. A spiritual giant, experiencing those difficult times, shared his prayer life with us when he wrote:

> Lord God, we lift to Thee a world hurt sore.
> Heal it and let it be wounded no more!

We live again in a world "hurt sore." We live in a world that is looking for and that desperately needs healing. We need someone who can make us whole, who can make us healthy, who can put us in touch with our spiritual roots, so that our tree of life isn't diseased and that we may bear the spiritual fruit we were meant to bear. We can't get ourselves another world; this is the only world we have. So we had better live here as the best people we can be and learn here how to be instruments of God's healing.

The anonymous, faceless woman in the crowd in our scripture lesson was interested in being made whole. Her particular problem was manifested in a blood disease that had bothered her for twelve long years. This didn't seem to be a terminal illness, but a chronic disease that she was having to learn to live with. Twelve years is a long time to struggle with a physical difficulty, especially when you figure that people did not live as long then as we do now. Twelve years, if adulthood commenced around the age of thirteen, could be one-third of one's whole adult life. Have you ever been sick for a long time? Have you ever felt weak, or been in pain, and had to struggle every moment of every day and every evening with discomfort? It can wear you down rather quickly. Pain for a week is a struggle. Pain for a month is more than a struggle. Pain for a year? For twelve years?

One of my associate ministers in another church was an older gentleman who became ill. He had experienced heart difficulties for a long time. As a matter of fact, that's why he was now an associate. He had been senior minister of a large church, but his heart acted up, and his doctors told him that he would live longer if he would get out from under the daily pressure of being the senior minister. Toward the end of his life, he was in much discomfort. I'm convinced that the daily pain, the daily struggle with ill health, the daily round of drugs and X-rays and medical appointments and the financial drain finally did him in. He just decided that as a man of faith, he had had enough, and he let go and let God. He wasn't going to struggle with this health problem for twelve years.

Fortunately, the woman who had the issue of blood did not give up hope, but she did seem to have every reason to do so. She "had suffered much under many physicians" (Mark 5:26). Matthew and Mark both refer to her difficulties with physicians, but Luke, who was himself a physician, does not mention this unfortunate aspect of the story. Medicine then was not the highly skilled science that it is now. It was half folk medicine and half "mumbo-jumbo." Ill persons probably suffered at the hands of many a physician in those days, and especially if they were ill for twelve years.

Not only was her health poor, but her finances were exhausted as well. She had no Blue-Cross and Blue-Shield, and Medicare and Medicaid had not yet been invented by a compassionate government. She "had spent all that she had" (v. 26).

What was worse was that she was getting worse. Nothing that she did seemed to make her any better. She could feel herself getting weaker and weaker. She could feel the complicated balance of health in her body becoming imbalanced. People who are ill often know the true state of their illness because of the changes taking place in their bodies. Sometimes we wonder whether we should tell our seriously ill loved ones about their grave condition, when in reality the sick are usually the first ones to know, for they feel the changes going on in their own bodies.

This woman had been ill for twelve long years and had visited doctor after doctor, seeking a cure. She had now spent all of her money, and every day she was getting worse and worse. She was penniless and defenseless. She was beginning to panic. She would try anything, and then she heard about Jesus, for news about someone who could heal people in a day of medical "mumbo-jumbo" spread like wildfire. You get the feeling that she was running out of time. This was the court of last resort for her.

Now as we look at her and the events that happened in this passage, certain spiritual lessons become available to us to help us to get things done.

First, it's all right for us to go to Jesus as a last resort, even late in life. Many of us spent our time in college discovering everything else but the spiritual truths of the Bible. We were on our own for the first time ever, and we were exploring our freedom. Many of us put on hold a response to God's call in Christ. Maybe some here have even delayed it into adulthood and into the mature years of their lives. One of the clear messages of this passage is that it's never too late to come to Jesus for healing. Early or late, he loves you and wants you to commit to him. When you do, that commitment will make you well.

In the shipwreck scene of *The Tempest,* the mariners speak for the whole company when they say, "All lost! To prayers, to prayers! All lost!" For this forgotten group of sailors, and for many others, prayer was not something to live with daily, but to die with. Religion was a last resort. When you reach a dead end, try prayer, but that's all right, says our scripture—better late than never.

Second, notice that a lot of people milled around Jesus. There was a crowd there. It was like leaving a football game, with everyone elbowing one another as they jockey for the nearest exit. The fact that the anonymous woman was even there in public was a scandal, for by definition a person with her kind of blood difficulty was unclean, and touching her would make one unclean. The fact that she then deliberately went out of her way to touch Jesus was an aggressive act—not a hostile act, but for an unclean woman, a very assertive one.

Many people, however, have touched Jesus over the years. They mill around him; they gaze at him; they listen to him; they judge him; they brush up against him. They enjoy being seen in his company, and then they go merrily on their way, and nothing happens in their lives that changes them into better people. This is sad, but the woman wasn't about to let that happen. This is why she thought, "If I touch even his garments, I shall be made well"

(v. 28). She came at him; she came to him; she approached him with faith in him.

Jesus knew he had been touched by someone, for he felt healing power go out of him. He asked his disciples who had touched his garment, and they responded by saying something like: "Are you kidding? Everybody is touching you. Don't you see the crowd around here? What's the big deal?" Jesus acknowledged that many had touched him, but this touch was different, for it was a touch of faith. This was a touch of belief. This was a touch of need. This was a touch of love. There was touching, and then there was touching, and this was the kind of touch that made a commitment. *If I touch even his garments, I shall be made well.*

John Greenleaf Whittier caught the impact of this event when he wrote:

> The healing of His seamless dress
>   Is by our beds of pain;
> We touch Him in life's throng and press,
>   And we are whole again.
> ("Our Master")

This is the difference between attending church and being the church. Just because we park something in the garage doesn't mean that it automatically becomes a car. This lady came with faith to Jesus as a last resort, and her faith made her well.

Let's look at that last thought again. In that crowd, many were touching Jesus, and nothing spiritual happened to them. Today many people worship in church, and they leave unmoved. Nothing happens, and they will probably blame the preacher or the choir or the choir director or the organist or the ushers or the greeters or the people in the pew beside them or the one who took their parking spot, but certainly not themselves. But the Bible says that you should start with yourself. You are to blame and no one else if, when you touch Jesus, you do not experience a rush of the Holy Spirit that will make you well, heal you, make you whole, restore you, and save you. You come to him with faith, and that will get things done, says the Bible. You come to him with commitment, and your life will change for the better, says the Bible. You come to him with love, and you will go away from him a more loving person. You come to him with humble confession, and you will go away from him, and from here, as one who is restored and renewed. When you take one step toward God, he takes two steps toward you.

The teacher was working faithfully to teach her pupils how to write correctly. As one little girl carefully and slowly wrote out each newly learned letter, the teacher asked in frustration, "But where is the dot over the 'i'?" The little girl giggled and said, "It's still inside the pencil, Teacher!"

For many of us, the full "i" is still in the pencil, for we have yet to let the "I" all out. We have yet to commit the full "I"—ourselves—and when we do, Jesus promises us that we will be whole persons: "Your faith has made you well; go in peace" (v. 34). A faithful life brings peace.

This woman, who really began as a nobody, became somebody when Christ turned to her. Then, in the grace of Christ, she became an everybody so that all bodies might be whole bodies.

Suggestions for Worship

Call to Worship:

Minister: Who may ascend the hill of the Lord?

People: The one who has clean hands and a pure heart.

Minister: Who may stand in this holy place?

People: The ones who do not lift their souls to an idol or swear by what is false.

Minister: Such is the generation of those who seek him. Let us worship and give thanks!

Prayer of Confession: O God of great compassion, grant us your favor as we confess our sin. We surround you with our needs for healing and restoration; yet, we fail to reach out to take your hand. We cry out to you to make our lives right again, but when you call us forth to faith, we shrink back into the refuge of the crowd. Forgive us for our lack of faith and our slowness to commit ourselves fully to you. Do not leave us comfortless, but receive us and make us whole. In Jesus' name we pray. Amen.

Suggested Hymns: "To God Be the Glory"; "Heal Us, Emmanuel, Hear Our Prayer"; "Precious Lord, Take My Hand"; "There's Something About That Name."

Pastoral Prayer: Eternal God, your power and might are beyond measure, your majesty beyond all that we can comprehend. We stand before your power, your might, and your majesty this day and praise your glorious name. Yet in all of this, O God, you chose to be among us as flesh. In all of our human suffering, in all of our temptations, in all of our fears and alienation, you have been there.

We give you our thanks this day for the healing touch of Jesus, which has calmed anxious minds, brought wholeness to diseased and broken bodies, and restored life to those bound by the cords of death. For this wholeness and peace given by Christ Jesus, we lift our voices together in triumphant song.

May the song of your saving be echoed in the everyday places of our lives. May your Spirit so fill us with the knowledge of your victory and peace that we may move from being merely spectators in the crowd to living witnesses of the power of Jesus Christ.

Receive our prayer and each of us, O God. Transform us each day anew to be your faithful followers, redeemed by Jesus Christ, for it is in his name that we pray. Amen.

JULY 7

□

Seventh Sunday After Pentecost

Rejection and hardship cause many to be resentful and defensive. For those who don't belong to this world, rejection becomes the power that bonds them to the eternal.

The Sunday Lessons

The Psalm: Psalm 89:20-37.

II Samuel 7:1-17: David expanded the boundaries of Israel from Egypt to the Euphrates and made Jerusalem a great city.

II Corinthians 12:1-10: Paul, telling of his visions and revelations, writes about being caught up into the third heaven. When he boasts, however, it is of his weakness.

Mark 6:1-6: When Jesus taught in the synagogue at Nazareth, he was rejected. Could an unskilled laboring handyman be trusted and honored? A prophet is respected everywhere except in his or her own city.

Interpretation and Imagination

There is something almost terrifying about a man or a woman so at home in the next world that he or she seeks none of the support and sympathy of this world. David was never welcome in Saul's court. Paul knew the kind of missionary loneliness that kept him in constant exile. He lived and preached among strangers, and as soon as they were friends, he was off on another missionary journey. The words "Jesus of Nazareth" suggest that the Messiah had a home in this world, but the text makes it plain that his own people rejected him. Even the Lord God, according to the prophet Nathan, does not seek a house of cedar.

It is not uncommon to find persons who do not live for money,

180

who willingly forsake personal comfort and do not indulge the appetites of their own flesh. But a life of solitary purpose that is unimpressed by opposition, distrust, and rejection, that needs none of the consolations of family and community, is too grand to imitate. Such a Savior and such a saint is so unlike any human we know that we are content to simply watch. It's like an eagle in flight: We don't ever expect to follow.

We know that there will always be opposition and rejection. Ambition, jealousy, and pride are so much a part of our games, our businesses, and our politics that nothing important goes unchallenged. We also know there will always be someone needing an ally who will be a friend. Some families never forsake their own.

Compromise is the necessity of community. When one comes among us who has established a separate space and is removed from praise and blame, watch and you will see the influence of a solitary life.

TOO CLOSE FOR COMFORT

Mark 6:1-6

A SERMON BY C. THOMAS HILTON

I know a minister who, after he went to a seminary and was ordained, went back to his hometown, his home people, his home church and carried on a ministry there for two years with his family and friends and people with whom he had grown up. It was, for him, quite an emotional time as he struggled to outgrow the boyhood image that many of the people had of him. As he strained to grow into his new role of "Reverend," many of them remembered him only as a little child growing up in the neighborhood. One day someone came up to him and said, "I remember when I had to call the police on you because you and your older brother were shooting 'twenty-twos' in the back yard." Another time someone said, "Do you remember when your dog, King, barked so long and loud when nobody was home that I had to call you out of class at college and ask you to come home and bring in your dog?" Other people would recall times when the minister had mowed their lawn, or shoveled their sidewalks, or driven around the corner too fast, screeching his tires. One man even remembered that the minister had been his daughter's first date. Another parishioner had even been his steady girl for two years.

By now you may have guessed that I was that minister who, after graduating from Princeton Seminary, returned to the House of Hope Presbyterian Church in St. Paul, and for two years was an assistant minister in my home church. "Isn't that nice? Tommy Hilton is back in town. You never know what a person will do when he grows up."

Mark tells us that Jesus went back home to minister in Nazareth. The fact that his disciples went with him indicates that this was a preaching mission and not just a nostalgic homecoming. On the Sabbath he went right to the synagogue where he had gone so many times before, only this time he did not come to listen and learn, but to teach and admonish. His friends and family assumed that he would sit in their pew with them and smile quietly, giving them an opportunity to show him off. It would be a little like what we have experienced when our college students or family return home at Christmas time. We expect them to spruce up, shine up, sit up, and shut up. We would be surprised if one of our returning children stood up on Sunday morning and began to preach. Jesus' hearers were astonished, and as one translation says, "amazed." The people were saying such things as: "Who does he think he is? Big man, all of a sudden. He leaves town and comes back, thinking he can tell us how to behave. He's no better than we are. He's just a local boy, Mary's son, a carpenter, not even a learned man. Why, I know his sisters and his brothers—James, Joseph, Judas, and Simeon—and they are no better than he is. Tell Mary's little boy to sit down." Actually, the Bible says that they were "deeply offended" with him. They "took offense" at what Jesus said, and the way he was behaving in the synagogue. Doesn't he know how to behave in church?

Jesus' response to this hostile reception was to say what was apparently obvious to everyone: "A prophet is not without honor, except in his own country, and among his own kin, and in his own house" (Mark 6:4). He was telling them, in the words of a contemporary American expression, "Familiarity breeds contempt." Remember Billy Carter's evaluation of his own family? He said, "My mother is a 'do gooder' who went overseas with the Peace Corps in her 70s. My sister is a traveling evangelist. My brother thinks he can be President. I'm the only normal member of this family." Sometimes you can be so close to greatness that you don't recognize it. You can be too close for comfort.

Jesus' experience with his family and friends back home can be instructive for us here back home in the church, lest the nearness of Jesus blind us to his greatness and we do not see the radical demands that he makes on our lives. We don't want to give Jesus' arrival the kind of hostile reception he got in Nazareth. For those of us who are intentionally trying to live close to Jesus, there are certain instructions here.

First, it's not wrong to minister and to witness to our family and friends, but it can be very difficult. Jesus tried to do it and was not too successful. There were some who were healed, although I must admit they seemed to be few and far between. Jesus' example here encourages us to share the faith with even our hometown friends and neighbors. Tell your family why you love them. Tell them about your love for Jesus and your desire for them to know him also. Tell them how you want them to be the best they can be. In your neighborhood, share your faith. Reach out and touch the heart of somebody who hurts. In the classroom, on the campus, on the bus, in the office, over the backyard fence, on the beach, on the golf course, share your faith in Christ. Be at least as enthusiastic about your faith as you are about your favorite ball team or your favorite stock or your car or your loved one.

Jesus shared the faith with those who meant the most to him. His responsibility was to plant the seed. Maybe others would water it, and who knows? Some day it could blossom into full faith. He knew the risks. He knew the dangers. As sharers of the faith, we should never let human barriers or risks deter us. In Jesus' situation, some were healed and that was enough. Our responsibility is to go where we are called and to leave the results to God.

Second, let's look at the flip side of this message. As listeners to the faith, we must be careful that we do not come too close for comfort and dismiss the claims of Christianity by analyzing away the faith. Sigmund Freud, in his book *The Future of an Illusion*, tried to make a case for Christianity as being merely a projection of humankind's needs. God is love because we need a loving God, Freud thought. God is powerful because we are weak and need a powerful God, he advocated. God is merciful because we are so sinful and need to be forgiven, he advanced. God is omnipresent and omniscient because we are limited to being in one place at a time and lack full knowledge. Freud would have us believe that God is but a figment of our psychological needs.

To dismiss Freud is not to say that we do not have special needs that the Christlike God can meet, but it is to say that God is more than just a projection of our needs. Freud thought that once he had analyzed our need, then God did not exist. To explain something is not to explain it away. To describe something psychologically is not to erase its existence. Educated people need to be reminded that the mind they are educating was given to them by God. The knowledge we are acquiring is knowledge placed there by a loving God who wants us to explore his universe and to use this knowledge in service to others.

Third, note that as listeners to the faith those who are "close to Jesus" may turn him off with clichés, with worn out assumptions that we think are true. The point is that we often function with quick and easy answers. Some of the answers we offer were valid years ago, but because of our fast changing world, old answers don't often fit our new world. Ninety percent of all scientists who ever lived on the face of the earth are alive today, and they are producing all kinds of new ethical challenges to our faith. Old clichés may not apply to new situations.

Jesus' listeners had analyzed the situation and decided that no good could come out of that little backward town of Nazareth. Jesus just wasn't what they had in mind for a Messiah, so, sorry Jesus, you lose out. You must fit into our way of thinking, or we will reject you. You must be what we expect, or we will be offended by you.

Fourth, there was also a certain snobbishness in their rejection of Jesus. He was, after all, a carpenter's son. He was not the educated rabbi's son or even an educated person in his own right. He never graduated from a theological seminary. He worked all his life with his hands. He was too ordinary for anyone to really expect extraordinary miracles from him. He's a nice man and does good work with wood, and I'd trust him with my most expensive piece of furniture, but with my soul? I don't think so.

The danger for us church people, for faithful Christians, is that we may be too close to Jesus for comfort. We may become smug, even snobbish. We think that we are the ones who define the categories in which the Holy Spirit operates. Just because we've never done it that way before doesn't mean that God doesn't want to do it that way now. We have to be ready for fresh revelations, for new winds, for different directions, for exciting futures in our own lives and in our own church's life. We must not rest on our past lest we embrace a false faith.

He was known as "Lefty." He was called LWK-173095 in federal prison. He was there for counterfeiting. Lefty was good at his profession. In fact, so good that he was called the Picasso of counterfeiting. He was such a perfectionist that he spent an entire year producing the finest set of engravings of fake twenty dollar bills ever carved. Yet, he got caught.

"I defy you to tell the difference between these two bills!" Lefty roared at the government men who held him in custody as he placed one of his fakes beside the bill he had copied.

"You're right, there's no difference," said the treasury agent agreeably. "You made an exact copy of this bill, but the bill you copied is also a phony."

There are many Lefties in the church, people who are copying counterfeit ideas and counterfeit ideologies, when they could be copying the true bill, Jesus Christ.

Suggestions for Worship

Call to Worship:

Minister: I will sing of the Lord's great love forever.

People: **I will make your faithfulness known through all generations.**

Minister: Righteousness and justice are the foundation of your throne; love and faithfulness go before you.

People: **Blessed are those who walk in the light of your presence, O Lord.**

Minister: We rejoice in your name together!

Prayer of Confession: O God, forgive us when we do not receive you in our midst. So often we miss your very presence and the nearness of your gracious love. We ask the wrong questions; we look for miraculous signs; we fail to see you in the ordinary of our days. Forgive us our slowness to accept you and receive you as Savior of our lives. Amen.

Suggested Hymns: "Lift High the Cross"; "I Know Not How That Bethlehem's Babe"; "Make Me a Captive, Lord"; "Jesus' Hands Were Kind Hands."

Pastoral Prayer: Our hearts are full, and we are proud this day, O Lord, for the bounty and fullness of this great land. We bow and once more give our humble thanks to you for blessing this land.

We are mindful that all things come from you, and without you nothing would be. Yet, how often we have forgotten your gracious bounty and providence, which have guided and shaped this land. We have broken our covenant with you; we have sinned against our neighbor and you. Help us, empower us, and forgive us, that we might move to a restoration of our relationship with you.

Our Lord showed us that even in his own home he was able to do his mighty work. We pray this hour that you would send your Spirit among us that we might experience anew the presence of the power and glory and love of Jesus. Help us to open our lives that Christ may make his home in our very hearts.

Bless us as the church. Keep us humble, so as not to be overly proud, and make us bold, that we may faithfully and effectively bear witness to our Savior, Jesus Christ, in whose precious name we pray. Amen.

July 14

□

Eighth Sunday After Pentecost

Prophets don't choose their roles. They are called and appointed and asked to trust themselves to God's providence.

The Sunday Lessons

The Psalm: Psalm 132:11-18.

II Samuel 7:18-29: David responded to the promise spoken by Nathan with a prayer acknowledging the sovereignty of God. He asked that God's blessing continue and "the house of thy servant be blessed for ever" (v. 29).

Ephesians 1:1-10: Paul notes the spiritual blessings that Christ brings to the church. He chose us; he destined us in love to be his children; he redeems and forgives. His plan for creation is to unite all things in him.

Mark 6:7-13: Jesus sent out the twelve without bread, bag, or money. The one thing given them was authority over evil. They preached, rebuked the demonic, and healed.

Interpretation and Imagination

The wish of humans does not determine the will of God. The more we discover about our world and the cosmos, the more we realize that some things are fixed and sure whether we like it or not. The economist sees this in the laws of supply and demand. The chemist sees it in marvelous affinities and proportions that never change. The astronomer sees it in the patterned movement of the planets. The harmony of God's universe is not altered as a convenience to any nation or any mortal.

Yet, we plan and pray and live as though a few things are decreed and most left to choice and chance. Thus we are sometimes more depressed than we ought to be and sometimes overly confident. Sometimes, we are duped by the hope hustlers of the church and sometimes beaten down by the prophets of doom. The adoring crowds make us high. Life's failures leave us feeling rejected and defeated.

We can learn from the saints. Their lives were not given to self-centered programs. Their prayers were not primarily petition and desire. Their style was one of patient dependency, not anxiety and haste. The saint waits on God.

When the gift of faith begins to have its way in us, it moderates our personal wishes, replaces desire with submission, and changes expectations into surrender.

When faith causes us to mistrust our own understanding and dread the promptings of self-interest; when love for God has us seeking the good of all and forgetting personal advantage, then desire becomes thanksgiving, and we begin to believe that all things are united in Christ.

COLD SHOULDERS AND SHAKING FEET

Mark 6:7-13

A SERMON BY C. THOMAS HILTON

A woman tells of attending her daughter's track meet:

> On the fourth and final lap of the mile run, everyone was clumped together except for the two front-runners, who were leading the pack. As the runners came toward the finish line, the crowd began cheering wildly. Just then, I happened to look back, and there, hopelessly last, was a short, portly kid who never should have walked a mile, let alone run one. His entire body was wobbling toward the finish line, and his bright red face was twisted in a kind of pain that made me wonder if death was near.
>
> Suddenly I was brushed by a frantic parent who was leaping down the bleachers to the railing around the track. She was obviously the poor boy's mother. She then yelled at the top of her lungs, "Johnny, run faster!" I will never forget that moment and the look of hopelessness on Johnny's face. He had to be thinking, "Run faster? Run faster? What am I? An idiot? What do you think the problem is here—I just forgot to run faster? I'm running as fast as I can."

Life is like that sometimes. We do our best. We try as hard as we can. We prepare, we pray, we plan, we study, we resource—and then we just can't seem to get it done. Our best laid plans are just not good enough. Everything comes apart, and the worst possible scenario develops. If only we could run faster, do better, be more persuasive.

But I'm getting ahead of the Scripture lesson. Jesus had just entered Nazareth and preached in his town, where he received a "cold shoulder." It began to dawn on Jesus that if he was ever going to get anywhere, he was going to have to trust the faith to his twelve human vessels, his disciples. They would now have to make the transition from being hearers to being doers. They would have to turn from pupils into teachers. They, who were once only receivers of the faith, must now become sharers of the faith. He "called to him the twelve, and began to send them out two by two" (Mark 6:7). This is always the movement of a Christian life. It parallels the movement of the ocean. The ocean beats upon the shore and spreads out, only to return to its source and gather momentum to once more form a wave and beat again on the shore—together and dispersing, coming and going.

To all of us, Jesus issues the call "Come to me, all who labor and are heavy laden" (Matt. 11:28). This is a personal call to all people everywhere. He created us all and loves us all and calls us all to come to him, to commit ourselves to him. But this is not the end of the call. This is not just a call to return to the womb to be safe and comfortable and secure. This is a call to service, to challenge, to growth. After the call to come to him, there is the call to go to others—first come, and then go. The life of the individual Christian is to come to Jesus and be saved, and then to go to others and serve. We are saved to serve. Coming and going, together and dispersing.

We see this when Jesus called the twelve disciples to himself and then sent them out two by two. I think it is instructive that he did not send them out separately. The Christian faith is meant to be lived in communion with other Christians. Individual Christianity is a contradiction in terms. The biblical faith clearly indicates that Christians must come together, or what we have is some other kind of faith. Jesus wanted to emphasize our spiritual need for each other when he sent out his witnesses two by two.

One of the interesting things of life is that everyone of us is a theologian, whether we realize it or not. A news announcer, describing the earthquake in Soviet Armenia, implied that God caused it at this time in the history of the world so that Gorbachev and his new policy of glasnost could be put to the test. Can you imagine a God like that? Playing with our lives as if we were toys? Yet, the well-known news announcer shared his shallow theology with millions of people, and millions of Americans probably thought, "Well that must be so, for he said it." That kind of faith is certainly not a biblical faith.

Another of secular America's favorite beliefs was recently expressed by an advice column writer when she told "Guilty Conscience" that "you need not belong to any church to communicate with God." Now that is a partial truth. It is true that you do not have to belong to a church to communicate with God, only the Christlike God. The biblical God calls us together to be his, together. When it came time to share the faith through human beings, Jesus sent us out two by two to emphasize the communal nature of our faith, which is demanded of a biblical Christian.

So, six groups of witnesses went out in pairs, and Jesus prepared them for the reality of the world by telling them that sometimes one just can't run fast enough: "Whenever a village won't accept you or listen to you, shake off the dust from your feet as you leave; it is a sign that you have abandoned it to its fate" (Mark 6:11 TLB). Sometimes your best will not be enough to make a difference, and when that happens, Jesus tells us that we are not responsible for the response of others to the gospel. They will be held accountable to God for their response, and not us. We are responsible for our own actions, our own witness.

Jesus says that when we get the cold shoulder, we should "shake off the dust from your feet as you leave." Now, that's a strange sounding expression to our modern ears. But to every Jew this phrase had special meaning, for the Rabbinic law said that the dust of a Gentile and a heathen country was defiled. Thus when a person entered Palestine from another country, he or she must shake off every particle of dust of the unclean land in order to remain pure. This "shaking off the dust" was a symbolic act, disclaiming responsibility for the actions of those who refuse to welcome the gospel of salvation. When you get the cold shoulder, shake your feet. Then get on with your work.

The message for us today is that when we are down we must get up. When we are defeated, go on. John Oman calls this the "sacrament of failure" and implies that it is a universal phenomenon, and it certainly is. We all experience down times. They are a part of life. When they come, then go on, for God is present in all his sacraments, even the "sacrament of failure."

A pastor was scheduled to be a visiting preacher in the prison chapel on Sunday afternoon. When he arrived, he went immediately to the chapel and ascended the steps to the pulpit in order to preach. On the way up to the pulpit, he tripped and fell flat on his face. This immediately got the attention of the inmates, many of whom were there simply to get out of their cells. Some were there in order to socialize. The preacher brushed himself off and strode onto the pulpit with every eye on him by now, and even some laughter. "Friends," he began, "we have just witnessed my sermon in brief. When you fall down, you can pick yourself up again." He went on to preach an eloquent message to an attentive congregation, who needed to hear that exact message.

That's all Jesus is saying here. You will fail. There will be times when you are given the cold shoulder. Nobody is liked by everybody. Jesus even said, "Woe to you, when all men speak well of you" (Luke 6:26). Nobody is always a success. When it happens, forget about it and get on with your high calling by God.

I suppose our natural inclination when somebody wrongs us is to seek revenge. We were personally wronged, and so, we think we ought to personally react to the person who has wronged us—an eye for an eye and a tooth for a tooth. When this concept was first introduced in the Old Testament, it was a great ethical leap forward, for people's behavior used to be governed by "you put my eye out, I'll put out both of yours. If you kill my ox, I'll kill five of yours." Jesus takes us even higher up that ladder in the New Testament. He says that when we get the cold shoulder we should forget it. Shake your feet of that place, of those people. It is not your job to rectify any so-called wrongs done to you.

The apostle Paul caught this message when he wrote to his Christian friends in Rome: "Dear friends, never avenge yourselves. Leave that to God, for he has said that he will repay those who deserve it" (Rom. 12:19 TLB). If we respond with revenge, then the other person has changed us into something less than we should be. We have become full of vengeance, rage, and jealousy, when we should be full of love, compassion, and care.

There is an expression that says "Time wounds all heels"—are you awake? I think that is often true. Look at the religious entertainers on television. They could not stand the test of time. It took a while, but everybody has caught on to the fact that many of them are crooked. Many church people knew that something was wrong from the beginning, but few people would listen to us, for they assumed we were jealous. We gently warned others that this was not a biblical faith, but we met many a deaf ear. It's like the warning we are now giving about the New Age Movement. Vengeance is not necessary, for these false prophets cannot stand the test of time. The Bible warns us that what we do in our closets will see the light of day, so we had better be sure that what we do in private is what we want the world to know, for it is simply a matter of time before we all "come out of the closet." Don't seek vengeance. The Lord is in control.

Annie Johnson Flint caught the importance of our being faithful to biblical witness when she wrote in "The World's Bible":

> Christ has no hands but our hands
> To do His work today.

Our hands, our feet, our tongues, the help we offer is the way God has of reaching others. Jesus wants us to share the faith with others through the community of the church, and that is our mission—to simply share. We must leave the outcome to him.

Suggestions for Worship

Call to Worship:

Minister: Grace to you and peace from God our Father and the Lord Jesus Christ.

People: Amen.

Minister: Praise be to the God and Father of our Lord Jesus Christ.

People: **Praise and thanksgiving be to God, for we have been blessed with every blessing in Christ.**

Prayer of Confession: Merciful God, hear us and receive us as we confess our sin before you.

We have heard the voice of Jesus, charging us to go out as witnesses for his kingdom; yet, often our hearts are only halfway in it. The temporal pleasures and possessions of this world are hard to let go of. The impressions of those about us often cause us to lose courage and the vision of your message.

Forgive us, we pray, and in your forgiving love charge each of us anew to be about the faithful work of your kingdom. Amen.

Suggested Hymns: "We've a Story to Tell to the Nations"; "God of Love and God of Power"; "Go, Make of All Disciples"; "Lord, You Give the Great Commission."

Pastoral Prayer: You amaze us, O God, with the vastness of your love for us. In the midst of our sinful lives, you have given us the gift of your Son, Jesus Christ. We give you thanks this day for the challenges his life sets before us as his followers. We thank you for the assurance we feel of his nearness when all others are far away and for the power he blesses us with to be witnesses of his kingdom. We stand amazed in the shadow of your grace, O God.

This day we are mindful of those who have not heard and those who refuse to hear the good news of the saving grace of Jesus Christ. Equip us in this hour to be swift and effective witnesses of Jesus to a world burdened by the weight of sin. Inspire our minds that we might catch a glimpse of new pathways and visions that will advance your kingdom.

Protect us, O God, when we encounter adversaries who are too powerful and great for us alone. May we feel the strength of your presence and the power of your truth.

When we find doors slamming in our faces and people telling us to leave them alone, help us to find peace in knowing that your presence has been near them. Help our spirits to remain unbroken as we are about the work of your kingdom. Help us to bear each other up, to pray for each other, and to be open constantly to the movement of the Holy Spirit.

This day, O God, help us to hear once more that charge of Jesus Christ to his followers. Open our eyes, our hearts, our minds, our very souls to your presence that we may faithfully receive and share the authority that has been given to us in Jesus' name. We make this prayer in the Spirit and name of Jesus Christ, our Lord and Savior. Amen.

JULY 21

□

The absence of compelling truth and goodness does not bring freedom. It brings confusion. Pity those persons and nations who are like sheep without a shepherd.

The Sunday Lessons

The Psalm: Psalm 53.

II Samuel 11:1-15: This record of David's scandalous sin—adultery and murder—reveals the self-serving and deceitful ways of the king.

Ephesians 2:11-22: Gentiles are reminded that they were "alienated from the commonwealth of Israel, and strangers to the covenants of [God's] promise" (v. 12). Christ has broken down "the dividing wall of hostility" (v. 14) and caused both Jews and Gentiles to be fellow citizens and members of the household of God.

Mark 6:30-34: Following the mission of the twelve, the disciples reported to Jesus what they had done and taught. He invited them to go with him to a solitary place to rest. The miraculous feeding of the five thousand follows.

Interpretation and Imagination

Christ's sorrow for the crowds was not because of their poverty and hunger. Yet, he fed them. It was not for their sickness and infirmities. Yet, he healed them. Christ sorrowed because of their lostness. They wandered like sheep without a shepherd.

Perhaps the disciples misunderstood their mission and the miraculous power associated with it. They reported "all that they had done and taught," not yet convinced that all authority belongs to Christ. Mark emphasized that they were sent, that they remained accountable.

There can be no doubt about the bewilderment and dependency of the crowds. Impressed by the miracles and wanting more, they followed Christ out to his private retreat. Without plans for provisions, they had come too far and stayed too long. They were without discipline and without a leader.

Mark's primary focus may be on the lostness and need of the disciples and the crowds. His final emphasis, however, is on the sufficiency of Jesus Christ. Christ teaches the crowd. He resists the disciples' intention to send them away. He brought order to their confusion. He uses the little they have to satisfy all that they need. Then, he lets them decide whether he is the Messiah, the one who has it right, or simply the source of bread for the hungry.

One evening I watched Israel's shepherds leading their flocks toward a sheepfold in the Golan Heights. Darkness was approaching. The tour bus and its intrusive tourists were menacingly close. The wilderness was bleak and empty of any safe hiding place. But those flocks had shepherds and all of the accompanying benefits. There were well fed. They moved with a sense of direction. They followed in confidence. They would soon rest in the safety of the fold.

SHEEP WITHOUT A SHEPHERD

Mark 6:31

A SERMON BY ROBERT ERIC BERGLAND

On the morning of November 22, 1963, Americans rose believing with buoyant hearts that there was peace in much of the world and that life was good, better than anywhere else. But as night fell, Americans were engulfed in uncertainty, grief, and suspicion, and they sensed that something was terribly wrong in America. That morning, President John F. Kennedy had been shot and killed in Dallas, Texas.

I remember that day as a child. Our teacher came into the room with tears in her eyes. She told us that the president was dead and that school was dismissed. We went home to find our parents listening to television reports with sobering interest. All wondered about what had happened and worried about what would happen. For weeks afterwards, there was a sense of lostness. We were like sheep without a shepherd.

All of us long for a leader. In homes, children look to parents for guidance. On our jobs, we seek direction and try to follow instructions. Every two to four years, we hold elections to surface those individuals who will be entrusted with government. People look for eternal truths in our churches through teaching and preaching that are faithful.

In Mark 6:30-34, we find Jesus in the midst of a people who were lost. Jesus' disciples had just come back from a mission among them. After preaching, teaching, and healing, the disciples were tired, both physically and spiritually. Jesus said to them, "Come away by yourselves to a lonely place, and rest a while" (v. 31).

Summer is a good time to gain perspective. We go to the mountains, the beach, or on a sightseeing trip. We call this time of getting away "vacation." It's a time of rest and renewal, a time to catch our breath. There's wisdom in Jesus' instruction for us to come away by ourselves. The disciples needed to regroup, to renew their loyalty.

Another reality present in the text is that Jesus and his disciples had just learned of the brutal death of John the Baptist at the hands of Herod. They were shocked and saddened, and they wondered about the cost of their discipleship. They needed to experience the confidence of the master.

But as Jesus and his disciples set out for that "lonely place," they were noticed. People saw them; crowds followed them. Solitude began to mix with shepherding.

The people who followed were desperately seeking. They were neglected, victimized, and without a trustworthy person to lead them. They wanted to belong. They longed for someone to provide, to protect, and to point the way.

Have you ever had someone follow you like a shadow? Someone who wanted so much to be with you and be like you that that person took every opportunity to find and follow you? There was a lonely boy who picked up on a pastor. He loved the pastor so much that he showed up on the pastor's doorstep every day. At times he appeared unannounced, which was awkward and disturbing. At first, the pastor took it in stride. But then as time when on and the visits became a nuisance, the pastor grew impatient and annoyed, and he sought ways to avoid the young boy.

This is a common response to intrusions. But in Mark's Gospel, Jesus' response is different. With all that burdened him and the disciples, one could expect Jesus to be impatient and annoyed by the crowd. Not so! Jesus saw the crowd coming and had compassion for them.

His compassion was not prompted by their poverty or hunger; it was not caused by their sickness or blindness or pain. Jesus had compassion for them because of their lostness, their confusion. In verse 34 we read: "He had compassion on them, because they were like sheep without a shepherd."

Jesus showed his love in a specific and surprising way: He began to teach them. No healings are mentioned here, no demons are exorcised, no missions are formed or plans of action devised. This needy and lost multitude is ministered to at their point of deepest need: knowing and being known by God. They needed to hear the good news of God's power and love, which was now being revealed in their midst. Perhaps, the thoughtful ones in the crowd found in Jesus' teaching a fulfillment of the prophecy of Jeremiah: "And I will give you shepherds after my own heart, who will feed you with knowledge and understanding" (Jer. 3:15). The crowd was not turned away. They were not rebuked. They were invited to belong and were called to become good citizens of the kingdom of Jesus Christ, the Son of God, the good shepherd.

Has the church today forgotten this style of compassion for lost and searching people in our world? Where is this sense of concern that will move us to a ministry of teaching the saving truths of Jesus Christ?

Paul's letter to the Ephesians teaches us that Christ breaks down the dividing walls and brings peace. He offers reconciliation to God. Those who were far off are brought near. Those who were separated and alienated are no longer strangers, but are members of the household of God. They belong. Both Jews and Gentiles are included.

There is a gift that comes with Christ's peace: *fellowship*. Jews and Gentiles, who had previously lived divided lives in the same towns, those who would not and could not sit at table together, were now "fellow citizens with the saints and members of the household of God" (Eph. 2:19). When the Shepherd comes, the lost, misguided, hungry, and searching crowd is brought together to become a part of the flock with one Lord, one Shepherd, one fold.

Dr. F. Belton Joyner, Jr., superintendent of the Raleigh District in North Carolina, tells an amusing story about belonging. One evening, when his family was living in Durham, North Carolina, where he was pastor at Old Trinity, he took his dog Snoopie for a late evening walk. It was quiet and very dark. Suddenly the serenity vanished. He and Snoopie saw a huge creature lumbering toward them. It looked like it was half elephant and half horse. Snoopie began to bark wildly and tug against his leash. Belton stopped, unsure of whether to tiptoe past with caution or flee in terror. The huge animal came closer. Then Belton saw that it was a Great Dane and that around its neck was a collar with a leash attached. He knew the dog belonged to someone.

Sure enough, not far behind was a small woman hurrying breathlessly after. Just before the Great Dane got to a quivering Snoopie, and just before he reached Belton, shaking in his shoes, she got hold of the leash. "You don't need to be frightened," she said. "He's as gentle as a kitten. He won't hurt you." He didn't and likely would not, especially if he was under her control. They exchanged some kind words and went their separate ways. A dog with its owner, like a sheep with its shepherd, is the picture of peace. When one belongs to a great truth or to a great God, there is a sense of order and direction, and all can rest in confidence.

When Jesus saw that huge multitude of lost people, his heart went out to them in compassion. He brought them in, he showed his love for them through his teaching, and he became for them a good shepherd. They were, to him, precious sheep.

If the church today would find new validity for its ministry of teaching, let it find it in this story from Mark's Gospel. We carry forward a ministry in the name of Christ and receive his gifts "that some [should be] pastors [shepherds] and teachers" (Eph. 4:11).

Suggestions for Worship

Call to Worship:

Minister: In Christ Jesus, we who were once far off have been brought near by the blood of Christ.

People: For he is our peace, who has made us one in him.

Minister: We are no longer strangers and sojourners, but members of the household of God!

People: We remember and give thanks!

Prayer of Confession: Almighty God, we confess you with bold statements of faith, but our lives are confused and in conflict. We are like sheep without a shepherd. We see around us lonely and hurting people, but we turn away in selfishness. We are called to be bearers of good news, but we fail to manifest it in our daily lives. Forgive us, we pray. Free us for joyful obedience in Jesus' name. Amen.

Suggested Hymns: "Only Trust Him"; "Savior, Like a Shepherd Lead Us"; "Guide Me, O Thou Great Jehovah"; "Jesus, Lover of My Soul."

Pastoral Prayer: Eternal God, some of us who come to you this day are very young, and some are very old. Some of us are strong and some weak. Some of us are on a true course, and some of us have lost our way. Now we bring before you all the joys and all the sorrows that encompass our lives. We come as your children, sheep of your fold, saved by the gracious gift of your Son, Jesus Christ.

We give you thanks today for the good gift of family and friends. We give thanks for the children, for whom life is filled with promise and hope. We give you thanks for neighbors and all who gather with us to lift prayers to you.

Help us also to remember those who do not have these blessings—those who are homeless and alone; children whose lives are filled with abuse, rejection, and despair; our sisters and brothers in this world who are oppressed and held captive. We pray that your presence, O Christ, will become real for them. Let your word compel us to become good witnesses of redemption and release.

Reform the church, O Christ, that we might become a faithful example of the goodness of mercy. Make us bold and able to share the good news with those who are searching for truth. Keep us from fear when we are faced with the power of evil in this world, and help us to live victorious lives so that all who meet us will want to share your nearness. In Jesus' name we pray. Amen.

JULY 28

☐

Tenth Sunday After Pentecost

Jesus Christ, Bread of Life, is the controlling theme of John 6. Passages from this chapter will provide the Gospel lessons for the next five Sundays.

The Sunday Lessons

The Psalm: Psalm 32.

II Samuel 12:1-14: The prophet Nathan confronted David with his sin. First he told the parable of a poor man's lamb, slain and served at a rich man's banquet. When David angrily declared, "The man who has done this deserves to die" (v. 5), the prophet answered, "You are the man" (v. 7). The king repented, and his life was spared.

Ephesians 3:14-21: Paul's intercession ends with a prayer that knowledge and comprehension may be granted to the church— not the kind of knowledge that is gained through special information, mere facts, and analytical thought, but that deep intuitive knowing that accompanies the indwelling of Christ.

John 6:1-15: Seeing the crowd, Jesus asked Philip, "Where can we buy enough food to feed all these people?" (v. 5 GNB). Philip ignored the question "Where can we buy?" and asked with what would they buy the food. Jesus fed the five thousand with five loaves of barley bread and two fish. Twelve baskets of broken pieces were left over.

Interpretation and Imagination

In a world where half the children will go to bed hungry tonight and parents won't know where to find bread enough to feed them; in a world where the overfed worry about keeping all they have and getting more; in a world where rich nations make trade agreements and build bombs to promote their wealth and protect their resources, it is hard to comprehend an economy of plenty. It seems impossible to provide for everyone.

The Lord asked, "Where can we get enough to feed them all?" Philip asked in return, "With what shall we pay for it?" One is a question of faith, the other a question of fear. One assumes that there is enough and that the problem is one of distribution. The other assumes that there is too little and that the problem is one of poverty.

When there isn't enough. Poverty and hunger are a reality in your town. The scenes of starvation from Ethiopia and the stories of need from Haiti have made us all conscious of starvation and poverty throughout the world. Social workers distributing food to the refugees and medical teams trying to save the dying know better than any of us that there simply is not enough.

Find a little. Five barley loaves are, in fact, quite insignificant. A lad who is willing to give away his lunch is not. He's the beginning of a miracle. Christ continues to seek those who will bring him what they have.

Share it with everyone. There's no lifeboat theory here. No one can justify feasting on a poor man's lamb. There is no word of encouragement for those who would turn the hungry away.

Count up the leftovers. If we carefully count our resources in the face of need—five loaves and two fish—we should not stop counting when there's more than enough—twelve baskets left over. But we do. A woman carefully harvested the first tomato from her garden, and within the week remarked, "I got three tomatoes today." At the height of harvest she said, "I've stopped counting. They're rotting on the vines."

GOD WITH A CAPITAL "G"

A SERMON BY H. MICHAEL BREWER

Joe glanced at the street sign and then studied once more the address on the little piece of paper in his hand. The store he was looking for should be on this block. Yes, there it was. He stopped before the tinted store window and read the Gothic lettering: The God Store. Beneath the name of the shop in smaller block letters was written: We Have Just the God for You.

This was the place all right. Joe swallowed his nervousness— it's not every day that you can go out to buy a god—and pushed the shop door open. As Joe stepped in, he heard the subdued chiming of a melody triggered by the opening door. The tune was familiar. It was the God Store jingle, the one they played on the radio. The words sprang to mind to accompany the music.

> We have so many gods from which to choose,
> From A to Z: Astarte to Zeus!
> We mean what we say, it's really true.
> We have just the god for you!

Scarcely had the chimes died away before a distinguished man approached Joe. He was wearing a blue pinstripe suit and had a warm smile. "My name is Underwood," he said, pumping Joe's hand. "Welcome to the God Store."

"Hi. My name's Joe." He looked around the store uneasily.

"There's no need to be nervous, Joe," Underwood assured him. "Sooner or later everyone feels the need for a god to worship. It's the way we're made. You just can't be really happy without a god. And you've come to the right place to find a suitable god. We carry all the most popular models. I'm sure we'll find a god that's perfect for you. Will you step this way?"

Joe followed Underwood down a plushly carpeted hallway and into an immense room. The walls were hung at regular intervals with long velvet draperies. Underwood gestured proudly at the cavernous room.

"This is our display area," he explained. "We used to work with a catalog, but we've found it's much more effective to let clients meet face-to-face with their prospective gods."

Underwood positioned Joe before a set of purple draperies.

"This is one of our oldest and most respected models," Underwood said. "We call it the Golden Calf." At that he yanked open the curtains. There on a spotlighted pedestal was a larger than life golden statue of a calf.

"I guess there's a lot of tradition behind this one," Joe mused.

"Oh my, yes," Underwood assured him. "Very old and

reliable. And very practical. The price of gold is simply bound to rise, you know."

Joe studied the golden idol. "Actually," he said, "this may be a a bit out of my price range."

"Don't you worry for a minute about that," Underwood said. "We're very helpful in arranging terms. Our primary goal is to see that you leave here with your very own god. We're willing to let you pay whatever you can, whenever you can. We have found that all of our customers eventually pay in full for their gods."

"That sounds good," said Joe. He laid one hand on the calf's neck. The metal was very cold.

"The Golden Calf model is versatile, too," Underwood told him. "We can cast it in a variety of shapes: a sheep, a bear, a horse. . . . Some people prefer the practicality of gold bars or coinage. Whatever your preference, we're glad to oblige."

"It's real pretty," Joe confessed. "But does it do anything?"

"Like what?" Underwood inquired.

"Well, does it, like, keep you company?"

Underwood chuckled, "With this model, you could buy all the company you want."

"I don't think the Golden Calf is what I'm looking for," said Joe.

"Fine," said Underwood. He closed the drapes. "It's a pleasure to serve a discriminating customer. Perhaps you'll like this next one better."

Underwood opened the next set of draperies to reveal an American flag. The red and white stripes undulated majestically as a hidden fan stirred the fabric.

"This is Old Glory," Underwood said with pride. "This is a perennial favorite."

"Oh, I don't think I need this one," Joe told him. "You see, I already own a flag, and I always fly it on holidays. In fact, I consider myself something of a patriot."

Underwood threw one arm around Joe's neck and dropped his voice to a conspiratorial whisper.

"Listen, Joe. You don't want to get mixed up with patriotism. Believe me. It's too much trouble. Keeping informed. Voting. Writing to your representatives. . . . Patriotism is a headache from beginning to end. It's never easy to get a country to live up to its ideals. You're in for a lot of disappointment and hard work if you decide to be a patriot."

Joe blinked in bewilderment. "But I thought that's what you were trying to sell me," he said.

"No, no, no!" Underwood admonished him. "There's a world of difference between patriotic loyalty, which is what you're talking about, and worship, which is what I'm talking about. If you decide to *worship* Old Glory, you're in for a good time. You'll be surrounded by like-minded people. You won't have to wrestle with any moral dilemmas because you can just shut your eyes to any shortcomings your country might have. It's much more fun to shout 'Love it or leave it' than it is to try to make a good country even better."

Seeing that Joe was unconvinced, Underwood hurried on with his sales pitch. "Of course, we have a variety of choices in this model. We could fix you up with a Russian flag or Canadian or—"

"No thanks," Joe interrupted. "I'm very happy with the country I've got."

Underwood rubbed his hands together. "Then it's a sale?" he asked.

"Uh, no," said Joe. "I don't think so. You see, I love my country, and I want to do my part to keep it healthy, but I don't want to love it above everything else in the world. I'm afraid Old Glory isn't big enough to be my god."

Underwood shrugged. "You are a challenge, Joe. But I like a challenge. I'm going to make you an offer you can't refuse. Let me introduce the most enjoyable god we have around here. We call this model Grab-the-Gusto."

As the next curtain slid back, Joe saw a statue with many arms, like one of those East Indian idols. Each hand of the statue held something different. In one hand was a pinup. In another, a bag of cocaine. Another hand held a pizza, and still another a video cassette. One hand was dribbling a basketball, and from the crooked finger of another hand dangled the keys to a Ferarri.

"This model," said Underwood, "is for people who worship a good time."

"You mean a basketball can be a god?" Joe wondered.

"Heavens, no! A basketball can't be a god. Neither can a pizza. But pleasure can be a god. And that's what makes the Grab-the-Gusto model so popular."

"You're putting me on," Joe protested. "Surely no one actually idolizes having a good time."

"Joe, my friend, you are hopelessly behind the times," Underwood told him. "A god is whatever you put first in your life. Whatever takes up most of your time and most of your energy and most of your money, that's what you worship. And that's why Grab-the-Gusto is one of our best sellers."

"It looks kind of chintzy," Joe said. "It's plastic, isn't it?" He tugged at one of the fingers, and the idol rocked back and forth. "And it's hollow, too!" he exclaimed.

"So we'll fill it with some sawdust," Underwood promised. "Joe, you don't know what you're missing."

"You really think this will make me happy?" Joe asked him.

"I can't guarantee *that*," Underwood hedged, "but it will show you a great time!"

Joe just shook his head.

"Joe, you're a hard nut to crack. But I've saved the most irresistible god for last." With a theatrical flourish, Underwood threw back the next curtain.

Joe found himself face-to-face with—himself. He stood looking into a large mirror in a gilt frame.

"Now admit it, Joe. Is that a face you could love? Is that the person you want to take care of through thick and thin? Of course, it is! Have it your way, Joe! That's the slogan that goes with the Numero Uno model. Who deserves your worship more than you do? Who's going to take care of you if you don't do it?"

"Well, that makes sense, Mr. Underwood. But this looks rather fragile. Does it come with any kind of guarantee?"

"I'm afraid not," Underwood confessed. "We take no responsibility for any god once you leave the store. Some people seem to think that a god should last a lifetime. How could we stay in business if that were true? No, Joe, nothing lasts forever."

"Well," said Joe, "actually I have heard about a god that sounded very durable. I heard about it on the radio."

"In one of our ads?" Underwood asked.

"No, I heard it in a sermon on the radio. I jotted it down. I have it here somewhere." Joe pulled a scrap of paper from his shirt pocket. "Here it is. This is what the preacher said: 'The king of ages, immortal, invisible, the only God.' Does that ring a bell?"

"Oh, yes," Underwood said with disdain. "I know the one. We call it the Capital G."

"Could I take a look at that one?" Joe asked.

"No, you can't because we don't carry that model."

"You don't? Why not?"

Underwood sighed. "The Big G is part of a family business, and the son has exclusive distribution rights on that particular God. Not that it's any great loss to our business. Most people wouldn't touch the Capital G with a ten-foot pole."

"How come?" Joe asked.

"It's a terribly expensive God," Underwood assured him. "Here at the God Store we keep our prices down, and we're always ready to dicker. But you practically have to sign your soul away to get the Capital G. And they insist on a contract. You have to promise to do this and not to do that. It's enough to make you wonder who's really calling the shots. Nobody likes a bossy God."

Underwood lowered his voice again. "And I hear it's a hard God to get rid of. Some people have tried to trade in their Capital G, and would you believe that the Capital G just kept on following them around until they took him back? It seems that the Capital G keeps on honoring the contract even if the client breaks it. Very unbusinesslike. And very ungodlike, if you know what I mean."

Underwood straightened his tie and said, "Come on, Joe. I have several more models to show you."

Joe stayed put. "I really think I ought to look at the Capital G before I make up my mind," he said.

"Joe, I wouldn't lie to you. You won't like the Capital G."

"Maybe," Joe admitted. "But I'd like to see for myself. Do you know where I can find him?"

Underwood shrugged. "You needn't try too hard," he said. "If you're serious about this, the Big G will find *you*." Under his breath he added, "He manages to get in touch with some of our very best customers."

"I beg your pardon?" Joe said.

"I was just saying that we have a great many satisfied customers. If the Big G doesn't measure up, just come on back to see us," Underwood urged him.

"Thanks, Mr. Underwood," said Joe. "But I have a feeling that I won't be back."

Suggestions for Worship

Call to Worship:

Minister: Come, let us bow down, and bend the knee, and kneel before the Lord, our Maker.

People: **For he is our God, and we are the people of his pasture and the sheep of his hand.**

Prayer of Confession: O God, apart from you nothing can satisfy, and nothing is strong. Increase your gifts of mercy and multiply the evidence of your love that there may be an increase of faith in the church today to the honor and glory of Jesus Christ, our Lord. Amen.

Suggested Hymns: "This Is My Father's World"; "Wonderful Words of Life"; "God of Our Life."

Pastoral Prayer: Thanks be to you, O God, for the gift of bread. We thank you that most of us have work to do and strength to do it. Our lives are lived out in a good land where bread is plentiful and fast-food is common. You have set us in pleasant places.

Look tenderly, we pray, toward those for whom life is hard: the children who know only hunger; the homeless who wait in bread lines; the poor who have no place to turn; the exploited and oppressed who only harvest for others. Gather us all to your banquet, O Lord, and teach us your way of giving. Nourish us with the bread and water of life given by you, O Christ, until we are made so strong in faith and joyful in hope that we may bring true gifts of charity.

Forgive us for thinking we have little to share. Place in our hands what we need to serve you. Then put in our hearts the will to obey. Through Jesus Christ our Lord. Amen.

AUGUST 4

□

Eleventh Sunday After Pentecost

The bread of life discourse begins with a contrast of food that perishes and food that endures.

The Sunday Lessons

The Psalm: Psalm 34:11-22.

II Samuel 12:15b-24: The child born to David and Bathsheba became sick. Fearing his son would die, David fasted and wept. On the seventh day, the child died.

Ephesians 4:1-6: Having written of the church's calling, Paul turns to the church's conduct with the word *therefore:* "I therefore . . . beg you to lead a life worthy of the calling" (v. 1).

John 6:24-35: Some of the five thousand who had been fed found Jesus on the other side of the lake. They sought bread to sustain physical life. He urged them to seek spiritual bread that imparts eternal life.

Interpretation and Imagination

An old story tells of a holy man who rested beneath a tree at the outskirts of a city. He was interrupted by a man who ran to him, saying, "The stone! Give me the stone! Please, give me the stone."

"What stone?" asked the holy man. Then the man told how an angel had appeared to him in a dream and told him that he would find a pilgrim just outside the city who would give him a stone and make him rich forever.

The holy man reached into his pocket and pulled out a great diamond. "The angel probably spoke of this," he said. "I found it on my journey here. If you truly want it, you may have it."

The diamond was as big as his fist and perfect in every way.

The man marveled at its beauty, clutched it eagerly, and walked away from the pilgrim. That night he could not sleep.

Before it was light, he went out to find the holy man. At dawn he woke the pilgrim, saying, "The wealth! Give me the wealth! Please, give me the wealth that lets you so easily give away the diamond."

BREAD THAT PERISHES

John 6:27

A SERMON BY JOHN K. BERGLAND

Do not labor for the food which perishes, but for the food which endures to eternal life. (John 6:27)

My grandson is five years old. He claims to be five and one-half now. Recently he showed me his report card. It did not reflect achievements in reading, writing, or arithmetic, but rather evaluated the personal qualities of this beginner in our educational system. "Ability to stay on task: satisfactory" was the category that caught my eye. His great-grandfather would have liked that. That rugged, pioneering man homesteaded in North Dakota and was fond of saying, "Work never hurt anyone!" Our Protestant ethic supports him in that view.

But the question remains, "What is worthy of human endeavor?" Why should one labor? For what good thing should we work? Rudyard Kipling's lines in "The Voortrekker" are true enough:

> Strong lust of gear shall drive him out
> and hunger arm his hand
> To wring food from desert nude,
> his foothold from the sand.

But what is the purpose of one's struggle to achieve?

The first answer is obvious to all of us: You have to keep bread on the table! I heard these words from a tenant farmer who fed and
clothed thirteen children by his hard work in tobacco fields in North Carolina. Those hot fields were home and work place for all of them. This farmer and I knew each other well and visited

together often. I stabled some Tennessee Walking horses in his old mule barn. One day, he did not have time for his lunch, so he wadded up his brown paper bag, tossed it aside and said, "Well, I'd better get back to work. You have to keep bread on the table." He's right about that, isn't he? The bottom line of what we must do with this given life of ours is "feed it." Without food, we die. No one ought to go hungry. Bread on the table—that's what it's all about!

Early tomorrow morning, the country roads, the village streets, and the city thoroughfares of this whole nation will bustle with traffic. We will be going to work. The food and clothing for which birds never toil, but which our heavenly Father knows we need (Matt. 6:32) will have us on task once again. But today is Sunday, and we are called from labor to rest. The text lifts up Christ's words: "Do not labor for the food which perishes" (John 6:27).

Have you ever felt like saying, "I hated all my labors"? The book of Ecclesiastes portrays King Solomon's reflecting on the emptiness and foolishness of his endeavors: "I hated all my toil in which I had toiled under the sun, seeing that I must leave it" (Eccles. 2:18).

The second answer is that money is compelling, with its claim on human endeavor. Most of us today don't labor for bread. We don't harvest wheat, mill flour, and bake two loaves every day. The hours and days of our work week are spent in working for wages or, better yet, in salaried positions. Money is the reward for which we labor.

Michael Quoist has written a book of prayers based on common things. A door, a rock, and a baby are some of the evident realities that prompt his prayers. One prayer meditates on a twenty-dollar bill. "It's heavy," he notes. Really it isn't unless one pays attention to the wrinkles of the twenty and their story of the men and women who have worried, worked, sacrificed, and compromised in order to have the twenty dollars and the pleasures the money can bring. What are those pleasures, those rewards that it can offer? The praying priest imagines what that twenty dollars had purchased: white roses for a fiancée, a dress for the baby's baptism, bread for the table, milk for the children, school books for a boy, a new dress for the prom, the saving visit of a doctor. It had paid the price of many wonderful things.

Then Quoist reflects on the destructiveness and tragic ways that are part of money, too. A boy taking it became a thief. A man wanting it turned to crime. It bought liquor for a drunk, drugs for an addict, a young body in prostitution, weapons for destruction and violence, the wood of the casket.

Money has no power of its own to bring the good that remains or the evil that perishes, just as it has no power to give life. We save money, buy annuities, build pension reserves, and plan insurance programs to provide for the future. Yet, in our best moments we know that the vanity of wealth is as real as the futility of labor. Money by itself cannot hurt and will not heal. Money, like bread that grows moldy and stale, comes under the judgment of our Lord: "Do not labor for bread that perishes."

What, then, shall we seek? What is the work that God would have us do? Is there anything that has a permanence, a lingering and lasting value that is worthy of the expenditure of the days and nights of one's life? "What must we do, to be doing the works of God?" (John 6:28). We must know. The Son of God helps us to know. Please God, let something remain.

The third answer is that there are some realities that remain, three things that last forever. The apostle Paul in his letter to the Corinthian church tells of the excellent ways that life may be lived. Thrilling speech, great knowledge, and the sacrifice of martyrs are examples of great gifts and notable achievement. But tongues cease, knowledge passes away, and martyrdom by itself gains nothing. Three things last forever, or as Paul says, three things *abide:* "So faith, hope, love abide, these three" (I Cor. 13:13).

You may trust the text. It is wise counsel. *Do not labor for bread that perishes.* You may trust the question, "What must we do to be doing the work of God?" You should rejoice in the truth. Christ gave the answer: "This is the work of God, that you believe in him whom he has sent" (John 6:29).

The Quakers have a spiritual quest that they refer to as "centering," or, more specifically, as "centering down." It begins as an idea, a meditation, but then moves to a consuming flame deep within human personality. Have you witnessed the strength of labor and the significance of life in one who is centered, one who has faith? There is no higher achievement, no grander labor, than being centered on the only One in all the long history of humankind who has it right, on Jesus Christ, who is the Bread of life.

Suggestions for Worship

Call to Worship:

Minister: I will bless the Lord at all times;

People: **His praise will continually be in my mouth.**

Minister: Glorify the Lord with me.

People: **Let us exalt his name together.**

Prayer of Confession: O Lord our God, you know the kind of people we are, and you know from whence we have come to this place. You know our transgressions. You know our failures. You know the emptiness that has followed us here. Be merciful, O God, and let your grace cover all our needs. Forgive our foolish ways. Heal the wounds we have caused. God, who is the Bread of life, have mercy on us. Amen.

Suggested Hymns: "Come, Thou Fount of Every Blessing"; "Guide Me O Thou Great Jehovah"; "All the Way My Savior Leads Me."

Pastoral Prayer: "Thou has called us to Thyself, most merciful Father, with love and with promises abundant; and we are witnesses that it is not in vain that we drew near to Thee. We bear witness to Thy faithfulness. Thy promises are Yea and Amen. Thy blessings are exceeding abundant more than we know or think. We thank Thee for the privilege of prayer, and for Thine answers to prayer; and we rejoice that Thou dost not answer according to our petitions. We are blind, and are constantly seeking things which are not best for us. If Thou didst grant all our desires according to our requests, we should be ruined. In dealing with our little children we give them, not the things which they ask for, but the things which we judge to be best for them; and Thou, our Father, art by Thy providence overruling our ignorance and our headlong mistakes, and are doing for us, not so much the things that we request of Thee as the things that we should ask; and we are, day by day, saved from peril and from ruin by Thy better knowledge and by Thy careful love. Amen." (Henry Ward Beecher, *A Book of Public Prayers*)

August 11

□

Twelfth Sunday After Pentecost

Jesus not only gives the bread of life, but he is that bread as well. He is both the giver and the gift. The bread is Word from heaven.

The Sunday Lessons

The Psalm: Psalm 143:1-8.

II Samuel 18:1, 5, 9-15: David organized his commanders to put down the rebellion led by his son Absalom, but he told them, "Deal gently for my sake with the young man" (v. 5). One man found Absalom and spared him; another killed him.

Ephesians 4:25–5:2: Vices to be put off are contrasted with the virtues to be put on. Falsehood, anger, stealing, slander, and attitudes that cause brokenness are to be replaced by a kind and forgiving spirit.

John 6:35, 41-51: The first of the "I am" sayings in John's Gospel is "I am the bread of life" (v. 35). The Father and the Son together feed the hungry. God prompts their seeking. Jesus receives all who come.

Interpretation and Imagination

Jesus taught that God forgives, and he himself forgave. Jesus taught that the kingdom is patient and gentle, and he himself was forbearance. Jesus taught that God is love, and he himself loved. Christ does not simply point to a reality or give a gift. He is the gift. The reality comes to expression through him.

Christ is not simply the agent of mercy. He is merciful. Christ is not simply the agent of life. He is the Bread of life, the staff of life. The lamb and the dove are familiar symbols in the church.

The symbol of the pelican is often found in Christian churches, but is less familiar. Legend tells that in time of famine the pelican parent will strip flesh and blood from her own breast to feed her young. "The bread which I shall give for the life of the world is my flesh" (John 6:51).

The importance of reconciliation and unity is apparent in all of the lessons. David was the only one who had true mercy for the rebel leader Absalom. One showed mercy because he thought he should. For others, it was unthinkable. For David, the father, there was only one wish: "Deal gently with the young man."

BREAD FROM HEAVEN

John 6:41-51

A SERMON BY JOHN K. BERGLAND

It was not Moses who gave you the bread from heaven. (John 6:32)

They had come too far. They had stayed too long. There was no place to buy bread. The little they had taken along and carefully rationed was gone. Hunger followed, and with hunger came their murmuring discontent. "You have brought us out into this wilderness to kill this whole assembly with hunger," they complained (Exod. 16:3). They remembered Egypt and their slavery. That day they would gladly have traded freedom for bread. "When we sat by the fleshpots [we] ate bread to the full" (Exod. 16:3). But neither the children of Israel nor the mighty Moses could find food in that desert place.

Their story is our story. Is it yours? I predict that if it is not your story now, the day will soon come when all your ability and reserves will not be enough. The bread will fail for you, too. And in some deeply significant area of life, you will need help.

In twentieth-century America the first request for assistance is directed toward family—"Dad, could you send a little money?"—or to friends—"Lend me a little of yours." When everyone needs bread, the bread lines form. Murmuring begins and rioting follows.

There had been good planning, and food was stockpiled in the Sudan before the rains came and made travel impossible. But even the most optimistic knew there would not be enough. An appeal had been made to governments and private citizens alike—"Unless you give and give generously, the children will die from hunger." But now the sobering truth was known. No human effort would save them. They needed a miracle. They needed bread from heaven.

There's a good market for miracles these days, not simply in desert places where folks are hungry, but in every dimension of life. The demand for miracles far exceeds the supply of them. It has always been that way. "Expect a miracle. Something good is going to happen to you," we have been told. Yet, in every age miracles are so extraordinary that persons associated with them become extraordinary, too. That's part of what made Moses famous. Pharisees were willing to give honor to Christ if he, like Moses, would work some miracles.

There is a market for miracle workers. Often we are not concerned that persons have supernatural powers. Recently I read about someone who "worked miracles" with a basketball team. He began by raising money for the program, recruiting extraordinary talent, and developing a good team concept. There was a good deal of cause and effect evident in that miracle-working coach. But that did not prevent him from receiving extraordinary respect. He was treated like a god, some said. Many colleges wanted him.

The question of what makes someone a miracle worker is interesting. Is it hard work or great talent? Is it being well born or being anointed? One of the social scientists of our age, Christopher Jencks, conducted studies to learn how competition and success factors actually function in our society. Most of us assume that education, a willingness to risk, and hard work are the things that make for success. Jencks, in his study *Inequality*, concluded that financial success is not explained simply by being well born or by achievements, but rather, by several unmeasured and unmeasurable variables that he called "luck."

I welcome good fortune and willingly acknowledge the reality of unpredictable luck. But I am not quick to speak openly or grandly about magic. Yet, show us a man or a woman who can confront impossible odds and with seeming magic overcome.

Are we not ready to hire, follow, and honor? There's a good market for miracles. There's also a good market for miracle workers. In Jesus' time, persons wanted him to be another Moses, or at least they wanted him to be a miracle worker like Moses.

Jesus said, "It was not Moses who gave you the bread from heaven; [it was] my Father" (John 6:32). On every hand we may witness the providence of God. We acknowledge the power of God. He numbers the hairs of our head. We cannot escape the creative authority of God. I like the prayer of the old mountain preacher who prayed for a parishioner, a seriously ill patient in a great medical center: "O God, you made his kidney in the first place. Now we just want you to make it well again." Yes, pray for miracles and expect them. Pray for the doctors and nurses who seemingly work miracles. Respect their ability. Thank God for them. But the text encourages us to seek something more than a miracle and something more than a miracle worker.

It is a good thing to take a penny from the Father's hand, but it is better to take the Father's hand. It is right to receive with thanksgiving miracle bread—bread of heaven. But there is a better gift of God to seek, to long for, to cherish. It is the power and the near presence of God. It is to come to know the God revealed by Christ, the one who is author and finisher of all things.

There came a day in my life when I needed a miracle. My father was sick. He went to a doctor and learned he was very sick. Then we tried to find the best doctors in the land. From those Montana prairies he went to the clinics of Rochester, Minnesota. There he learned that he had acute leukemia.

I had been praying, but now I knew he needed a miracle and a miracle worker. Just as we had gone for better doctors, we now sought better people of prayer. We sent for a man of faith, and he came with his disciples to pray and to anoint. He quoted the book of James: "Is any among you sick? Let him call for the elders of the church, and let them pray over him, anointing him with oil in the name of the Lord; and the prayer of faith will save the sick" (James 5:14-15).

They anointed my father, laid hands on him, and prayed for his healing. But there was no miracle. The leukemia kept winning. The men of prayer came back again and again. Like the comforters of Job, they came, until one day they tried to explain why there was no evident miracle. "If you had more faith, G. K.," they said to my father, "our prayers would be effective." Is that right? If one has faith can one use it as currency to gain miracles? A dollar worth of faith for a dollar worth of miracle; a hundred dollars worth of faith for a hundred dollar miracle. A whole heart full of faith so that you need never die? Can one earn or buy the bread of heaven and the miracles of God?

My father was my teacher that day. "Oh, no," he said. "Faith is not telling God what to give me or what to do with me. Faith is trusting my life and offering my death to the faithfulness and love of God." Then he spoke these mighty words of Job, "Though he slay me, yet will I trust him."

There are many signs and wonders recorded in holy scriptures. They are not recorded to encourage us to seek miracles. Miracles are recorded for the same reason that God sent them—to increase faith. Pray, brothers and sisters. Pray. Pray that God may come into your life through the mystery of the indwelling of Christ, the Bread of life. Amen.

Suggestions for Worship

Call to Worship:

> Minister: Let us exalt our Lord and praise God.

> **People:** **For he is perfect in faithfulness and has done marvelous things.**

> Minister: The Lord Almighty will provide a feast of lasting food for all people.

> **People:** **Therefore, today let us say, "Surely this is our God; we trusted in him and he saved us."**

Prayer of Confession: Quiet the distressing noise within our hearts and minds, O God. Help us to be still and know you. Quiet the distressing sounds of our fear, the sobbing of our grief, the murmuring of our suspicions, the complaints of our suffering, the shuffle of our tired souls. Then give us ears to hear the whispers of your peace and love. To every listening heart, speak the good news of Christ's victory over sin and death. Save us and help us, we pray, through Jesus Christ our Lord. Amen.

Suggested Hymns: "Praise to the Lord, the Almighty"; "Jesus, Thine All-Victorious Love"; "God Will Take Care of You."

Pastoral Prayer: O God, you are more ready to give than we are to receive. You have better gifts for us than we are able to desire. You know our needs before we know how to ask. Now be for us the prayer we should pray and the blessing we should receive.

You have filled our world with many good things, O God, and we are thankful—bright mornings filled with the songs of birds; a shade tree when the sun is hot; flaming sunsets at evening; moonlight and music that begin with the dark. Mountains and sea shores, fields and gardens, cities and villages, great art and good books, the love of family and the fellowship of friends cause life to be filled with joy, and we are thankful, O Lord.

We thank you, too, for the sadness and sickness, the failure and defeat, the brokenness and loneliness, the farewells and final partings that remind us of our need for the greater gifts that you can give.

Help us not to love this given life so much that we fail to receive even richer and more glorious life that our Lord gained for us through suffering.

Take then our thanks, O God, for every token of your love and thus prepare us to receive with faith and thanksgiving the bread of life. To seek you is life; to serve you is freedom; to praise you is our soul's joy. Therefore, we bless you through Jesus Christ our Lord. Amen.

August 18

□

Thirteenth Sunday After Pentecost

Living bread delivers those who receive it from the power of death.

The Sunday Lessons

The Psalm: Psalm 102:1-12.

II Samuel 18:24-33: Two runners raced to carry news of the battle to the king. Ahimaz told of the victory but not about Absalom's death. The Cushite brought the news of Absalom's death. David wept.

Ephesians 5:15-20: Paul adds to the church's principles for conduct, noting the influence of Christian character in days that are evil. Impulsive foolishness and drunken dissipation are set aside by knowing the will of God and the fullness of the Spirit.

John 6:51-58: Christ says that those who eat of this bread will live forever. The Jews asked, "How can this man give us his flesh to eat?" (v. 52)—by offering his own body. Both cross and Eucharist are seen here.

Interpretation and Imagination

Living with the sixth chapter of the Gospel of John, I have discovered three truths. First, I noted that the secret of life is to discover the certainty of death. Then, one will not be charmed by that which is perishable and will labor to leave his or her mark in the world.

Still dissatisfied with the importance of that idea, I gleaned from the bread of life discourse another truth: The Lord God provides bread for our bellies and spiritual food that satisfies a deeper hunger, hunger for the Word of God. I remember that the rabbis interpreted manna in the wilderness to be both physical and spiritual food.

221

Still not comfortable and at peace with any human dimension of life, either ordinary or extraordinary, I began to struggle with a third insight. John's Gospel speaks of eternal life—life that is infinitely beyond and infinitely better than anything we can know in this world. He speaks of it as the gift from Christ, bread of life.

The enlightened saints in the church, who see beyond this world to the light of eternity, bear witness of an indwelling presence. It comes mysteriously as bread of the Eucharist and as living Word. Its gift is the assurance of eternal life.

BREAD OF ALWAYS

John 6:51-58

A SERMON BY JOHN K. BERGLAND

I am the living bread which came down from heaven; if any one eats of this bread, he will live for ever. (John 6:51)

Sir Thomas Browne, a medical doctor of the seventeenth century, describes human personality as being ruled by three competing powers: affection, faith, and reason. Reason rebels against faith. Passion rebels against reason. "As the propositions of faith seem absurd unto reason, so the theories of reason unto passion, and both unto faith."

Perhaps the nature of humankind is too complex to fit into three such categories; yet, somehow—long before I read Thomas Browne's essay "Religio Medici"—I had to be convinced that the way one feels makes little real difference. One day in a discussion of the meaning of things I said, "I *feel* that. . . . " My perceptive colleague interrupted, saying, "How you feel about it really doesn't matter. Two plus two equals four whether you like it or not."

Then going hat in hand to the academy, I became convinced that being rational was the highest goal in the quest for truth. "Trust thought more than feeling," became my standard of measure. Yet, that did not satisfy the deep yearning I had to reach out for a reality that seemed to be just beyond anything I could touch or think. "Fact more than feeling—faith beyond facts" now describes my perception of an ascending order of human responses to eternal realities.

Aldous Huxley has observed that as the island of knowledge grows, the shoreline of wonder will also increase. There is more to discover. Yes! There is also an increasing mystery with every new meaning.

The Bread of Life discourse reflects these human responses. First is the feeling of hunger and it's concern for bread for one's belly—bread that perishes. Our feelings prompt primitive response. Second is the interest in evidence—a sign like manna from heaven—that will convince the skeptic. This is an earthbound response.

What our Lord seeks is an increase of faith, suggested in the word *abide*. "He who eats my flesh and drinks my blood abides in me, and I in him" (John 6:56). There is a lasting and eternal quality in faith. It shares the life and revelations of the eternal God. It is an increase of faith that I want for each of you and for myself today. But let's begin with what we feel and see.

Nothing lasts forever. I have a boyhood friend who came off the blocks quickly. He had vigor to match his vision, and his dreams often became realities. By the time he was thirty, he was president of the company he had started and employed more than a hundred people. Soon he was a recognized leader in the industry. He became wealthy. We stayed in touch and sometimes vacationed together. He took our family to the beaches of Florida. I was with him in Atlanta, Chicago, and Philadelphia. His long distance calls came from London and Tokyo.

Then came the day when he called me from Greensboro, North Carolina. "Can you come over and have breakfast with me? My flight leaves at 9:30 A.M." I knew there had been some reverses in his life. The business had failed. New ventures were heavy with stress. His three sons—once all part of the business—were now scattered across the nation. He and his lovely wife were estranged. But the noticeable change was his pain, his physical pain. It came from rheumatoid arthritis, which made it difficult for him to get dressed, to eat, to walk, or just to sit and visit.

We spoke of change. "You chose well, John," he said. The university lasts longer than the market."

"But knowledge passes away, too. The apostle Paul wrote of that," I mused.

Later, with a wonderful candor that was bold through faith, he said, "Nothing lasts forever, does it?"

The bread and the miracle bread are reminders of that. The bread for which we labor is bread that perishes. The miracle bread from heaven—manna in the wilderness—had to be gathered fresh every morning. And those saved by the miracle, those who ate heaven's bread, and even those who fed on the word of God—all died. Nothing lasts forever.

Please God, let something remain. A young woman stood on the shores of Normandy. She thought of all the long history that had been lived out on those shifting sands before rolling waves. Many battles had been waged there, many kingdoms established and defeated. Her grandfather had died there during the invasion of Europe in the Second World War. She had visited his grave and saw the long rows of crosses and the green grass of the cemetery. The grass seemed more permanent than the bodies buried there. The shifting sands and rolling seas seemed more permanent than the rise and fall of civilizations. Looking out across the sands, she whispered, "Please God, let something remain." Then she screamed at heaven, "Please God, let something remain."

That's the heart cry of most of us, if not all of us. When we begin to know that the strength in a hand is giving way to weakness; when the vitality of our physical being is slowed by age; when we are sobered by the reality that death is as natural as birth, we cry, "Please God, let something remain." The most important thing in all the world to me is the good gift of those who love me and the ones whom I love—the good gift of family and friends. But every relationship ends, either with my death or with the death of the one I love. The words of an anonymous poem are true, "I spare none, says Death." Please God, let something remain.

The Bread of Always is offered by Christ. It's God's best gift to us. It provides food enough to feed all of us—not just once, but always. It is received through faith—faith that enables one to hear the Word of God as the very presence of the Incarnate Word—faith that enables one to receive simple things like bread and wine and so receive into the mystery of one's own flesh the very presence of the risen, living Christ.

There are thousands of things that seem more lasting than human personality. This building in which we gather stands secure today, but many of our fathers and mothers who labored to build it are gone. The sandhills and Piedmont forests of North Carolina are home for today, just as they have been for the generations that have lived here before us.

Across this land flow the rivers. The Native Americans fished their banks even before our ancestors traveled them. The rivers seem to flow eternally to the sea. Beyond them stand the hills and the mountains. They stand there, eternal hills and everlasting mountains. They have towered over all the generations of humankind that have inhabited this continent. Do these created things last forever?

A man of faith had learned that he had a terminal illness. With a last bit of strength, he went out to visit the redwood forests of the Pacific Northwest, where he lived. Some of those trees, still growing, had been growing since the birth of Christ. The redwoods had always been God's poetry to this man's soul. He spoke to the trees, "I may not see you many times more, trees, but when you are gone I'll be alive in God's presence." He looked beyond the trees to the mountains, "I may not see you many times more, you mountains, but when you have crumbled into dust and have been carried away by the eternally rolling rivers, I'll be alive in God's presence." And above the mountains he called out to the sun, moon, and stars: "I may not see you many times more, oh stars, but one day when you have been wrenched from your sockets by the mighty down-pulling of the universe, I will be alive in God's presence."

We sing of this great faith in Handel's *Messiah*: "And he shall live forever, and ever and ever and ever." Jesus said: I am the living bread which came down from heaven; if any one eats of this bread, he will live for ever."

Suggestions for Worship

Call to Worship:

> Incline your ear, and come to me;
>   hear, that your soul may live;
> and I will make with you an
>   everlasting covenant,
>   my steadfast, sure love.
> (Isa. 55:3)

Prayer of Confession: Good Father of us all, we have strayed too far; we have stayed too long. Now from the desolate places of our wilderness journeys, we cry to you. With deepness and the lingering emptiness of our sin, we seek your mercy. Only you, God, can provide the food we need. Therefore, it is for you alone that our souls wait. Receive us again to yourself and provide for us the bread of life through Jesus Christ, our Lord. Amen.

Suggested Hymns: "Joyful, Joyful We Adore Thee"; "'Tis So Sweet to Trust in Jesus"; "The King of Heaven, His Table Spreads."

Pastoral Prayer: O God, you are from eternity to eternity and are not set in one place at one time. O God, you are before and beyond every day and your immensity cannot be contained in the heaven of heavens, much less in the small areas of our lives. We now seek to know our destinies as your children. We are poor; we are weak; we are mortal. Yet, you have made us in your image. In our frail flesh, you have placed a longing for eternal life.

Please God, in this small room and in this short hour, give us the bread of always. Turn us away from all that is transient. Save us from trusting in things that cannot save. Drive from among us all earthbound goals and be for us, today, the bread of life.

We know how uncertain our date with time is. We know that we are strangers and sinners in this world and that we will soon pass as all our forbears have.

Please God, let something remain. O God, who did raise Jesus Christ from the tomb and has established him in everlasting glory; who has given faith and courage to all your saints; who has enabled some among us to see beyond the shadows of mortal life—enlighten all our souls, satisfy our hungry hearts, and keep us for eternity through the forever victory of the risen Christ. Amen.

AUGUST 25

□

Fourteenth Sunday After Pentecost

The offer of bread of life is both gracious and compelling. It forces one to choose.

The Sunday Lessons

The Psalm: Psalm 67.

II Samuel 23:1-7: This hymn is referred to as David's last words. The passage praises David's dynasty, noting God's covenant with him. It likens a just king to sun on a cloudless morning and to life-giving rain. The last verses (6-7) tell of "godless men" who, like thorns, are thrown away and burned.

Ephesians 5:21-33: The Christian grace of submission is set forth in this analogy of family and church. Mutual submission is the first word: "Be subject to one another" (v. 21). Wives are told to "be subject to your husbands" (v. 22). Husbands are told to "love your wives" (v. 25). Reverence for Christ who humbled himself moves Christians to offer themselves to one another's disposal.

John 6:55-69: The flesh and blood metaphor offended not only Jews from the synagogue at Capernaum, but also some of Christ's disciples. "This is a hard saying; who can listen to it?" (v. 60). Many turned away and no longer accompanied him. Jesus asked the twelve if they wanted to leave him. Peter answered, "Lord, to whom shall we go? You have the words of eternal life" (v. 68).

Interpretation and Imagination

Anthony de Mello, the mystic priest, tells the story of five monks. A request came to the great Lama of the North from the Lama of the South to send a wise and holy monk to initiate the novices in the spiritual life. Instead of one monk, he sent five. Asked why, he said, "We will be lucky if one of them finally reaches the Lama."

227

One dropped out to be a parish priest. Another, offered the chance to succeed a king, seized the opportunity. A third turned aside to care for a child whose parents had been killed. The two remaining monks stopped in a village where a false teacher had misled the people. One stayed on to win them back to true faith. Finally, the fifth monk reached the Lama of the South.

Commenting on the story, de Mello said, "Religious activity is my favorite escape from God."

The text suggests that Christ is so unique and compelling that he is at the same time offensive and attractive. Some turn aside, favoring familiar and comfortable values and styles. Some follow, saying, "To whom shall we go? You're the one who offers life."

Whether we renew our vows today or simply go away, Christ remains among us, never compromising himself or his mission, yet never forcing anyone to follow.

A HARD SAYING

John 6:55-69

A SERMON BY MICHAEL T. McEWEN

"This is a hard saying. Who can listen to it?" That's what the disciples said to Jesus in our Gospel lesson for today. Did they mean that they just did not understand the meaning of Christ's words, or was it that they were not willing to do as he was commanding? The text itself does not answer those questions, but it certainly invites us to consider just how we respond today to the Lord's teaching about himself as the Bread of life.

When you think about it, the idea of Jesus as food and wine to be consumed must have sounded pretty strange to his followers. Almost certainly some of them must have had immediate images of some kind of ritual cannibalism, which was as repugnant to the Jews of Jesus' day as it is to us. Jesus didn't mean that, of course, but he may have been misunderstood, and he was rejected by some of his followers because of that, just as he is still misunderstood and rejected by some of us today.

A few years ago, I was doing clinical pastoral training at Walter Reed Army Medical Center in Washington, DC. As one of the major military hospital facilities, Walter Reed is the referral center for a number of the most difficult and deadly diseases, including AIDS. We had dozens of AIDS patients in various wards of the hospital, but the most serious and soon-to-be fatal cases were kept on one corridor where their special needs could be most managed.

Ted, one of my best friends that summer, had primary responsibility as chaplain for the AIDS ward and would often talk about his efforts to minister to these gravely ill patients. Ben and Roger were two young men in the final stages of their illness, and both were in essentially the same condition and had the same prognosis of just a few weeks to live at most. In virtually every aspect of their case histories, the two men were similar. Both had been baptized as children, but had been basically "lukewarm" in their faith for all of their adult lives.

As Ted began to minister to the spiritual needs of these two dying young men, he found it quite natural to offer them the opportunity to receive Holy Communion each week. Both Roger and Ben came from denominational backgrounds in which Holy Communion was offered regularly, so it seemed logical to Ted for his ministry to include the body and blood of Christ in the bread and wine of the Lord's Supper.

At this point, the lives of Ben and Roger began to go on very separate and distinct tracks. Both men told Ted that they did not feel worthy to receive Communion, but when Ted reminded them that Christ died to guarantee forgiveness for the sins we truly confess, they both decided to begin taking the sacrament each week. For Ben, the experience became the focus for a beautiful time of spiritual healing that sustained him in peace and a sense of being loved for the last few weeks of his life. For Roger, nothing really happened.

Roger told Ted on several occasions that he just could not believe that Christ was really coming to him in the Communion, and he did not choose to receive it after the first couple of Sundays. His death was physically painless, and it was absolutely devoid of the spiritual peace and grace that marked Ben's final weeks.

Ben and Roger had been raised in basically the same faith, had lived the same kind of lives, suffered the same disease, and were ministered to by the same chaplain, who gave them both the same sacramental bread and wine. Yet, the result for them was so obviously and dramatically different.

It seems to me that Roger was like the disciple who felt that

Jesus was offering a teaching that was too hard to accept. Ben, on the other hand, had no problem in accepting Christ's love in and through the bread and wine that had become for him the body and blood of our Lord. For Ben, Christ had become the real food of eternal life in both tangible and spiritual forms.

I'm sure it was not the receiving of Communion alone that made such an incredible impact on Ben. But I'm equally confident that Ben was renewed and transformed by the clear and certain faith that he was receiving Christ in a mysterious and miraculous way when he ate and drank the bread and wine.

One of my favorite definitions of the word *sacrament* says that it is "an outward and visible sign of an inward and spiritual grace." It is not the physical property of the Communion bread and wine that makes a difference. It is God working through those elements in his miraculous way that, as the Gospels tell us, is the work of the Holy Spirit. We can accept this or reject it, but the offer from God remains.

Because some found Christ's teaching to be a hard one, they rejected him both when he was physically in their presence and when he was spiritually present in the sacrament of the Holy Communion that he left them. All they could see was the outward and visible sign. They didn't even bother to ask God for the inward and spiritual grace that would make bread and wine into the food of eternal life.

These doubters were right in one regard: It is very hard to understand how we can be strengthened and sustained eternally by something as ordinary as bread and wine, or how some mysterious change occurs to fundamentally and completely transform the elements in a real, but physically and scientifically undetectable way. Let's face it, this is indeed a hard teaching and is pretty difficult to accept.

Over the long history of the Christian church thousands of theologians have tried to come up with a suitable explanation of just how and when Christ is present when we celebrate the Lord's supper. Perhaps you have heard of some of the classical theories. They have names like "transubstantiation," "transessentiation," "memorialism," and "the doctrine of real presence." Although long and hard battles have been fought over these theories, they are, after all, only human attempts to explain a divine mystery.

In the final analysis, it really doesn't matter which, if any, theological explanation is correct because theology is human enterprise, not God's. What matters is that Christ does come to us in the Holy Communion and that he is the bread of eternal life. He is the only food that can really sustain us. All we have to do is open ourselves to the Lord, ask God to grant us the grace to know him in the breaking of the bread, and believe that Christ is indeed in us when we reverently receive his body and blood. God is offering us an incredible gift, if we will just accept it.

To the skeptics who say this teaching is too hard to accept, I would point to the incredibly different endings of the lives of Ben and Roger. Both lives ran parallel with common experiences of sin, pain, and suffering until one decided to accept the food and drink of eternal life.

One group of disciples said to Jesus in John 6:34: "Lord, give us this bread always." Let us also pray to our Father: Dear God who sent your Son to be the bread of eternal life, feed us now and always. Amen.

Suggestions for Worship

Call to Worship: Dear heavenly Father, you gave your Son, our Lord, to be the perfect sacrifice for the sin of the world and to feed us eternally as the food of everlasting life. Give us the grace to know Christ in every way that you have made him manifest, and grant us the desire to seek him in all people and all places. Amen.

Prayer of Confession: Dear heavenly Father, we confess that we have not always been open to the sustaining nourishment you have given us in the body and blood of our Lord, Jesus Christ. Give us the grace to accept and be fed with the spiritual food that is sufficient now and forever. Amen.

Suggested Hymns: "Amazing Grace"; "Blessed Assurance"; "Love Divine, All Loves Excelling"; "Remember Me, the Master Said."

Pastoral Prayer: Father, you have called us over and over again to accept your gift of forgiveness and love. Help us to live as your Son has called us to live. Let us forgive all those who have hurt us. Let us help all those who need our love and care. Let us learn to focus more on you and less on ourselves. And in all this, feed us with the only real food that you gave so that we can be nourished even when we cannot fully understand. Amen.

SEPTEMBER 1

☐

Fifteenth Sunday After Pentecost

Pseudo-holiness that embraces legalism as a means of gaining approval is called hypocrisy.

The Sunday Lessons

The Psalm: Psalm 121.

I Kings 2:1-4, 10-12: David's time to die was near. He charged his son Solomon to: "Be strong, and show yourself a man, and keep the charge of the Lord your God . . . [keep] his commandments" (vv. 2-3). David reigned for forty years. His dynasty was firmly established.

Ephesians 6:10-20: From his prison cell, Paul observed his guard's armor and wrote: "Put on the whole armor of God" (v. 11). The battle is with "spiritual hosts of wickedness" (v. 12); therefore, the armor is made of spiritual strengths.

Mark 7:1-8, 14-15, 21-23: Purification laws, important to the Pharisees, were ignored by Jesus' disciples. The scribes asked: "Why do your disciples . . . eat with hands defiled?" (v. 5). Jesus quotes Isaiah 20:13 to answer them, contrasting human laws with God's commandments.

Interpretation and Imagination

Fascination with old religious forms is a plague on every generation. Ralph Waldo Emerson's address to the senior class of Divinity College, Cambridge, in 1838 reminds us of that: "It is still true that tradition characterizes the preaching of this country; that it comes out of the memory and not out of the soul; that it aims at what is usual and not at what is necessary and eternal; that thus historical Christianity destroys the power of preaching." Emerson went on to observe that this absence of intellectual and spiritual vigor caused a "decaying church and a wasting unbelief."

When the church is committed only to old doctrines, along with old codes of conduct that seek the approval associated with honored traditions, the whole of society is shortchanged. The soul of the community shrivels. Worship fades. Genius forsakes the places of prayer and wonder. Inquiry hides in laboratories and tracking stations. Science becomes cold, analytical reductionism. Insight is stored in computers rather than in the muse. Old men no longer dream dreams, and young men are without vision. The church surrenders to trifles and bickers over petty religious practices until no one cares.

THE HIGHEST AND THE BEST

Philippians 1:1-11

A SERMON BY EUGENE BRICE

Start with a timely question as September comes: What kind of goals should our team have for the upcoming football season? There have been some good seasons and some bad in the past, but a new season is about to begin. What kinds of goals should we have?

Suppose the coach announces to all that his goal is the championship. Suppose we win ten games and lose six and just miss the play-offs. This is much better than last year, but the goal was not reached. Would that be cause for despair?

Or suppose the coach reminds us that this is a rebuilding year and says that the goal is four victories and twelve defeats. Suppose that in December we exactly reach that goal. Would that be occasion for great rejoicing?

Our question is whether it is better to set low goals and reach them or high goals and risk not quite making it. This is a stubbornly persistent question that faces us in every area of life. As a parent, how do you help teenagers set goals? Do you advise easy goals that do not test the youth, or high goals that may subject him or her to disappointment? How does a preacher address a congregation in setting a budget for a new year? Do you set easy goals that give everyone a sense of accomplishment, or tough goals that stretch us, cause us to grow, and yet might not be reached?

Paul faced that in writing to his friends in Philippi. He knew how hard a battle they faced. They were a new religion in a corrupt town—a minority, an unimportant, powerless minority. Wouldn't he have been justified in suggesting easy goals for them? Knowing full well the reality of the situation, Paul's advice was unequivocal: "I want you to be able always to recognise the highest and the best" (Phil. 1:10 JBP). His advice about goal setting? The highest and the best!

But back from Philippi to our town and to us. What kind of goals do we set for ourselves? In our own personal lives, what kind of target do we aim for? When I face this question in my own life, I am helped greatly by recognizing three facts about life itself. See if they help you in your own task of goal setting.

First, *recognize the attraction of easy goals.* Believing myself to be getting a little out of shape, I decide to take up jogging, and my goal is to jog out to the end of the driveway every morning to pick up the paper, and then, after a short rest, to jog back. Seeing pudginess as a part of my problem, I resolve that between now and next Christmas, I will lose one pound. I am standing in the need of prayer, so my goal is that I will say grace before at least one meal a week. Feeling the need for Bible study, I resolve that sometime within the next two weeks, I will read John 3:16.

Easy goals! Now these may be exaggerated, but they symbolize what we do all the time. It would have been easy for Paul to do this for his friends at Philippi. "Listen," he might have said, "I know your situation, so I don't expect too much from you. A few of us who had personal experiences with Jesus have high obligations. But I can't expect too much of you. So just hang in there. If you can't be too good, at least don't be too bad. I want you to aim toward being moderately good and fairly decent."

There is something appealing about easy goals. They seduce us quickly. Why do people respond to those incredible ads in the newspaper that say, "Eat all you want, and still lose weight!"? Should we reach for the best? That's too hard. The moderately good and the fairly decent—that's for me.

So we yield to easy goals, struggling feverishly toward four and twelve seasons, aiming toward mediocrity and achieving it, and gaining a small amount of satisfaction with being moderately good and fairly decent. Sadly, in this world we live in, being moderately good and fairly decent stands out. It's a long way from reaching for the best, but it's better than most. Remember what someone said: "In the kingdom of the blind, the one-eyed man is king."

The attraction of easy goals. Listen, young people, you watch this especially—don't learn this lesson from us. Don't be satisfied with mediocrity just because we are. Jessie Rittenhouse's poem advises us well:

> I bargained with Life for a penny,
>   And Life would pay no more
> However I begged at evening,
>   When I counted my scanty store.
> For Life is a just employer,
>   She gives you what you ask
> But once you have set the wages
>   You're left with your chosen task.
> I worked for a servant's hire,
>   Only to learn, dismayed
> That any age I had asked of life,
>   Life would have gladly paid.

When I think of targets for my own life, I remember frequently the attraction of easy goals.

The second warning thought for setting goals is *the illusion of apparent excellence.* I tell you with all the force I can muster that this is a trademark of much of our culture today. If we cannot, if we *will not*, reach for the best, we can at least pretend to be there.

Try on for size these two curious examples of the kind of thing we do today in creating the illusion of apparent excellence. Have you ever seen a Bradley G-T driving down the street? The most popular model has an old Rolls-Royce appearance—an open touring car body, chrome plate, exposed piping, low, sleek. It looks as though it ought to be driven by Aristotle Onassis or Prince Rainier. I first saw it displayed in airport lobbies several years ago. Wouldn't it be fun to drive that up to a party at a friend's house, or into the minister's parking place at church?

The Bradley G-T company manufactures fiber glass car

bodies, complete with chrome piping and all the fancies. You can buy a Volkswagon Bug of almost any vintage, remove the VW body from the chassis, lower the beautiful fiber glass body onto it, make all the proper connections, and suddenly as you drive down main street, heads are turning. You've got something that may not be the best, but it sure looks like it! People think you're driving a $75,000 sports car, and only you know that it is nothing more than a VW Beetle with a wig on.

Or consider an advertisement aimed at those who serve a glass of wine occasionally to their guests. If the bottle you serve from looks as though it has come only this afternoon from Safeway, it loses some of its allure. But if it looks as if it has just been carefully brought up from some deep wine cellar, it naturally tastes better.

Therefore, a company manufactures and sells phony wine bottle dust. Before your guests come, sprinkle the dust liberally over the unopened bottle and at the proper time bring out the bottle of wine "besprinkled with the dust of centuries." It may not be the best, but it looks it!

These are ridiculous, but real, examples, and they hint at what may well be a growing inner weakness of our nation today: the willingness to accept the illusion of excellence without its reality.

This is the Sunday before Labor Day, and in no other field than our work does this national malaise show up. Our labor is the basic fiber of our nation. Our nation was founded on hard work, sacrifice, sweat, and tears. Behind the facade of our nation was the reality of quality in what we did, in our reach for the best of hard work, labor, technology, and industry. In all the world, there was no need for illusion. It was the best. But now, in so many fields, we settle for the illusion of apparent excellence.

In the field of education, for example, a great debate now centers on the question of whether students have a right to receive a high school diploma without doing the work to earn it. The phrase the educators use to define the question is "entitlement without qualification." Are students entitled to a high school diploma without being qualified for it? The illusion of apparent excellence comes as we are declaring people to be educated, when they, in fact, are not. To claim excellence without creating it is vain!

But we see it in other fields, too—in labor, where we demand high wages without hard work; in professions in which we receive great honor and out-of-balance income without demon-strating a balancing personal responsibility to go with it; in the military, where we often have power without true patriotism; in politics, where we have influence without integrity. This is the malaise in American life today, and on this Labor Sunday. It stands out clearly—the illusion of apparent excellence.

There remains, then, only the need to state positively the idea we have been entertaining: There is power in high goals. There is a dynamic power in setting the highest and the best as our goal, for the very act of reaching for excellence strengthens us and remakes us beyond our expectation. We tend to become what we aim at!

Say that again, and keep saying it. *We tend to become what we aim at.* Say that for young people making plans for their lives. Aim low, and you'll likely hit low. Aim high, and that's likely where you'll end. When you choose a goal, you determine a destination.

Say it for marriage—if our goal is a life of shared joy, lived together, then the very act of reaching for that will enrich our lives, and we will be the chief benefactors of our own high goals. But if our goal is simply to make do, to endure, if our goal in marriage is enduring mediocrity, then we will be sentenced to sharing the misery of that achievement.

Say it for a church program. What do we want our church to be? What kind of enthusiasm and joy in giving and serving and worshiping do we want? We will become whatever we aim at.

We are putting our finger on the very essence of religion. God is the highest and the best, drawing us out of our lesser selves. Jesus Christ is the highest and the best example of what human life can be. This is why we come to worship. It is our reach for the best, drawing us up, making us leave our porches and breakfast tables and newspapers, drawing us to worship.

The act of worship is an act of responding to the highest and the best. I am convinced that the French theologian Teilhard de Chardin was right. From the dawn of time, humanity has been moving upward, drawn by the magnetic power of God, pulled upward by a distant Best, drawn out of the primordial slime, out of the swamps, out of primitive chaos. We are being drawn upward, pulled along by God's goodness, by Jesus Christ, upward toward the stars of a fulfillment that God in good time will give us.

And every offering we make of the best, everything that is good and beautiful, everything that is rich in excellence—music that soars and poetry that inspires, radiant windows that shimmer with light, experiences in worship that stir us, profound literature and deep prayer, great acts of heroism and little acts of courage, love offered freely and received joyfully, little children singing and older folk praying and giving—all are examples of reaching for the best. All of them lift us up anew, lift us up daily out of little personal swamps of despair and into the presence of God.

This is a contest that will go on as long as we live, pulled between the highest and the lowest, between the best and the worst. In our setting of personal goals, we decide how the game comes out. Because in every area of life we tend to become just what we reach for, I urge you with every once of persuasiveness I can muster, in every moment, make your goal the highest and the best!

Suggestions for Worship

Call to Worship:

> Minister: Lift up your eyes to the hills, from whence does our help come?

> **People:** **My help comes from the Lord, who made heaven and earth.**

Prayer of Confession: O Lord, our God, you have taught us that in returning and rest we shall be saved, that in quietness and trust we shall find strength. Incline our hearts to love you and our voices to praise you. Increase faith among us and with it the other gifts of hope and love. Then, bring forth in us the goodness and peace that are promised by Christ, in whose name we pray. Amen.

Suggested Hymns: "Not Alone for Mighty Empire"; "Ask Ye What Great Thing I Know"; "I Need Thee Every Hour."

Pastoral Prayer: Almighty God, our Father in the beginning.
You, eternal and uncreated, made all things out of nothing.
You called forth light from darkness
Established space and time,
You put the ground beneath us
And the sky above us.
You created everything that lives:
   birds, fish, and the beasts of the field.
And last you made humankind in your own image.
And you have called it good.
We praise you, O God, for all that you have made, for all that you provide. We thank you for giving us dominion over the earth and for work to do and strength to do it.

Today we pray that no opportunity for true service may be neglected and that all the emptiness of meaningless work and idle days shall be repaired by your grace. Let us face what you appoint us to do with the strength you provide. When we have prospered in any endeavor, let us earnestly desire to grow in grace and favor with you through Jesus Christ, our Lord. Amen.

SEPTEMBER 8

□

Sixteenth Sunday After Pentecost

How shall we know God? By rational inquiry (works)? By intuitive awareness (faith)? Where is the true church? Where the Word of God is heard, or where works of love are manifest?

The Sunday Lessons

The Psalm: Psalm 119:129-36.

Proverbs 2:1-8: This instruction teaches one to seek wisdom, "making your ear attentive . . . inclining your heart to understanding . . . [crying] out for insight" (vv. 2-3). It describes the reward of wisdom: "the fear of the Lord . . . knowledge of God" (v. 5). Notice the reversal of "the fear of the Lord is the beginning of wisdom" (Ps. 111:10).

James 1:17-27: James has many similarities to Old Testament wisdom literature. Its pithy sayings are often quoted: "Be quick to hear, slow to speak, slow to anger" (v. 19); "Be doers of the word, and not hearers only" (v. 22). The theological assumptions of the book emphasize works righteousness.

Mark 7:31-37: A man who could neither hear nor speak was brought to Jesus. With gestures (his fingers in his ears and touching his tongue), Jesus addressed the man privately. Then looking to heaven, he sighed and said " 'Ephphatha,' that is, 'Be opened' " (v. 34). The miracle story reflects Mark's emphasis on the new ability to hear and speak that was given the disciples.

Interpretation and Imagination

Where is the true church? Is it found where there is faith—where people gather around Word and sacrament, hearing, believing, praying? Or is the true church found where there are works of love, where good is desired for everyone and slander and selfish ambition are put aside and each person speaks positively of his or her neighbor and works for love and justice?

Helmut Thielicke, in volume three of his systematic theology *Evangelical Faith*, notes that even Luther assumes that the "where" of the church may be defined by the rule of love as well as faith. Thielicke's comment sharpens the issue:

> Love in the power of the Spirit can never be an objective sign of the being of the church, for the basis of love—that we are first loved and can pass on only what we have received—is not manifest to sight but only to faith. Hence love is not a sign but a witness and it thus shares its unavoidable ambivalence for a neutral observer. . . . The witness of love does not in itself produce faith but lack of this witness can rob the church of its credibility.

The importance of hearing the Word of God cannot be overstated. There can be no faithful witness or redemptive service apart from it. A young rabbi once asked an old rabbi, "How may I preach and teach the Torah?" His terse answer was, "Turn yourself into a giant ear."

LANGUAGE OF THE BOUNDARY

Mark 7:31-37

A SERMON BY JOHN K. BERGLAND

He could not hear. He could hardly talk. The people who shared the burden of his handicaps brought him to Jesus. "Lay your hand on him," they begged, hoping the deafness might be healed. Jesus took the man away from the crowd, put his fingers into the man's, and touched the man's tongue with spit. "Ephphatha be opened," he sighed.

The deaf man's ears were opened and his tongue loosed. The news went out: "He even makes the deaf hear and the mute speak" (Mark 7:37).

What should we expect to hear from this New Testament story today? This healing story is not new. Does it hold anything worth telling? Worth hearing? Does it hold a good word for us?

For those who lose interest in religion when it is not filled with miracles, one might emphasize the dramatic, magical formulas of the story—fingers in the ears, spittle on the tongue, a deep sigh, and the "abracadabra" word in Aramaic. But don't give your attention to this, or you will miss the main message.

For those who like to show how Jesus does everything well, there is the opportunity to note how considerate he was. So as not to embarrass the deaf man, Jesus healed him in private—away from the crowd, away from a "downfront" preaching place, and a long way from television cameras. But don't give your attention to this, or you will miss the main message.

For those who like to spiritualize and moralize miracle stories, here is a story that offers a beginning place to proclaim the importance of communication—in marriages, in friendship, in international affairs, in church business. "Be open" is a possible theme. But don't give your attention to this, or you will miss the main message. You won't hear it, so you can't tell it.

What is the main point? The Gospel of Mark begins with the words: "The beginning of good news about God." Is that not the important clue for hearing and understanding this text? Karl Barth has pointed out that serious persons come to church with the question: "Is there any Word from God today?" Can the preacher speak it? Can the hearers hear?

If a deaf man could hear for the first time, what is the important thing he should hear? If a person who stutters could speak plainly, what would he or she tell? Moreover, who's the other party in the conversation? You have ears to hear. What do you hear? For what message should one listen? Are ears opened so that we may listen to the six o'clock news, hear neighborhood gossip, tune in the radio for a disc jockey's chatter and the jarring sounds of hard rock music?

A devoted mother had cared for her handicapped child for eighteen years. She loved him as a baby. She tried desperately to call him forth as a child, and now patiently, day in and day out, she cared for every need of an eighteen-year-old youth who could not even say her name, Mama. "I don't know if he can hear me say I love him. I'm not sure that he can understand at all," she said.

Now that is more important. The sounds we take for granted

are those that make the world safer and warmer. These are things we need to hear—a baby's cry, a child's excited report of a new adventure, a parent's familiar voice with wonderful tones of love and assurance. We need to hear the approaching footsteps, the word of warning, the doorbell or telephone ringing. Ordinary sounds are extraordinary for those who never hear.

The most important conversation going on anywhere today is happening right here in church, right now. It's not this preacher's words that are important. It is rather the nature of the conversation. Language of the boundary may describe it. "The Other Voice speaking" is a definition.

I once asked Billy Graham, who preaches boldly as though he were proclaiming the very Word of God, how he knew that what he said was the Word of God and not simply his own idea. He didn't hesitate a moment. He responded: "It's when one person there, all the people there, twenty people there but at least one person no longer hears the voice of the preacher, but hears the other voice speaking." Have you experienced that anywhere? Some of us have, and all of us want to. How may we hear this other voice?

Prayer is a gift. When we speak of talking with God or talking *to* God we call it prayer. True prayer is not only begging and asking, but it is also communion with God, and such prayer is a gift of God's grace. John Wesley—like Luther, Calvin, and other reformers—emphasized that every part of salvation is a gift of God. One cannot earn the right to hear and speak in the presence of God. One cannot demand an audience with the Almighty.

The healing of the deaf man shows that Jesus was in charge. It was by his authority and through his grace that the gift of hearing was given. It was by his power that the man's speech was made clear and the proclamation compelling. Communion with God, the most important conversation of all, is a gift. If the word of God is preached and heard, that is a gift, too.

When we forget this, we often feel guilty about the shallowness of our faith. We're embarrassed because we sense so little power in God's presence and know so poorly the mysterium. Sometimes we pretend at prayer and faith. We fake an understanding and try to make the church conversations comfortable. Underneath we are lonely, discouraged, afraid, and not very hopeful. Can we receive the gifts of hearing and speaking; the gift of communion with God; the good news of Jesus Christ?

We have the ability to respond. "She has a wonderful ability to hear and respond." The words left me with a paradox. If prayer is a gift, like love is a gift, what must I do to get it? Is there a discipline that achieves it? A holiness that deserves it? Are there works of piety and styles of obedience that can merit the gift of hearing the other voice?

I think the answer is yes. Yes! Prayer is a gift of God's grace. Yes! We have a need to respond. Yes! We can respond. But the response may be little more than turning aside to be alone, in solitude, with the Christ.

Anthony the Great is the often quoted mentor of Christian monastics. A devotee asked him, "What thing is so good that I may do it and live by it?" Anthony did not reply with a prescription of what one must do. Neither did he provide a way to pray. He did not say, "This is the message you must hear, and these are the words you must speak." The holy man answered, "Cannot all works please God equally? Scripture says, Abraham was hospitable and God was with him. And Elijah loved quiet and God was with him. And David was humble and God was with him. So what ever you find your soul wills in following God's will, do it, and speak your heart."

Suggestions for Worship

Call to Worship:

Minister: With my whole heart I cry; answer me O Lord.

People: **Thou art near, O Lord, and all thy commandments are true.**

Prayer of Confession: O Lord, prepare our hearts to reverence you, to adore you, to love you. O Christ, cause our hearts to hate all our pride, our envy, our selfishness, and our cold emptiness. O Christ, have mercy and give us a sorrow for our sins and a longing for your grace, that we may hear and praise your saving Word today. Amen.

Suggested Hymns: "O For a Thousand Tongues to Sing"; "Master, Speak! Thy Servant Heareth"; "Talk with Us, Lord"; "Open My Eyes, That I May See."

Pastoral Prayer: "Gracious Father, who givest the hunger of desire, and satisfiest our hunger with good things; quicken the heart of Thy servant who mourns because he cannot speak to Thee, nor hear Thee speak to him. Refresh, we beseech Thee, the dulness and dryness of his inner life. Grant him perseverance that he may never abandon the effort to pray, even though it brings for a time no comfort or joy. Enlarge his soul's desires that he may be drawn unto Thee. Send forth Thy Spirit into his heart to help his infirmities; to give him freedom of utterance, and warmth of feeling. Let him muse upon Thy goodness; upon the blessings with which Thou hast strewn his path; upon the mystery of the world, and the shame of sin, and the sadness of death—until the fire kindles and the heart melts in prayer and praise and supplication.

Lord, teach him to pray the prayer that relieves the burdened spirit, and brings Thy blessing, which maketh rich and addeth no sorrow. Hear us, for Jesus' sake. Amen." (Samuel McComb, *The Meaning of Prayer*)

September 15

□

Seventeenth Sunday After Pentecost

To name Jesus "the Christ" (Greek) or "the Messiah" (Hebrew) is to know that he has come from God. Yet, he comes to serve and to die.

The Sunday Lessons

The Psalm: Psalm 125.

Proverbs 22:1-2, 8-9: Thematic unity is not a primary concern of the Proverbs. These verses begin, "A good name is to be chosen rather than great riches" (v. 1). They warn, "He who sows injustice will reap calamity" (v. 8).

James 2:1-5, 8-10, 14-17: The passage teaches that true religion is impartial. It contrasts treatments of a rich man and a poor man in the synagogue: The rich man is given a seat of honor; the poor man is left standing.

Mark 8:27-38: At Caesarea Philippi on the northern boundary of the Holy Land, Jesus asked, "Who do [they] say that I am?" (v. 27). Peter made the first confession of Christian faith: "You are the Christ" (v. 29).

Interpretation and Imagination

It is not hard to honor Christ. His life, teaching, and sacrificial death are indeed honorable. It costs little to name him Christ or Messiah—the one who comes from God. For the most part, we accept that. The radical demand still comes through his cross and an invitation to be like him—to become servants who willingly suffer for others.

To really believe in Christ, in the church, in justification by faith, and in love as the best way of all one must have brought all of these mysteries into one's daily life and made them part and parcel of one's values, commitments, and hopes.

246

The question the preacher faces in these lessons is how to speak of Christ to secular people. Harvey Cox, attentive to Bonhoeffer's worldly religion, made three observations: (1) A divided church will not speak to a secular age—unity is not something for Christians to enjoy; it is a prerequisite of mission; (2) a church that uses politics to shore up its own position in the world will never speak to secular society; and (3) a church whose ethical pronouncements remain abstract will never speak to the secular humans.

A deeper question than how to offer Christ to our twentieth-century world is "Who is Christ for us today?"

SO WHAT?

Mark 8:27-38

A SERMON BY W. C. TAYLOR, JR.

"What are they saying about me?" Jesus asked his disciples. This is a perfectly good question. Every public figure needs a valued, updated readout on his or her standing. It is essential for a politician to know the temperament and temperature of his or her constituency. Performers are the first to read their reviews. Television producers check their ratings. Market researchers continuously analyze the needs and whims of the masses.

But Jesus' question is not to get comparative ratings for himself, the prophet Elijah, and John the Baptist. His is a query of reality, not of personal preferences.

And so it is with Jesus' follow-up question: "Who do you say that I am?" Jesus listens for an answer of "is-ness," rather than of who or what is the "biggest," the "best," or the "most."

In answering "You are the Christ of God," Simon Peter is really saying, "You're the one who is going to rescue me and remove all the suffering, frustration, and failure of my life!"

We know the feeling, don't we? Who hasn't perked up at the occupational appeals of the media, which promise success, security, self-esteem, and the good life. Business, personal, and help wanted ads in the newspapers offer the alluring message: "Earn $60,000 per year in a position with a future. Work basically interesting and rewarding. Pleasant surroundings."

Maybe, just maybe, Peter's answer is directed more toward

the future than to the present. Possibly, Peter means: "Jesus, you are somebody whose hand I can hold when I get the need, somebody who can take care of me when I get old." His model for a Messiah isn't so bad. Just think, such a savior is someone to make life all we long for it to be; someone to take away all the world's aches and pains; someone to erase all that diminishes the well-being of good people; someone to transform our lives into a huge, healthy, beautiful rose-garden! Who wouldn't like to get hold of a "good genie" to supply our wants, a protector to shield us from unpleasant things? To put it another way, who wouldn't feel safer if we could be absolutely sure that a Christian gets on better in business or sports or marriage or whatever endeavor he or she takes on?

There's a flaw, though, in banking on this type of insurance. Nowhere does this position take into consideration that the One we're supposed to be following ended up on death row and was executed as a common criminal, instead of rising to the enviable position of being the toast of the town, favorite son.

In fairness, though, hear Jesus' explanation of things past, present, and future to Peter and all the Lord's other disciples:

> "The Son of man must suffer many things, and be rejected . . . and be killed, and after three days rise again. . . . If [anyone] would come after me, let him deny himself and take up his cross and follow me. For whoever would save his life will lose it; and whoever loses his life for my sake and the gospel's will save it. (Mark 8:34-35)

What are Peter's emotions? He blushes or he bristles or he backs away. And so do we. We silently protest, saying: "If Jesus is merely that kind of Messiah, Christ, Savior, Lord, Master, or whatever, then, so what? After all, we have our own troubles!" We quietly argue: "Wouldn't it be so much nicer, Jesus, if we could lay down all those crosses rather than having to keep up with them all, plus having to pick up a new one every time we turn around? Wouldn't it be easier for everyone concerned if we didn't have to bother with such pain and threatening predicaments, or things like race and color and religion and life-styles? Couldn't you just stay away from bothersome things like these?"

Christ Jesus faces us eye-to-eye in this time and place. He comes in what the world calls "weakness" rather than in the power we usually associate with "almightiness." The power of God does not exempt us from pain and suffering and death; it helps us to cope with them and to get through them. Faith in Christ doesn't put us on Easy Street; it enables us to walk Rough Street with our heads held high. The way of Jesus casts us into the thick and thin of life, not only with all its obstacles and hurts and pains, but also with its joy and laughter and wonder. After all, faith is not feathering one's nest, it is laying hold of and being held in the power of God. There are no miracles to pop us out of problems; but something more than a miracle saved Jesus from final defeat on the cross. And, thanks be to God, the risen Christ provides us with that same power to live above whatever life offers or casts upon us. Our resurrected Lord enables us to give freely of ourselves to and for others without fear or despair.

Isn't this what parenthood is all about? Here is a father changing his baby's diaper. Can he be entering the kingdom of God? There is a father who is free from all his adult and male stereotype inhibitions, free from his fears of looking and sounding foolish to others, on all fours, laughing and chasing his one-year-old across the family room. Here is a grandfather, already tired from all his labors—in the garden, the lawn, the garage workshop—with still more to do, taking an opportunity to play catch with his grandson, all as if he had nothing more important to do. In a sense, he really doesn't, does he?

You have heard statements like those that follow, many times, in fact. "He gave his life to research." "She gave herself to her students." "This community and the world are better because of persons like her and him." These tributes confirm that life, real life, is found not in saving one's own skin, but in losing oneself in service to others.

"Learn to give your life away," a pastor advised a young person who was in search of the meaning of life. Those who have tested the wisdom of that statement seldom complain about boredom or loneliness.

"Safety first" is excellent counsel for swimmers, boaters, hikers, whittlers, and the like, but it is a self-defeating, even self-destructing cliché for anyone who proposes to live, really live.

"If [anyone] would come after me, let him deny himself and take up his cross and follow me. For whoever would save his life will lose it; and whoever loses his life for my sake and the gospel's will save it" (Mark 8:35). Our Lord speaks this same word of caution and promise to us today, just as he spoke it to Simon Peter and the other disciples. His challenge makes some bold.

Nathan Allen, a hero of the Revolutionary War, was pursuing a certain young lady. To reach her home in the evening, Allen frequently cut across a local cemetery. Soon tiring of Nathan's seeming disregard for their dead, his neighbors decided to help him alter this habit.

One night, upon Nathan's usual leap over the cemetery fence, he was surprised to land in a freshly dug grave—one that just happened to be located at the exact spot in the fenced area where his shortcut ordinarily began.

That very moment, an imposing figure draped in a white sheet appeared above him and rasped in a ghostly, ghastly voice: "Nathan Allen, what are you doing in my grave?"

Not at all distraught, Allen retorted: "What in the thunder are you doing out of your grave!"

Thank God that by his grace we enter and continue the way of following Jesus as Lord by faith—our absolute trust and utter obedience of him. The life of a disciple is not feathering one's nest. Faith is laying hold of and being held in the power of God. Faith in Christ won't likely put us on Easy Street; rather, it enables us to walk Rough Street with our heads held high.

The Master asks us, as he did Peter and the other disciples, "Who do you say that I am?" In our answer, we say something about not only our knowledge of the historical Jesus, but even more vitally, we divulge the truth about our self-perception, our personal relationship with God and our neighbors, and even our destiny as well. Jesus, the Christ of God, is more than willing to call us his disciples. May the heavenly Father help us to say "my Lord" about—and to—him.

Suggestions for Worship

Call to Worship:

Minister: Trust in the Lord and do good.

People: Live in the land and be safe.

Minister: Seek your happiness in the Lord.

People: And he will give you your heart's desire.

Minister: Put your hope in the Lord and obey his commands.

People: He will honor you, help you, and save you.

Prayer of Confession: Almighty God, Father of our Lord Jesus Christ, you have revealed your truth to us through his life and teaching. You have revealed your love through his cross. You have shown power by his resurrection victory. Forgive our foolish ways and turn us once more toward our Savior, Jesus Christ, in whose name we pray. Amen.

Suggested Hymns: "There's a Wideness in God's Mercy"; "Ask Ye What Great Thing I Know"; "How Firm a Foundation."

Pastoral Prayer: Lord God of freedom, of mercy, and of life, teach us, we pray, to turn toward you and others without fear with open hands, trusting that this life is, indeed, a wonderful gift and that others, in spite of differences, are here for us to love.

Help us, Creator and Redeemer God, to see your world and ourselves through the eyes of your Son, Jesus, so that we might be truly thankful and compassionate to our families, our fellow workers and students, our fellow Christians, and our neighbors—close at hand and afar.

Seeking to become one with your love and mercy, O God, we pray for others—ones that suffer in spirit or mind or body, that they may have relief and wholeness; ones who grieve, that they may know the value of the ones or the other losses they mourn; ones who are anxious or afraid, that they may experience the peace to be found in trusting you. We pray also for persons who are lonely, that they may find satisfying companionship; and for all who are oppressed or excluded by barriers or labels, that they may know themselves to be a part of your Body, and find freedom to live a full and rich life.

Master, you have made our lives the occasion for new beginnings, if only we have eyes to see. This hour marks such an opportunity for many of us. Provide us with strength and direction to meet the challenges of our present day discipleship. Through your Son and our Lord, Jesus Christ, who became weak that we might become strong, we offer our thanks and our longings as we continue to pray: (the Lord's Prayer). Amen.

SEPTEMBER 22

☐

Eighteenth Sunday After Pentecost

Desire for greatness makes one blind to the significance of meekness and wisdom.

The Sunday Lesson

The Psalm: Psalm 27:1-6.

Job 28:20-28: In preceding verses, this poem that praises wisdom states that humans cannot find it or buy it. Only God knows the source. Therefore, fear of the Lord is wisdom.

James 3:13-18: True wisdom is seen "in the meekness of wisdom" (v. 13). The marks of false wisdom are jealousy and selfish ambition. The marks of "wisdom from above" are purity, peace, gentleness, mercy, sincerity.

Mark 9:30-37: Jesus told his disciples again that he would be killed. They discussed who was the greatest among them. Calling the twelve to him, he said, "If any one would be first, he must be last of all and servant of all" (v. 35). Readiness to serve is the beginning of discipleship.

Interpretation and Imagination

To accept Christ as Lord is to accept the closest possible identification with those he serves and saves. It is to demonstrate our oneness with them; to draw near to them and be with them as one stays with a child while babysitting. The humility and servility of Christ are his offer of greatness. When we think of climbing the ladder of success, we think of ascending positions of power, wealth, and prestige. When we think of social climbing, we think of increasingly genteel occasions surrounded by the refined and elite.

Jesus identified with the least, the outcast, the beggars, and the poor. He gathered his followers from tax collectors and fishermen. One might say that he was a social climber, but not like any we know. Jesus climbed downward, stepping to lower social orders and nearer to those who needed to be helped, healed, and saved.

The hymn "Come, Christians, Join to Sing," has a powerful line: "He is our guide and friend; to us he'll condescend." That means he will stoop down to us. Those who discover such meekness discover true wisdom and greatness.

THROUGH JESUS CHRIST OUR LORD*

Mark 9:50

ABRIDGED SERMON BY RALPH W. SOCKMAN

A good many years ago a Hebrew lad was learning to read his sacred Scriptures. He struggled through the sentences, picking out one by one the words in the ancient characters. By and by he would come to a word of four letters, and, boylike, he would begin to spell. "No," his father would say, "do not say that. That word is not said. Say *Adonai.*" For centuries the Jew has never said that sacred name of four letters, but always *Adonai,* which means "the Lord."

Then one appeared who was worthy to bear the name of Lord, the word which stood for those four letters too sacred to pronounce as a Jew. Paul, a Pharisee of the Pharisees, wrote the New Testament letters that are filled with references to the worthy name that could be said: Lord Jesus Christ.

Nineteen centuries have passed since Paul's day. People have pondered this tangled skein of experience called life. The world in which we live wears an enigmatic face—a face as ugly as sin and as beautiful as an angel, as cruel as a sea in storm and as tender as a woman in love. It is a world of snakes and stars, of laughter and tears, a world of contradictions and confusion.

---

* Adapted from *Now to Live* by Ralph W. Sockman. Copyright © 1946 by Abingdon Press. Used by permission.

Some have said this world's life is "a tale told by an idiot." But better judgment has contended that this medley of events has behind it a Creator with a purpose and a program.

And out of this confusing sequence of history, centuries of seasoned thought have selected one flaming section as the key of the whole book of life. It is the biography of Jesus, that strange man on the cross, who from his blood-stained throne has so ruled the hearts of men that they, like Paul, say "the Lord Jesus Christ." In his character we see the highest we know or can imagine, and therefore we too believe that in beholding him we see the Father also. In his life of love we see the most heavenly revelation of life's possibilities. Therefore we conclude that God must be like him. And so we begin our Apostles' Creed with the statement, "I believe in God the Father Almighty, Maker of heaven and earth; and in Jesus Christ his only Son, our Lord." And the prayers which we repeat in our rituals we conclude with the words "through Jesus Christ our Lord."

What does it do for our prayers to conclude them with the words "through Jesus Christ our Lord"?

First of all, when we pray "through Jesus Christ our Lord," the words give us an invitation to pray.

Does it ever seem to you that prayer is a rather presumptuous thing on our part? Here is God with a whole world on his hands, a world of some [four] billion souls. Moreover, he has millions of other heavenly planets in his universe. Why should I presume to bother him with my little personal problems? When we think of the Creator with his innumerable concerns, we feel perhaps as did the little boy who said, "God is like my father; he is too busy to listen." Is it not presumptuous for us to take our affairs to God in prayer?

Furthermore, is not prayer a sign of weakness on my part? Here am I, an adult. Ought I not to handle my own affairs and not childishly carry them to God for his help? A minister some years ago said that the only person in the community who can talk about God without causing something of a sensation is the preacher. If, for instance, at a directors' meeting in a business office the president of the board should say, "Let us ask God's guidance," the suspicion would spread that the business must be heading for the rocks. Yes, for us to stop and pray in the midst of a business meeting or a social gathering would create a mild sensation—an awkward pause, to say the least. Some of us blush to be caught at prayers. To many it seems presumptuous, or weak, or pious.

But not when we pray "through Jesus Christ our Lord." Christ invites us to pray. He makes it as natural as a child's turning to a father. He teaches us to pray, saying, "Our Father." When we close our eyes in prayer, of what or of whom do we think? Dale Carnegie has said that one reason why we do not better remember the names of the persons we meet is that when we meet them we are thinking of ourselves rather than of them. Perhaps that is one trouble with our praying. When we meet God in prayer we are thinking of ourselves. But Christ taught us when we pray to say, "Our Father," and to think of God and not of ourselves.

And when we do think of God, how do we behold him? I confess frankly that God becomes vivid and personal to me only as I think of him in the image and spirit of Christ. When I see God "through Jesus Christ our Lord," I see a God who cares—cares as did the father of the prodigal who longed for his boy's return. I see not only a God who cares but one who also knows me. A college student once said to her professor of religion, "What I really want to know is this: Does God know my name?" Well, our gospel says that the very hairs of our head are all numbered. The God who notes the sparrow's fall takes notice of us, for we are of more value than many sparrows. When I pray, I am not pleading my case before an implacable judge in a cold court of justice; I am talking to a Heavenly Father who knows and understands.

Secondly, when we pray through Jesus Christ our Lord, we have a test for our praying.

We read that in the wilderness Jesus fasted and prayed. In Gethsemane, Jesus sweat great drops of blood. Prayer, as Jesus taught it, means surrendering our wills to God's will, and that means more than relaxing the muscles and stretching out the body. It means saying, "Not my will but thine be done," and that's a pretty hard struggle sometimes.

So much of the current talk about prayer leaves Christ out of the process. Prayer is treated as a power after the analogy of the radio. Here God's power pervades the universe as the ether waves penetrate the air. Just tune in. Just desire hard enough, and you can get anything you want. Well now, suppose we could.

Suppose that each of us could by wishing strongly enough, and invoking God hard enough, receive anything we wanted. What a confusion we should have!

But when we pray "through Jesus Christ our Lord," we cannot ask for just anything our hearts desire. Christ said, "Whatsoever ye shall ask in my name, that will I do." Not everything can be asked for in Christ's name, can it? I can pray for help in my business problem "through Jesus Christ our Lord" provided my business is designed to further the good of men and the program of Christ on earth. I can pray for health "through Jesus Christ our Lord" provided I desire that strength not merely to prolong my own self-indulgence, but to serve my fellow men. I can pray for victory in war "through Jesus Christ our Lord" provided I believe that the victory will further the reign of righteousness and good will on the earth. I can pray "through Jesus Christ our Lord" for the safety of my boy or girl provided I am not selfishly thinking of my own family's welfare and forgetting the welfare of other parents' sons and daughters. When we pray "through Jesus Christ our Lord," it sifts the selfish motives from our petitions.

More than that, it lifts the sights of our prayers. When we pray in the name of Christ, our horizons are enlarged toward the unattainable. His perfection makes us aim at the impossible. He said: "Be ye therefore perfect even as your Father which is in heaven is perfect." Of course, we cannot be perfect in this life, but we can pray and strive toward perfection. He taught us to pray, "Thy kingdom come. Thy will be done in earth, as it is in heaven." Of course, God's Kingdom will not come fully here on this earth. But if we stop striving for it, what happens? The paradox of life is this, that unless we strive toward the impossible, we never realize the possible. Recall King David. He desired to conquer the enemies of his people, to establish his capital at Jerusalem, to unite his nation, and to build a worthy temple to his God. David never built the temple, but because he strove for that which was beyond him he was enabled to achieve that which was within his reach. Great lives are never self-contained.

When we pray "through Jesus Christ Our Lord," our reach exceeds our grasp, but that is what heaven is for. And that is what will make earth more and more like heaven. We need Christ to sift our prayers and lift their sights toward perfection.

Thirdly, when we pray "through Jesus Christ our Lord," we

get power in our praying. For one thing, we get the strength which comes through confidence in the rightness of Christ. If you have ever had the experience of being lost in a strange region, you know how much difference it makes to feel that your guide knows the way. If you have confidence in your guide, a strength comes into your limbs to keep you going. But if you doubt your guide's knowledge, then you lose heart and weariness overtakes you. However bewildered we are by the confusion of our world, we at least know that Christ is right. He is our Lord, the Son of God. Other leaders may falter and change, but Jesus Christ is "the same yesterday, and today, and for ever." Men may think him wrong. Every generation has those who call Christ a foolish dreamer, but eventually men wake up to find that it was they who were dreaming while Christ saw the truth. One generation turns from Christ, but the force of circumstance pulls their children back to him as the one hope.

Moreover, Christ gives us power not only through his own rightness but also by imparting to us a faith that we too can reach toward his rightness. Dr. Harold Walker, of Oklahoma City, says that his own father once gave him a glimpse into the meaning of Christ's redemptive love. In his boyhood he had taken piano lessons. His teacher was giving a program with her pupils as the participants. He himself was to play a few chords and then swing into a little piece entitled "Moonlight on the Waters." He sat down at the piano. In his fright he struck the chords in rather miserable fashion. He looked over at his father, whose face was glum, and at his mother, who was on the verge of tears. His performance was pretty bad, and he finished with a feeling of mortification. On the way home his father said to him, "Son, I know you can play those chords in 'Moonlight on the Waters,' and as long as we know it, what do we care about anybody else?"

When we pray "through Jesus Christ our Lord," we feel ourselves in the presence of a heavenly Father who believes in us, who banks on us, who so loved us "that he gave his only begotten Son, that whosoever believeth in him should not perish, but have everlasting life." In that feeling we can do all things through Him who strengthens us. A modern novel makes a devoted wife say to her faithless husband: "We will face this thing together, you and I, until we win over it." That is what Jesus Christ our Lord says to us.

September 29

□

True discipleship seeks to be free from anything that may hinder fellowship with God.

The Sunday Lessons

The Psalm: Psalm 27:7-14.

Job 42:1-6: Recognizing his human limitations, Job humbles himself before God, despising himself and repenting in dust and ashes. He is in awe before God and "things too wonderful for me." The suffering Job sought answers, but was given faith.

James 4:13-17; 5:7-11: Don't presume that the future will work out according to your plans. Because you know so little about tomorrow, say, "If the Lord wills, we shall do this or that." Don't be impatient about the future. The steadfastness of Job is an example of patience.

Mark 9:38-50: True discipleship is outlined in a collection of sayings. Hard sayings about cutting off hand and foot or plucking out an eye that causes one to sin reflect the radical way in which Jesus values friendship with God. It is to be cherished more than the members of one's body.

Interpretation and Imagination

We're accustomed to the idea of accepting discipline as the means of Christian growth. The desert fathers deliberately cut themselves off from the joys and comforts of life in their search for an encounter with the living God.

Even secular arenas, such as athletics, business, and the military teach us the ethic of self-denial. Diets and exercise programs help us to get in shape. The regimen of climbing the corporate ladder and the severity of boot camp are not strange to us. We expect the radical demand in Christian obedience.

Sometimes, the claims of Christ come in other ways that may be foreign to our expectations. The story is told of two men who met at a bar. One asked the other, "Do you pray?"

"No," said the man.

Then the first man asked, "Have you ever prayed?"

Again the answer was, "No."

"How much will you take to promise never to pray in the future?" the first man asked.

"Five bucks," the second man answered. The questioner put five dollars on the bar, and the second man put it in his pocket. Then he began thinking. "That must have been the devil," he reasoned. "I just sold my soul for five dollars." He rushed out to return the money and be free of the promise.

THE GREEN-EYED MONSTER

Mark 9:50b

A SERMON BY WALLACE E. FISHER

The Gospel lesson today, in its opening verses, alerts Christians to the danger of teaching explicitly or implicitly that Christ's work is limited to the Christian community alone or primarily to any single segment of it. The text also lights up another relevant theme: taking ourselves so seriously as Christians that we focus on ourselves doing Christ's ministry rather than on Christ doing his ministry through our converted selves. Indeed, the whole lesson is crammed with truths waiting for proclaimers!

We shall focus on the last part of the last verse of the lesson: "Have the salt of friendship among yourselves, and live in peace with one another" (Mark 9:50b GNB). That is a marvelous prospect—the salt of friendship flavoring and preserving the whole Christian community. It is the only way for us to live in peace with one another. But it appears to be an unattainable ideal. When we read Paul's letters to the young churches, especially his two letters to the church in Corinth, we come face-to-face with personal enmities, personal theological controversy, and crass immorality, tearing that little congregation to shreds. The salt of friendship, rooted in the gospel, was rare in the Corinthian congregation; peace was a distant goal.

That disappointed and angered Paul, but it did not dissuade him from setting before the Corinthian church members what they could become in Christ. The harsh situation there pulled from the apostle his most celebrated piece of writing, what has come to be called "The Hymn of Love" (I Cor. 13)! Reflecting on Paul's experience, we are moved to turn to Christian hymnody and sing somberly, the cross in our minds' eye, "Greater good because of evil . . . " and to sing joyously, the empty tomb in our minds' eye, "There's a wideness in God's mercy like the wideness of the sea." God surrounds us with a love that never lets us go, even as he surrounded those self-willed, quarrelling Christians at Corinth long ago.

And well he must. The salt of friendship, rooted in the demands and promises of God, is rare enough in many congregations. If we are not majoring on mundane details of parish administration, we are beating the drums over some new church growth program, devised by experts far removed from the daily stresses and strains that characterize grass roots Christianity. Many congregations will do almost anything to escape the demands of God! In the searching light of the whole counsel of God, we can identify a score of reasons for this state of affairs. This morning we shall examine only one: envy. Simply defined, envy is sorrow at another person's good fortune. That puts this sin of the spirit on our doorsteps. Envy causes the salt of friendship to lose its power to flavor and preserve. Envy turns one person against another. It divides; it does not unite. But envy is not a "little evil." It is a big sin that corrupts the sinner, damages the one sinned against, and wounds the gallant heart of Christ himself. Envy is demonic. It lays waste to life.

One would expect the church to be wrestling valiantly against envy. That is not the case. Rarely is it addressed head-on among the laity and clergy. In fact, there are few serious treatments of envy anywhere in theological, philosophical, or psychological literature. Psychiatrist Leslie H. Farber, an astute observer of society, comments on this lack: "The protean character of envy and its talent for disguise account, I believe, for the infrequency of studies on the subject. Because of the variety of forms it may take, it is often simply impossible to recognize."

Our task today is to recognize the nature of envy and discover what we can do about it.

The shifting faces of envy. Envy is indeed difficult to pin down, but the damage it does is readily apparent. Envy imprisons us in self-absorption. It destroys our capacity to appreciate other persons. Allowed to roam at will through our imaginations, envy contributes to our natural self-centeredness even as it springs initially from it. It is at home in persons like the gifted novelist, Edith Wharton. A contemporary said of her: "Edith is a little country bounded on the north, east, south and west by Edith."

Envy is a hydra-headed monster, hard to identify, harder yet to kill. Like the famous silent film actor Lon Chaney, evil has "a thousand faces." For envy, Cain murdered Abel. For envy, Saul attempted to kill David. For envy, the Pharisees railroaded Jesus to the cross. Francis Bacon observed in the fifteenth century that "only death can extinguish envy." To be human is to envy. Envy respects no person, class, ethnic group, race, or nation. All humans are infected; all humans are its victims. It often takes the form of covetousness. The Nazis coveted Czechoslovakia's territory. The American colonists coveted the land of the Native Americans. The Western world covets the Arabs' oil. The Third World covets the Western world's affluence, technology, and power. Covetousness, like greed and false witness, has its roots in envy.

Envy, disguised as covetousness, is rampant in America these days. We covet one another's mates, children, jobs, houses, cars, clothes, education, culture. The dispossessed clamor for what the affluent enjoy, while the affluent dig in greedily to keep what they inherited, earned, or stole. American political parties have played to this human sin since the beginning of the Republic. Jefferson and Jackson and Roosevelt were no less guilty of actively exploiting human envy than Hoover and Nixon and Reagan were of exploiting it passively. Our American Revolution was a mean-spirited civil war in which envy, covetousness, and greed were mixed with passionate love of liberty and honest concern for justice and hope for a republican society.

Let the focus on envy be widened at the person-to-person level of human experience. Scientists, for example, are not immune to envy. Robert Oppenheimer's distinguished career was ended abruptly and his character vilified in the 1950s. There are several reasons why that happened. One of them is professional jealousy intertwined with ideological differences. Envy, like the common cold, assails medical doctors and truckers, lawyers and file clerks, teachers and children, executives and secretaries, clergy and laypersons. Many congregations are victimized by envy, especially those fighting to survive institutionally. Authors are particularly vulnerable to envy. F. Scott Fitzgerald simply could not accept that his literary star was falling while Ernest Hemingway's star was rising. In time, the aging Hemingway came to envy the young Hemingway!

Shakespeare's Iago, speaking of Othello, provides a description of envy that is sharper than a dozen case studies:

> He hath a daily beauty in his life
> That makes me ugly . . .
> O! beware, my Lord, of jealousy;
> It is the green-eyed monster which doth mock
> The meat it feeds on.

Jean Jacques Rousseau, influential French philosopher of the eighteenth century, describes with raw honesty an elemental cause of envy: "I pretended to despise what I could not emulate."

Coping with envy. How does one get at this sin of the spirit? How does one rip out an attitude in one's mind? How shall we cope with the envy in us that sends us forth on mean missions that destroy human relationships, rob us of self-respect, and offend God?

Jesus points the way. At every turn he alerts us to reality: the deep issues of life originate in the heart, the human imagination. First there is desire, conscious or unconscious. Next there is decision, calculated or spontaneous. Finally there is the deed, rational or impulsive. Our Redeemer liberates us from wrong desires. He alone can cleanse our hearts and purify our imaginations. So we pray, "Create in us, O Lord, clean desires." We pray, "Let the thoughts in our hearts be acceptable in your sight." Apart from his saving grace, we shall be driven to despair and sink deeper and deeper into the envy that alienates us from others and curtails our growth in the likeness of our Lord.

Paul takes up this theme, too. He urged the scattered Christian communities to "rejoice with those who rejoice, weep with those who weep" (Rom. 12:15). The second part of his exhortation calls for sensitivity and compassion; the first, alerting us to envy, encourages us to rely on God's grace. Decent people are sensitive to others in need; they sorrow with those who sorrow. But few enter eagerly and gladly into their neighbor's joy.

It is difficult to rejoice with others who have stable, happy marriages when our marriage is a mess; to rejoice with a neighbor whose teenaged daughter has her head on straight, when our daughter shows no signs of maturing as an authentic person; to rejoice when another person gets the promotion we wanted; to rejoice with people who are more talented, better educated, more prosperous. It is indeed difficult to rejoice with those who rejoice—especially when they have more reason to rejoice than we do! We need God's grace every step of the way. "Create in me a clean heart, O God, and put a new and right spirit within me" (Ps. 51:10) is a prayer that his followers pray every day.

Envy is not a "little evil" that any of us can afford to wink at. "It is the green-eyed monster which doth mock the meat it feeds on." In short, envy can eat us, body and spirit. Envy breeds covetousness, greed, and false witness. It robs the salt of friendship of its flavor. It holds at bay the abiding peace God yearns to give his people. He expects us to go to the mat with our adversary—envy—everyday. The life that is liberated will be our own. God does not neglect anyone who pleads, "Create in me a clean heart." Amen.

Suggestions for Worship

Call to Worship:

Minister: Let us confess our sins before God and in the presence of one another.

People: God, our Father, we have resisted the new humanity, revealed to us in Jesus. Because you have sought to know us we can know ourselves: in contrast to your immortality, we are aware of our mortality; against the background of your goodness, we recognize our wickedness; in the light of your truth, we see our ignorance. Lift up the burden of our guilt; blot out the effects of our sins; teach us to live without pretense; help us to accept your love; open our hearts to see the needs of others so that, by serving them, we may express your love. Amen.

Minister: By claiming God's mighty act through Jesus, we are free and forgiven persons with an open future. Let us live out that future with boldness and hope.

People: Amen.

Prayer of Confession: O God, forasmuch as without you we are not able to please you, mercifully grant that your Holy Spirit may in all things direct and rule our hearts, through your Son, Jesus Christ our Lord, who lives and reigns with you and the Holy Spirit, one God, world without end. Amen.

Suggested Hymns: "Spirit of God, Descend upon My Heart"; "Dear Lord and Father of Mankind"; "He Who Would Valiant Be."

Pastoral Prayer: Almighty God, gracious Father of our Lord, Jesus Christ, and in him, the loving Father of us all: Forgive our feverish ways. "Early and late, getting and spending we lay waste our powers." Long and hard have we sinned against You in grievous ways that we do not fully understand. We neglect daily to do the good we know and persist in doing the evil we know You abhor and, when done, makes us ugly. We do not search the scriptures as we should, nor pray with the diligence that we should, nor worship as faithfully as we should, nor give as generously as we should. Day-in-day-out, we place comfort above character; we honor convenience above conscience; we insist that our will, not thine, be done. We are at best poor sticks that boast loudly of our achievements one week only to brood desperately over our failures a week or so later.

Yet You have not left us to wander in these wastelands alone, O God. You have come among us in Your only Son, Jesus of Nazareth, to share our common lot. You are with us now, "nearer than breathing, closer than hands and feet," as the Resurrection Christ, still sharing our common lot, eager to share with us Your victory over the sin that makes us ugly, the demonic forces that terrorize us and our society, the death that wipes us out. Help us to repent and claim the gift of Your victory. Enable us to share our substance and our persons with the under-loved masses in this tangled world of sin. Look mercifully on them and us. Guard us against growing weary in well-doing. Give us grace to rely on You. Keep us ever mindful that there is that point in God's "end-time" when Christ welcomes the faithful into His kingdom where all tears are wiped away, all wrongs are righted and our fragmented selves are made whole.

We ask these gifts in the name of Him who taught us to pray simply and directly: (The Lord's Prayer).

OCTOBER 6

□

Twentieth Sunday After Pentecost

The primary human relationship, that of man and woman, is rooted in God's purposes in creation.

The Sunday Lessons

The Psalm: Psalm 128.

Genesis 2:18-24: The Lord God said: "It is not good that the man should be alone" (v. 18). God made a woman from Adam's rib.

Hebrews 1:1-4; 2:9-11: Telling of Christ's superiority in all things, this ancient hymn claims that Christ is the Son and heir, the agent in creation, the revelation of God, the sustainer of the universe, and purification for sins.

Mark 10:2-16: Some Pharisees asked Jesus whether divorce was lawful. The law of Moses provides for bills of divorce whereby a man, but not a woman, could legally set aside a marriage. Jesus said that this was a concession to human wickedness and spoke of God's intention that two become one. The importance and acceptance of children—"Let the children come to me" (v. 14)—is joined to the teaching regarding marriage.

Interpretation and Imagination

We try to find fulfillment and happiness in many ways, such as travel, friends, work, play, gardening, and the arts. Is there one source of satisfaction that outranks all others in bringing entertainment? Some surveys suggest that marriage is still the most important basis for happiness in the modern world.

An article titled "The Contribution of Marital Happiness to Global Happiness" was published in February 1981 in *The Journal of Marriage and the Family*. Glenn and Weber report:

"The estimated contribution of marital happiness is far greater than the estimated contribution of any of the kinds of satisfaction, including satisfaction with work." This was found to be true for both men and women.

The importance of homes and family, of marital adjustment and growth, cannot be overstated. The pain of divorce, however, can be and likely will be decried and lamented from the pulpit in judgmental ways that only add guilt to the unhappiness and grief of broken families.

The lessons are about marriage and family. Divorce is not the primary theme.

WAS THIS MARRIAGE MADE IN HEAVEN?

Mark 10:2-16

A SERMON BY RONALD E. DIETRICH

". . . and they lived happily ever after." That familiar line from children's stories unfortunately has not held true for millions of marriages today. The incidence of divorce in the United States remains among the highest in the world. Increasingly, problems arising in a marriage are being settled in a court of law and end in divorce. Latest statistics predict that half of all recent first-time marriages will end in divorce. One out of three white children and two out of three black children born in the late 1970s will watch their parents' marriage break up before they reach their sixteenth birthday. Of the 3.6 million children in the United States who began school in September of 1988, 40 percent will live in broken homes by the age of eighteen.

And what of the children who are the products of all these broken marriages? Do you know what it is like to lie in bed at night, frozen in fear as your parents, in the midst of a vicious verbal fight, threaten to end their marriage and destroy your family? Have you ever had to live with that gnawing, empty feeling in your stomach, knowing that your mom and dad were splitting up? It's a terrible feeling! Your security, your sense of trust, your ability to concentrate in school, and many times your faith in God crumble in a heap at your feet. While the deteriorating marriage and the resultant breakup and divorce are extremely painful to the children at that time, we are now discovering that the effects linger on in the lives of those children. Psychologist Judith Wallerstein has been studying divorce and its effect on children since the early 1970s. Her findings indicate that almost half of all children studied entered adulthood as "worried, underachieving, self-deprecating, and sometimes, angry young men and women." Divorce placed so many demands on them that they lost their childhood.

So what should the church say about divorce? Isn't there enough evidence to classify divorce as a major problem of society, and therefore, make it the object of serious study?

Children, youth, and parents alike are frantically searching for help. What is God's word at this point? Is there some clear-cut direction that we can communicate out of our faith? While it is not an easy answer or a simplistic solution or a legalistic directive, I believe that Jesus, through his confrontation with the Pharisees in today's Gospel lesson, has provided a message for us. That message can be stated briefly as this: Marriage is not a matter of temporary convenience or pleasure, it is a matter of God's holy purpose and design.

The Pharisees once again attempted to openly expose Jesus, to discredit his teachings and thereby either provide evidence against him sufficient to remove him from their presence or to develop enough public ridicule and embarrassment that his following would be destroyed. Jesus took the opportunity to provide clarity on the subject of divorce and to lift up several profound teachings concerning God's plans for his creation.

First, Jesus says that the Pharisees (and those who are like them) do not understand the spirit of marriage as God intended in the story of creation.

The rightness and wrongness of divorce can be debated forever, but God's purposes remain firmly established. An individual male and an individual female leave their families and become one. However, the relationship must begin with a recognition of God's purpose for it if it is ever to have meaning, worth, and if it is to last. True marriage is not only physical, but also spiritual. A woman and a man join together their different gifts in equal honor and in equal exercise. This spiritual aspect of marriage is present in the Hebrew creation story. Two distinct sexes were created by God for the purpose of marriage. The two become one (actually the Hebrew word seems to indicate that they even become one personality), and that relationship is permanent. Society and/or the individuals may dissolve the marriage, but the relationship remains forever. Divorce cannot change that. The words in the marriage ceremony about "leaving" and "cleaving" may appear to be outdated, but they still represent the divine purpose of the Creator God. "One flesh" may sound restrictive in a permissive society, but it is still God's intent.

Second, Jesus not only uses the opportunity to call attention to the unique place of marriage in God's plan for the world, but he also teaches a profound lesson on our affinity for legalism. I do not see this as an absolute teaching on divorce. Jesus transformed the question from "Is it lawful?" to the much more significant setting of the purposes of God and the moral and spiritual realities of the marriage relationships. Jesus refuses to be trapped into a new legalism. He chooses to deal with the spirit of the law rather than the letter of the law. In doing this, he exposes our tendency to establish an absolute only to search later for ways to manipulate its application to suit our pleasure of the moment. In the past, the church has taken this word from Jesus and taught that divorce is not permitted; this is an unfair misuse of his larger teaching. As a result, thousands of persons have considered themselves outside of God's grace and have separated themselves from the church.

What message can the church communicate to the divorced person, to the person with a disintegrating marriage, to the young person considering marriage, to the child experiencing the devastation of the divorce of his or her parents? James Efird says, "The most important point is that which emphasizes the importance of and the intention of God for marriage. Marriage must never be taken lightly. The ideal is for one man and one woman to be united in such a way that they become one. Where that occurs there can be no divorce. This is the ideal, the way God intended. There is emphasis on monogamy and unity."

So part of its essential nature is the permanence of marriage. When they do not begin the marriage with a sense of the solemn, the holy, persons do not bring the necessary attitudes and dedication. When there is not an element of permanence, the security of the home and of the society is gone. The permanence of the relationship has implications far beyond the pleasure of two individuals.

However, divorce is not forbidden; although it is strongly discouraged. Rather than legalistic pronouncements, we in the church should do all in our power to teach the Creator's purpose for marriage and to elevate this man/woman relationship, which has the potential of being secondary in importance only to one's relationship with God. The church can provide more adequate preparation before marriage takes place. The church can put an emphasis on marital counseling in the early years of marriage when disappointments, discouragement, and difficulties arise. The church must demonstrate a caring, loving acceptance of persons involved in divorce. The church needs to be the vehicle by which healing and redemption may take place. And the church can provide meaningful programs of support for persons living as singles following divorce.

There is no new legalism in this teaching of Jesus. When the spiritual concept of marriage is absent, when life has become fear and brutality, when the safety and welfare of children are threatened, to deny the possibility of divorce on the basis of Jesus' words in Mark is to distort the consistent, loving, life-enriching message of his life throughout the Gospels.

Although divorce is not part of God's purpose, we in the church can and must demonstrate God's love and grace, which forgives in spite of any failure on our part. Then we must lift up the beauty, the sanctity, the holiness, and the life-fulfilling possibilities of marriage.

In the end, the final question is not "Is it legally permitted?" but "Is it God's intention, and will it help to accomplish his purposes?"

Suggestions for Worship

Call to Worship: Welcome to this gathering of God's people for worship. His goodness and grace challenge us to offer praise that is sincere and heartfelt. Raise your voices in praise and thanksgiving for God's goodness and mercy.

Prayer of Confession: Holy God, with reluctance we open our lives to your examination. Our love of self and immature competitive jealousy of each other are an embarrassment to us. Speak words of acceptance and forgiveness to us. Reclaim us as your own. Empower us to a holy living that will bring glory to you, our Creator. Purify us, strengthen us, and motivate us.

Suggested Hymns: "Praise to the Lord, the Almighty"; "Children of the Heavenly Father"; "As Man and Woman We Were Made."

Pastoral Prayer: Gracious, loving, purposeful Creator God, accept our worship this day. Speak through word, song, sight, presence, and person. Surround us with arms that accept, expose, illuminate, encourage, and forgive. Keep us far from those things that we would substitute for a right relationship with you.

Family relationships are of special concern this day. Speak your word of purpose and intention for your institution of marriage. Help us to use marriage rightfully and sacredly. Use this closest of all personal relationships to bring us our highest degree of worth and development. Use it to provide the setting where children may flourish in safety and love; where our recognition of your will gives such importance to our being that harm and destruction to any of your children becomes an impossibility.

Lead us this day to an active understanding of the purpose of relationships. Take from us any sense of pride in our relationships that have not failed. Remove any sense of superiority and condemnation of persons whose relationships have failed.

Strengthen our marriages. Place them where growth and understanding of life in its fullest may take place; where we may become more than we can be by ourselves; where life is affirmed and joyously celebrated; and where those childlike qualities of trust, openness, dependence, and receptivity will be the ideals we strive for in all relationships.

Send your Spirit among us. Quicken our minds, purify our thoughts, inspire our motives, bless us, and use us to accomplish that day when justice, mercy, and peace will be established, to the honor and glory of your name. Amen.

OCTOBER 13

□

Twenty-first Sunday After Pentecost

A person's sense of vocation and the values that enable him or her to discern the way are often compromised.

The Sunday Lessons

The Psalm: Psalm 90:1-12.

Genesis 3:8-19: Following their disobedience and sin, Adam and Eve hid among the trees in the garden. God asked three questions: Where are you? Who told you that you are naked? What is this that you have done? The consequences of sin—alienation, suffering, and meaningless toil—are graphically demonstrated.

Hebrews 4:1-3, 9-13: Promised rest is the theme. The author first warns that some will miss its benefits. Then he exhorts all to strive for it. The living active word of God, "sharper than any two-edged sword" (v. 12), takes the measure of every seeker. All are naked before it.

Mark 10:17-30: A wealthy, yet dissatisfied, man knelt to ask, "What must I do to inherit eternal life?" (v. 17). He had obeyed the laws of Moses, but he lacked one thing: the ability to center his life around something other than his possessions. Teachings concerning discipleship and wealth show that riches present real difficulties for those who want to follow. "It is easier for a camel to go through the eye of a needle" (v. 25).

Interpretation and Imagination

When asked what hell is like, I fastened on to the "endless holiday" theme and answered, "It is eternal emptiness; it is time neverending and nothing to do; it is money inexhaustible and nothing to buy." Most of us are not convinced of that. We, like the rich young ruler, find affluence and leisure the goals that determine the way we spend our time and energies.

Preachers who decide to preach from the Old Testament

lesson will be helped by reading William Willmon's book *Sighing for Eden*. In it he tells of the time Carlyle Marney was asked, "Where is the Garden of Eden?" When Marney answered, "Two-fifteen Elm Street, Knoxville, Tennessee," the questioner responded, "I thought it was someplace in Asia."

Marney explained that it was in Knoxville on Elm Street where he lived as a boy. He had stolen a quarter from his mother's purse, bought candy, ate it, and then hid. His mother found him out and asked, "Where are you? Why are you hiding? What have you done?"

GO AND SELL *ALL*

Mark 10:17-30

A SERMON BY JAMES H. BAILEY

If we were honest, we would have to admit that we all want to be rich. There is nothing wrong with wanting to be rich. The issue is what is your definition of riches and how do you acquire them?

The rich young ruler had a desire to acquire more riches when he came to Jesus, asking, "What must I do to inherit [obtain] eternal life?" (Mark 10:17). When people talk about an inheritance, usually they mean to acquire riches. The word *inherit* carried the same kind of connotations in Jesus' day as it does today.

We identify with the rich young ruler because by the standards of the rest of the world all of us here in America are rich rulers. We compose one-eighth of the world's population; yet, we control fifty percent of the wealth. By the standards of Jesus' day, we would all be rich rulers. To have more than two suits of clothing, more food than you could eat in one day and reside in more than a two-room house was to be rich. So all of us can relate to this young man who had much but desired more, who though rich was still poor, who though well educated had discovered that right thinking would not satisfy his needs or questions. So he was asking what he must do to inherit life. To that question, Jesus responded, "Go, sell what you have, and give to the poor" (Mark 10:21).

Go and sell *all*! Now let's not be so literal that we fail to see what Jesus is asking, for the emphasis is not on money. The emphasis is on the all. Our reaction is to say, "Hey, man, do you know who you are talking to? Now if you were talking to someone in Haiti or Ethiopia or Bangladesh, you wouldn't be asking so much because they don't have much. You are asking this of an affluent twentieth-century American. We have a lot to give up!" But if you read the New Testament, you will discover that Jesus always demands a radical obedience. You must come and give all. That is threatening, isn't it? We miss the point if we think that how much we have is the issue in question. The important thing is how much Jesus demanded. We all want to run our own lives. The rich young ruler, like most of us, turned away with sagging shoulders and dropped head because he wasn't willing to surrender all to Jesus. It means putting God and others first. The first time I visited a state mental hospital, I asked the attendant who was directing the tour, "I suppose these people here are not themselves." To which he answered, "Oh, no sir. Just the opposite. In fact, that is all they think of is themselves. That's why they're here." Jesus understood what was necessary for good mental and spiritual health: to surrender ourselves. Did he not say, "He who finds his life will lose it, and he who loses his life for my sake shall find it" (Matt. 10:39). That scared this young man away because he couldn't understand how, by surrendering all, you can make yourself rich. To him, that seemed like the fastest way to get poor. And he was interested in getting more, because he used the terminology, "What must I do to inherit?" "How can I find riches I do not have?" Jesus knew he was interested in riches. So he responded, "If you go and sell all, then you will become rich in heaven." But he could not understand that. That was not the kind of riches he had in mind.

A young man feeling a call to the ministry called me from the college he was attending and asked, "What must I give up to be a minister?" I knew what he meant—beer, girls, cigarettes, and so on. He wanted some easy things he could do. So I responded, "You do not have to give up anything to be a Christian or a minister. In fact, as long as you are still asking that question, you are not ready to make that decision. I sensed he was confused when he hung up the phone. About a year later, the same young man called me to say, "I have surrendered my life to Christ to be used in ministry." Enthusiastically he went on to say, "I discovered what you meant when you said as long as I asked what must I give up that I was not ready. I have discovered that what I get is so wonderful and valuable compared to what I will give up that the cost seems insignificant."

I was talking to a young man who had extended himself in a rather extravagant way. He was heavily in debt, trying to start a new business. But he was extremely generous with his money to the church. Once I said to him, "You can't afford to do that." He became irritated and said, "Preacher, don't tell me I can't afford it. I have a rich heavenly Father who says to me, 'All I have is yours.' " That was what Jesus was saying to the rich young ruler. In Mark 10:30, Jesus says that if we give our all, he will multiply it "a hundredfold." That's why he said that if we go and sell and give all, then we "will have treasure in heaven" (Mark 10:21).

That is hard to do, isn't it? We want to run our own lives, even if they are terrible messes. I heard a story of a peanut vendor who pushed a wooden cart through Brooklyn, selling peanuts. One day he began to realize that he was losing money, so he decided to end his life. He shoved his cart in an alley, went to his one-room flat and put on his only suit. With his last fifty dollars, he decided that before he ended his life he would blow all his money on a swanky meal. Entering a prestigious restaurant, he was met by the head waiter, who told him, "I'm sorry, sir, but all the tables are taken." The peanut vendor turned away sorrowfully, and the head waiter sensed that something was wrong. He stopped the man as he prepared to leave and said, "But if you wouldn't mind sharing a table with another gentleman, I can seat you."

"Oh, that would be all right," responded the peanut vendor. The waiter ushered him to a table where a man was seated by himself. The man struck up a conversation with the peanut vendor by asking him, "Well, what kind of business are you in?" The peanut vendor said, "I'm in merchandising." The man asked, "What is your position?" The vendor said, "I'm a chairman of the board and treasurer." Well, this was very impressive sounding, and he liked the guy's ideas the more they talked. So the man said, "Well, I am in the same kind of business. I like your ideas, and I need a partner. Let me propose that we merge our corporations and form a conglomeration." The peanut vendor thought that sounded like a pretty good offer, so he asked, "What is your name?" The man said, "My name is Mr. Rockefeller."

Well, you know what went through the peanut vendor's mind right away: "This is the wealthiest man in the world. If I merge my corporation I might not be chairman of the board. I might have to be vice-chairman." Immediately, he stood up and said, "You'll have to excuse me. I cannot accept your offer." He left the restaurant and went back, pulled his little cart out of the alley, and resumed selling peanuts.

How like most of us that is. God offers us a chance to merge with him, to jointly share in the richest kingdom there is, if we will only surrender our all to him. But you and I would rather handle our little peanut business and be the head of a bankrupt life than to merge with God and share in the unsearchable riches of Christ. The rich young ruler couldn't understand how by surrendering all he could become rich. Do you?

Suggestions for Worship

Call to Worship:

Minister: We come to worship and to inquire of God.

People: **We come to find out what we need to do.**

Minister: If you learn what you need to do, will you do it?

People: **We will do whatever Jesus tells us. Amen.**

Prayer of Confession: Father, we confess that often we know what you desire of us, but we have been reluctant to give it. We have been obsessed with wanting to be the boss and manager of our lives. We have made a mess of our lives and now desire you to forgive us our mistakes and sins and enable us to turn our all over to your control. Amen.

Suggested Hymns: "This Is My Father's World"; "Jesus Is All the World to Me"; "Take My Life, and Let It Be."

Pastoral Prayer: Father, we praise you for all you have given us. We acknowledge that it all belongs to you. However, we confess that we have managed our lives as though it all belonged to us. We rejoice that you understand as well as forgive our grasping and hoarding. We pray that you will enable us to surrender all we have and are to you and that you will use us to feed the hungry, care for the hurting, and minister to the poor.

We especially pray that each member of the church will find meaning in his or her stewardship, that it will strengthen the church, and that they will experience a new joy through it. Pour down the generosity of your Holy Spirit over all of us who profess to serve you. Amen.

OCTOBER 20

□

Twenty-second Sunday After Pentecost

The suffering servant is a common motif in the lections for today. It is the mark of greatness.

The Sunday Lessons

The Psalm: Psalm 35:17-28.

Isaiah 53:7-12: The servant's life is described as one of humiliation and suffering. Although he was neither violent nor deceitful, he was "cut off out of the land of the living" (v. 8). His death, as seen by God, was for others. The servant "bore the sin of many" (v. 12), and his humiliation became honor.

Hebrews 4:14-16: Christ, the great high priest, provides a way to approach God. Moreover he is able to sympathize with our weaknesses because he has known human suffering. "Let us then with confidence draw near to the throne of grace, that we may receive mercy" (v. 16).

Mark 10:35-45: James and John came to Jesus, asking to sit "one at your right hand and one at your left, in your glory" (v. 37). "Are you able to drink the cup that I drink?" (v. 38), he asked in return. Then he responded to the other disciples who were indignant at James and John: "Whoever would be great among you must be your servant" (v. 43). The Son of man gave his life as a ransom for many.

Interpretation and Imagination

Numerous sermons and books have challenged the self-reali-zation, look-out-for-number-one cults that abound in our society. One of the most imaginative and refreshing is Charles Swindoll's *Improving Your Serve*. In the second chapter, he makes a case for unselfishness and begins by quoting the sarcasm of Wilbur Rees:

> I would like to buy $3 worth of God, please, not enough to explode my soul or disturb my sleep, but just enough to equal a cup of warm milk or a snooze in the sunshine. I don't want enough of him to make me love a black man or pick beets with a migrant. I want ecstasy, not transformation; I want the warmth of the womb, not a new birth. I want a pound of the Eternal in a paper sack. I would like to buy $3 worth of God, please.

James and John were asking for a part of Christ and his kingdom. Our Lord challenged them and the disciples and all who may want to follow to drink his bitter cup of suffering and to take his servant style. He did not suggest following at a safe distance or offer seats in attractive places.

NEEDED: MORE MEMBERS LIKE LUTHER

John 8:31-36

A SERMON BY RICHARD ANDERSEN

While Martin Luther represents many different things to different people, to those of us who rejoice in his discovery of scripture's emphasis on salvation by grace through faith, we would welcome more members like him. He was more than courageous; he was a careful student. He was more than conscientious; he was perceptive. Indeed, Martin Luther was more than determined; he was faithful. He loved the church, but he loved Christ and his Word more. What we need are more members like Luther.

Somehow, from the first to the sixteenth centuries, Christianity became overgrown with the weeds of heresy. It took Luther to yank them out, roots and all, from the garden of faith. Others had tried to do so before, but were overcome by the forces inured in error. Jan Hus made the attempt in Prague, Savonarola in Florence, John Wyclif in merry old England a hundred years before Luther. All four of these reformers were condemned to death, but only with the first three was the order accomplished.

Some have dared to call the man of Wittenberg "the thirteenth apostle," but I am certain he would back off from such a title. He was an ardent Christian, to whom faith was not static like the electrical snap that happens in dry air when one moves over a plush carpet, a momentary shock, a temporary tingle, and nothing more. To him, faith was a living, thriving, constantly growing thing. He believed Jesus when he said the truth would make people free. Here was a dynamic that could not be tied down and bound up by human rules and ceremonial laws. Swept up by the surging force of divine love, Luther rode the crest, declaring God's boundless love to the whole world.

What is needed by this church in this age, as well as by every congregation of believers in every time, is more members like Luther. And it's possible.

When we continue in the Word, we become free disciples; we become like Luther. When we continue to be faithful to Christ, we are free forever, just as was that peasant scholar who spread the news the just shall live by faith!

What we need is not more Luthers, but more members like him, by whom God's published Word—the Bible—and God's living Word—his Son—are not ignored, but explored; not abhored, but adored. Jesus said it plainly: "If you continue in my word, you are truly my disciples, and you will know the truth, and the truth will make you free" (John 8:31-32).

In the sixteenth century, many professors, prelates, popes, priests had been fooled by the thin layers of apostasy that veiled apostolic faith. Like the many-layered textures of French pastry, the fruit of the good news was obscured by tasteless dough, by misguided pronouncements and ignorant interpretations, the rules and rituals, the superstition and superimposed legalism. They got wrapped up in logic and liturgies without searching the scriptures. Guilt heavy handedly was pounded into the populace.

Martin Luther suffered from it himself. It was years before he discovered the loving God. He beat his body and did penance for the most absurd infractions of the tiniest laws. All he perceived was a God of judgment, vengeance, and determined meanness. It was only as Luther dug into the Word, into the Bible, and studied its magnificent truths that his soul was liberated from the bondage ignorance had imposed. He studied the Word with such ardor that he mastered its original languages, Hebrew and Greek, and then proceeded to put its message in the vernacular of the German peasants. Until he died, he was still revising this translation to make it more in keeping with the original. As Shakespeare and the King James Bible made English soar, so Luther's German Bible gave splendor to the heretofore disparaged German language. He was deep in the Word of God.

What we need are more members like Luther who study the Bible and apply it to life, who know its joy and not just its judgment, who find they are loved by God rather than loathed, who cannot keep their freedom to themselves, but gladly share it, as they publish its glad tidings by word and deed. Such people become Jesus' freed disciples, freed from the notion that they must save themselves and free from the hopelessness the concept of a tyrannical God imposes. They find Jesus removing the shackles of uncertainty and ripping out the separating walls of misunderstanding. And, like a zealous Luther, they liberate others, simply because the wondrous joy breaking forth within will not permit them to keep silent as others stew in the pot of fear and feudalism.

Luther once wrote an imagined conversation with the devil. Old Nick speaks to the reformer and taunts him: "Luther, you are a great sinner and you will be damned." Luther was startled not for one moment before he replied: "That is not good reasoning. It is true that I am a great sinner, but it is written that Jesus Christ came to save sinners. Therefore I shall be saved." What we need are more members who have read God's Word and understand this thrilling truth.

Get into the Word and free yourself from the devil's destructive powers. Get into the Bible and find love in a person, God reaching out to all of us to rescue us through Christ from sin's numbing power. Like Martin Luther, continue in the Word, as Jesus urges. If you're not the thirteenth apostle, you will nevertheless be a free one, no longer bound by the ropes and chains of unsatisfied law and unforgiven sin. If there is one ounce of doubt or one fragment of fear, continue in God's Word to find the truth and be set free. What we need in this world are more Christians like Luther who get into the Word and are set free to set others free as well.

But a pure scholasticism that examines the Word and

intellectualizes faith is a pale ghost of the freedom God wants us to have and Luther manifested. Let the Word deepen you in Christ and then continue in him to be free forever.

The Jews were puzzled by Jesus' words. They thought that because they were the heirs of Abraham they were free, even though they had been conquered numerous times by enemies around them. Even at this time, they were a puppet state of Rome. Jesus answered their query with a profound concept: "Truly, truly, I say to you, every one who commits sin is a slave to sin. The slave does not continue in the house for ever; the son continues for ever. So if the Son makes you free, you will be free indeed" (John 8:34-36). That was Luther's experience and the reason he went to great lengths to share this good news with everyone from prince to emperor to peasants to pope.

When a new lad moved into the neighborhood, he struck fear in the hearts of all the other kids. He was a pompous bully. Only one small child was unafraid. "What's the matter with you? Ain't you scared of me?" the bully bellowed.

"Course not," was the speedy retort. "My big brother's the boxing champeen, and if you touch me he'll tear you apart." So the devil, the world, and our own flesh swagger cockily up to us and demand, "Ain't you afraid?" Martin Luther penned our answer in "A Mighty Fortress Is Our God":

> No strength of ours can match his might!
> We would be lost, rejected.
> But now a champion comes to fight,
> Whom God himself elected.
> Ask who this may be:
> Lord of hosts is he!
> Jesus Christ, our Lord,
> God's only Son, adored.
> He holds the field victorious.

Luther, in his exposition of John 17, said:

> I do not know how strong in the Spirit others are. But I cannot become as holy as some imagine themselves to be, however learned and full of the Spirit I might be. I still constantly find that when I am without the Word, Christ is gone, yes, and so are joy and the Spirit. But as soon as I look at a psalm or a passage of Scripture, it so shines and burns into my heart that I gain a different spirit and mind. Moreover, I know that everybody may daily experience this in his own life.

He was saying that the living Jesus is resurrected from the tombs of biblical study when we continue in him, letting the joy he gives pulsate in our words and actions.

Jesus Christ, arising from the grave in which the law buries him, inspires us to love as he loves, to aid others as he does, to counsel the foolish and caution the ridiculous as he did as he went from village to village in the Israel of his days on earth. When you continue in Christ, there is no doubt about contributing to agencies that help the truly needy, that provide food and shelter for the homeless and assistance for those dying of AIDS, shriveling from cancer, weakening from advancing years. There is no hesitancy to befriend others or encourage the frightened. Christ within us frees us from bondage to the self that makes serving him by serving others no longer a hated obligation, but the natural response of love. That is to be more like the reformer by letting Christ live within us. It's then that freedom is a reality instead of a theory.

But Martin Luther was a sinner. He did not assume more of a role than to be a teacher. He did not presume to instruct others, as Paul did, to "be imitators of me." It was not for his life that he wanted to be heard, but for his doctrine, the message of salvation by grace through faith, which was not his invention, but the rediscovered truth from the pages of Holy Writ. Luther's hope was that humankind would come to trust God's grace, his love, and become loving themselves by continuing in Christ. "God can make himself known only through those works which he manifests in us, and which we feel and experience within ourselves," said the reformer. "But where there is this experience, there, a hearty love for him is born, the heart overflows with gladness, and goes leaping and dancing for the great pleasure it has found in God."

To the people of Wittenberg, where Luther taught in the university and celebrated mass in the town church, he said in 1522: "Through love we must do unto one another as God has done unto us through faith. A faith without love is not enough—rather it is not faith at all, but a counterfeit." To him, to be a Christian was always a developing factor. No one ever completely reached it, but the Spirit of God was constantly cultivating that quality as the believer continued in Christ. The Christian is being freed more and more from those devilish things that enslaved him or her.

That's why we need more members like Luther. He made mistakes. He wrote some terrible things about Jews and got involved in some controversies that tainted his reputation at times. And yet, when we examine him more closely, we discover that it is not these unfortunate frailties that are uppermost, but his contrition at having failed his Lord and his resolve to deepen himself in Christ anew, that the Savior might more brightly shine through him.

Like the pair of California gray whales that Eskimos, scientists, and Soviet icebreakers released from impending death in a frozen sea, Jesus Christ has set us free forever by not only breaking up the ice of sin and law, but also melting it so that we may swim on to eternity with him. Luther rediscovered this truth, and to God we owe thanks that one awakened Christian could break through the frozen ice once more.

Do we not need this kind of humility, which resounds from error through grace, to live graciously all over again as a freed slave and a disciple of Christ? If not the "thirteenth apostle," Martin Luther echoed the good news of the other twelve so that the world has not forgotten it.

What is that good news? It is Jesus, God's Son, who, though sinless, became enslaved to our need for salvation and took our sins upon himself, so that God's love might make the one pure sacrifice required to atone for them. He was nailed to the cross as firmly as Luther nailed his ninety-five theses to the Wittenberg door sixteen centuries later. Jesus Christ is the truth who sets us free, who conquered death and enables us to master life with a sense of joy that comes from knowing grace has saved us.

Friend, it's not that we need more Luthers—there was only one. What we need are more members like him who feed their souls daily on generous helpings of God's Word and, therefore, are set free and who, in discovering Christ, continue in him to an ever expanding freedom from sin that makes them free indeed until the day eternity happens.

What this church and the church at large need are more members who trust the Word and follow Christ as sincerely as that German theologian who nailed down hope when he nailed up the ninety-five theses. Friend, pursue grace by getting into the Word, and then follow Christ as a freed soul forever, endlessly rejoicing. Amen.

Suggestions for Worship

Call to Worship:

Minister: He was oppressed, and he was afflicted.

People: **Yet he opened not his mouth.**

Minister: Like a lamb that is led to the slaughter.

People: **So he opened not his mouth.**

All: **Let us take on his likeness.**

Prayer of Confession: O holy and merciful God, we confess that we have not always taken upon ourselves with joy the yoke of obedience, nor been willing to seek and to do your perfect will. We have not loved you with all our heart and mind and soul and strength, neither have we loved our neighbors as ourselves. You have called us in the need of our fellows, and we have passed unheeding on our way. In the pride of our hearts and our willingness to repent, we have turned away from the cross of Christ and have grieved your Holy Spirit. Amen.

Suggested Hymns: "Praise to the Living God"; "O Jesus, I Have Promised"; "Are Ye Able."

Pastoral Prayer: Master, you taught us not only with words, but also with the giving of your life, that it is more blessed to give than to receive. We praise you for your example, and for your strength and spiritual power, which can enable us to become like you. May we learn to take our discipleship seriously—the demands as gifts, the sacrifices as privileges, and the calling as being loved and chosen. May we drink deeply of the cup and be extravagant with our service. Amen.

OCTOBER 27

□

Twenty-third Sunday After Pentecost

Hopelessness is set aside by these lessons, which proclaim salvation.

The Sunday Lessons

The Psalm: Psalm 126.

Jeremiah 31:7-9: The prophet Jeremiah proclaimed salvation: "The Lord has saved his people, the remnant of Israel" (v. 7). From the farthest corners of the earth will gather the blind, the lame, the women with child, and those who weep. "With consolations I will lead them back" (v. 9).

Hebrews 5:1-6: Christ, like a priest after the order of Melchizedek (great high priest) was divinely chosen to act on behalf of others in relations to God. Called to this service by God, he does not set himself apart for it, nor is he elected to it. His sacrifices are for the sins of the people.

Mark 10:46-52: Outside Jericho, a blind beggar named Bartimaeus called out, "Jesus, Son of David, have mercy on me!" (v. 47). Told to be quiet, he cried all the more until Jesus stopped and said, "Call him" (v. 49). The blind man was given sight and "followed him on the way" (v. 52).

Interpretation and Imagination

Bartimaeus was a man who was determined to be heard. Once heard, he was told to ask for what he wanted. Jesus commended him for his faith, which was neither hesitant nor timid.

Depression has become a familiar illness in our society. In vernacular expression, it is spoken as "being in the pits" or "being down." It is the most common kind of mental illness. One

285

counselor has estimated that half of his patients come to him because they are depressed.

Severe depression requires professional counsel. Some normal depression will soon give way to one's willingness to "get out of the ditch." Roland Bainton reports that Luther, no stranger to despair, once gave the earthy counsel, "A good way to exorcise the devil was to harness the horse and spread manure on the fields."

HEALED ON THE WAY

Mark 10:46-52

A SERMON BY ROBERT ERIC BERGLAND

People love parades. It is exciting and fun to see all of the floats, to listen to the bands, and to laugh at the clowns as they pass by. In our lessons this morning, there are parades passing by.

First, turn your attention to Jeremiah 31. Most times when we think of Jeremiah, we envision a prophet of consolation—the man who preached repentance through tears. In chapter 31, Jeremiah proclaims salvation for the children of Israel. How strange it must have sounded: Instead of doom and judgment, a message of hope. And there was no reason for God to save, he just sows. And so, Jeremiah is prompted to describe a kind of "victory parade."

What a strange kind of parade it was. There were the blind, slowly tapping along with their canes, and the lame, limping along with feet and legs that no longer worked very well, and old women with aching bones and young women, heavy with child. This is the victory parade Jeremiah describes. It is completely different from the opening ceremonies of the Olympics. There you see the healthy, young bodies of athletes, well conditioned athletes who jump with joy or march with strength.

Jeremiah's parade reminds me of a movie's portrayal of a Salvation Army band. Have you seen one like it? They were trying their best to play together and march together, but the harder they tried, the more their efforts appeared like confusion.

One would never confuse them with the Marine Corps band.

Another parade, or more likely a procession, is recorded in the Gospel of Mark. Here we meet the blind man named Bartimaeus. Jesus and his disciples were on their way to Jerusalem from Jericho. As Jesus and his band made their way along the road, a crowd followed—the lost, the lonely, the sick, the dying, and the curious. Among them was Bartimaeus, whom the text tells us was blind. But there is nothing wrong with his hearing. From where he had been begging for many long years, he heard that Jesus passed by. When Jesus drew near, he cried out, "Jesus, Son of David, have mercy on me!"

At big parades, especially when someone like the president is involved, you will notice that police officers line the way. They are there to keep a watchful eye on the crowd so that no one will interfere and so that no one will attempt to interrupt those in the procession. That is as it should be.

The disciples were keeping things moving on the road from Jericho to Jerusalem that day. They knew they were headed somewhere important, and they didn't want anyone to get in the way. But a blind beggar who had nothing to give and everything to gain, who had nothing to see and all to hear, was told that Jesus was passing by.

This is the first time Mark allows someone to name Jesus as the Messiah, and it is a beggar. Peter had named Jesus the Messiah, but Jesus told him to tell no one. Others had said Jesus was the Christ, but he charged them to keep silent. But poor, blind Bartimaeus cried out from the crowd, "Jesus, Son of David, have mercy!" and the crowd told him to be quiet!

Jesus stopped. He told his disciples to bring Bartimaeus to him and then asked him, "What do you want me to do?" We read that Bartimaeus asked for his sight and that Jesus healed him because of his faith.

My sisters and brothers, I suggest to you today that this is our story. First of all, some of you here today have nothing to give and everything to gain. You feel that you are not a part of this community of faith, that you are outcast and forgotten and passed by. You are the beggar. The text should encourage you to cry out from where you are, "Jesus, Son of David, have mercy on me!"

Others of you here today are part of the established community. You are well trained in quieting the beggars of this world. You know how to look over the hungry and how to hide the needs of the forgotten from visitors and from your own conscience. This is your story, too. If you find yourself telling the poor, the hungry, the outcast, and the lost to be quiet, if you are one who silences the crowd, hear this: That is not God's way!

Some of you are also like the disciples in this passage. You are content with what you have now, the little vision of God's salvation you have already received. My friends, do not be satisfied with what you have now, for God has an abundance of light and revelation to offer us through Jesus Christ. Give up your false contentment and cry out like the beggar, "Jesus, Son of David, have mercy on me!"

Finally, remember this about the story from Mark: Blind Bartimaeus, whose sight was restored, did not remain where he was. He got up and followed Jesus "on the way."

Some beggars only wanted sight for their blind eyes. When they received that, they remained where they were. Bartimaeus wanted to be with the light of the world. He left the ditch and followed.

Listening to this familiar passage today, some of you might think it is encouraging a save-yourself-sufficiency. Others may find in it the promise of a quick fix. All you have to do is pray, "Jesus, have mercy," and that is all of it. The lessons show our need. They proclaim Christ power.

Then let the text remind us of the one who makes healing possible. Let the story remind us of the one who brings sight to the blind. His name is Jesus, Son of David; Jesus, the Christ; Jesus, the Son of God! And we are called to follow with faith. The next step is obedience.

There is a sculptor named Gutzar Borglum. He has some thoughts regarding his art that may have application for us today. He says: "Don't cut too deep. Don't carve too hard. Don't paint the picture too much yourself." If you look closely at his work, you will find that his sculptures and paintings are simple. He says that he only cuts away the pieces that don't belong there and presently a figure comes to view.

Let the wise among us do the same. Rely on the grace of God in this moment to save and transform your life into the creature he intended you to be. Christ does the healing. We are called to follow.

Suggestions for Worship

Call to Worship:

Minister: Sing aloud with gladness, proclaim, give praise and say,

People: **The Lord has saved his people, the remnant of Israel!**

Minister: They shall come and sing aloud on the height of Zion,

People: **And they shall be radiant over the goodness of the Lord.**

Prayer of Confession: Most merciful God, we confess that we have sinned against you in thought, word, and deed, by what we have done and what we have left undone. We have not loved you with our whole hearts; we have not loved our neighbors as ourselves. We are truly sorry and humbly repentant. For the sake of your Son, Jesus Christ, have mercy on us and forgive us that we may delight in your will and walk in your ways to the glory of your name. Amen.

Suggested Hymns: "O For a Thousand Tongues to Sing"; "Open My Eyes, That I May See"; "Pass Me Not, O Gentle Savior."

Pastoral Prayer: Almighty God, from a world of hurry and care, we come, seeking your presence. As you brought out of captivity the children of Israel and gave sight to those who were blind, so make us to know your presence among us now and open our eyes that we may see with eyes of faith.

We give you thanks for the gift of the seasons, for all the splendor and beauty of creation, for the cool breezes of autumn and the wonder of the trees painted in glorious colors. We thank you for your love, which extends to all the corners of this world. You seek out those who are lame, that they might follow you. Those who are hungry, you fill with the eternal bread of life. You offer to those held captive by sin the promise of release. For all your many kindnesses, we give you thanks.

We would not let this hour pass without remembering the needs of our sisters and brothers in this world—those whose eyes are blinded from the beauty of your creation by selfish desires and greed; those who refuse to follow you because fear has paralyzed their bodies; those who have built prisons around themselves to escape the realities of life. May they come to know you as Lord, that their eyes might be opened, their bodies strengthened, and their lives made free in Jesus Christ.

Empower us as the church, that we might faithfully follow you along pathways that lead to caring for the needs of those fallen in spirit and reaching out to those seeking your truth.

This is our prayer, O Lord. We make it in the Spirit and name of Jesus Christ, our Savior. Amen.

NOVEMBER 3

□

Twenty-fourth Sunday After Pentecost

The greatest commandment is the theme of these lessons.

The Sunday Lessons

The Psalm: Psalm 119:33-48.

Deuteronomy 6:1-9: This sum of the law, "You shall love the Lord your God with all your heart" (v. 5), is the beginning of the *Shema,* the Jews' daily profession of faith. It is to be remembered, taught, discussed, carried about, and inscribed. The New Testament also teaches total love to God alone.

Hebrews 7:23-28: Christ is able to save those who draw near to God through him. He is different from other priests, being perfectly holy and having a priesthood of permanence.

Mark 12:28-34: One of the scribes (the best paid professionals in first-century culture) heard the disputes with Pharisees and Sadducees. He asked which law was most important—there were more than six hundred. To desire God above all things and all others with wholehearted devotion is the first commandment. The second asks for complete dedication to one's neighbor.

Interpretation and Imagination

Six hundred laws to obey or even to remember is a bit much. The apostle Paul found the law to be burdensome. Modern Christians hear Paul's desire for freedom in Christ, but for the most part choose their favorite precepts like they pick their favorite foods.

Not all Israelites found the law to be "oppressive, breeding despair and hypocritical displays of religion." Jesus affirmed its basic tenets, as did Paul. And these lections reflect reverence for law.

Often, our reverence for the law is reflected by a concern for "What is the great commandment that we should honor above all?" Jesus showed his respect for the law by commanding us to love God and neighbor. But this law can never be enforced. Tax laws can be. Traffic laws become habits. We demand pure food and drugs. Yet, the centering and saving law above all laws will always be an invitation more than a summons, a "right way" more than a rule.

THE FIRE THAT BURNS IS LOVE

Mark 12:28-34

A SERMON BY SAMUEL WYNN

The scripture lesson from Mark reveals the uniqueness and simplicity of the gospel in the word *love*. It is descriptive and inclusive in scope and focus. The text is a summation of the law. It reflects upon the fire of love that burns within the tenets of the Christian faith.

One cannot easily ignore or overlook the importance of the obligation of love. Nor should the implications of its message vacate the pews of our churches and the corridors of our society. The law of love, therefore, calls us to a life of tension between a message that embraces the world and a bond with Christ and his church that dares to speak to the complexities and perplexing issues of our day. The obligations of love might best be summed up in the saga of the Native American, which is articulated in the words of Peggie McIntosh (the wife of William McIntosh, Chief of the Creek Nation), who signed the treaty relinquishing the land of the Creek tribe:

> I do not blame the Creeks, the Creeks treat me well, the Cherokee treat me well—it was Government caused me to suffer, it was by Government my husband lost his life—Government say to my husband, "Go to Arkansas, Go to Arkansas and you will be better off." My husband wished to please the Government—my home is burned, myself and children run—my children naked—no bread—one blanket, is all—like some stray dog, I suffer; with one blanket I cover my three children and myself—Government say "Go!" The Indians kill him; *between two fires my husband dies;* I wander—Government does not feed

me—Creed does not feed me—no home, no bread, nothing!
nothing! (Grant Foreman, *Indian Removal: The Emigration of the
Five Civilized Tribes*)

William McIntosh lost his life trying to stand between the
"fires" of the federal government and the "fires" of his own
people. It is ironic, to say the least, that those fires confront us
and challenge us within contemporary society as well as in the
gospel. Jesus stood between the fire of the law and the new
covenant. His response to the young scribe's question addressed
Israel as well as the Gentile world. Christ defused and disarmed
the legalism of tradition and law. His message claims us today
because it speaks in the universal language of love.

A long time ago, a great teacher, Jesus, said: "He who has my
commandments and keeps them, he it is who loves me; and he
who loves me will be loved by my Father, and I will love and
manifest myself to him" (John 14:21). I invite you to wrestle with
me as we seek to digest the principles locked behind the message
in the teaching of Jesus recorded in Mark's Gospel. For me,
there are several lessons to be learned.

First, we are charged to love God first and foremost. Jesus
responds to the young scribe's question by quoting the Old
Testament passage from Deuteronomy. He couples the Shema
(Deut. 6:4) with the law of neighborly love (Lev. 19:18): "The
first is, 'Hear, O Israel: The Lord our God, the Lord is one; and
you shall love the Lord your God'" (Mark 12:29-30). Jesus
reminds the young scribe that Israel is exhorted to "do" and to
"keep" God's law and to "reverence" him as Israel responds to
the law of Moses. Jesus does not ask Israel to consider, nor does
he coach Israel to reconsider, loving God, but he charges Israel
to love God foremost. The charge that is locked behind centuries
of biblical reflection hounds us like an eagle in pursuit of prey.
The only way we may fulfill this charge is to love God and to love
our neighbor. In his book *Guerillas of Grace: Prayers for the
Battle*,* Ted Loder teaches us to pray when he writes:

> O Holy and Haunting Presence
> whose spirit moves quietly

---

* "Prayer from *Guerrillas of Grace* by Ted Loder. Copyright © 1984 by Lura
Media, Inc., San Diego, California. Used by permission.

but surely
in the sound and fury of the world
and of my life,
you know me as rushing water knows the rock
and releases its beauty to reflect new light.
Open me
to the insistent abrasiveness of your grace, for
I often trivialize love by abandoning the struggles
which accompany its joys and rejecting
the changes which lead to its fulfillments.
Release me
from the dark fury of assuming
I am unloved when the day calls
for sacrifice and the night for
courage
Release me . . .
from being possessed by riches I do
not need and grievance that weary me
when you call me to share my very
self with neighbors and to
reflect for the world
the light of the kingdom
within me

If we love God, we will choose to do God's will. The charge embedded in the law of Moses has yet to lose its implicit and explicit value. Love must be internalized and lived out daily. To love God and neighbor is more than all the observance of the law. The love of your neighbor as yourself is the fire that burns the brightest.

The Hopi have a legend called the "New Fire Ceremony," a sacred ritual practiced at the beginning of the new year. This ritual has been passed down from one generation to another for centuries:

New life, new fire.
In the Hopi kivas, the new fires bring life for a new year, perhaps for a new era, as prophecies have said! The rite of life, the rite of hope. This is the same ritual which makes the stars stay where they are, the sun shine and the moon glow. . . .
For as long as we stay on this cradle, this arbor, prepared for us to make us of, we will follow the sacred writing on the rock as they remind us to do. (Robert Boissiere, *Meditations with the Hopi*)

The sacred writing of the scripture reminds us to live out the double law of love, and it is superior to sacrifice. The Shema (Deut. 6:4) also reminds us to remember that the God of Israel is "one," but the warmth of the law is rekindled when we add love. Bring new life to a new day, a new hope that embraces all people and binds us to Christ and his church. The love of God and the love of neighbor are required for a holy life.

Second, we are invited to love our neighbor: "The second is this, 'You shall love your neighbor as yourself' " (Mark 12:31). Part of the history of North America is well documented and reminds this nation of the many struggles it has overcome. Yet, there are bits and pieces left out of history books. One such incident is the story of Tsali, a brave Cherokee man who gave his life so that his people might have a chance to remain in their homeland in the Great Smokey Mountains. The story is told by Jeannette Henry and Rupert Costo in *A Thousand Years of American Indian Storytelling*.

> In 1838, Tsali and his sons were faced with the time when they were told they must leave their old homeland and go west, to Indian Territory. This area later became the state of Oklahoma.
> There were more than 17,000 Cherokees who were sent out of their homes and forced to travel to the west. Many died on that forced march.
> The Indians were rounded up like cattle and a squad of Georgian soldiers took Tsali and his family. They were taking them down a steep train to be put into a concentration camp before being shipped to the west. The state of Georgia . . . wanted their land.
> As she walked, Tsali's wife grew tired. A soldier pricked her in the back with bayonet. She screamed. Tsali and others in the group became very angry. They attacked the soldiers and took away their guns. Then they ran into the mountains. One soldier was killed in the fight.
> So Tsali and about two thousand of his countrymen remained in the mountains, hiding from the soldiers. The white people were told, "Find Tsali." So a white man, named Will Thomas, was sent to find the Cherokees.
> The Army Commander told Thomas, "Tell Tsali that if he will surrender and pay the penalty for the death of the American soldier, I will help the other fugitives and will convince the government to let them remain in the mountains."
> Thomas took the message to Tsali. So he took his sons, one of whom was a mere boy, and went to the Army Camp and gave himself up. The Army men shot Tsali and his two older sons. The younger son was spared because he was still a child. That is how Tsali saved his people.

Jesus said: "Greater love has no man than this, that a man lay down his life for his friends" (John 15:13). The essence of the lesson from Mark is that the love of God and love of one's neighbor are inseparable, and when its obligations are lived out, it provides fulfillment and purpose for life.

Suggestions for Worship

Call to Worship:

> Leader: Our mouths were filled with laughter, our tongues with songs of joy. . . .

> **People: The Lord has done great things for us, and we are filled with joy.**

> Leader: Restore our fortunes, O Lord, like streams in the [desert].

> **People: Those who sow in tears will reap with songs of joy. (Ps. 126:2-5 NIV)**

Prayer of Confession:

> Minister: O Great God of Spirit,

> **People: Whose voice I hear in the winds, and whose breath gives life to all the world, Hear me! I am small and weak, I need your strength and wisdom.**

> Minister: Let me walk in beauty,

> **People: And make my eyes ever behold your creation.**

> Minister: Make my hands

> **People: Respect the things you have made and my ears sharp to hear the voice of my neighbors when they cry for help.**

> Minister: Make me wise

> **People: So that I may understand the things you have taught my people.**

> Minister: Make me always ready

People: To come to you with clean hands and straight eyes. So when life fades, as the sunset, my spirit may come to you without shame. Amen.

Suggested Hymns: "Many and Great, O God"; "How Great Thou Art"; "God Is Love, by Him Upholden"; "More Love to Thee, O Christ."

Pastoral Prayer: Let us pray for our neighbor who lives in a world of brokenness and confusion.

O God of our ancestors, it is with humility we seek your attention at this hour. We are reminded, O Lord that you are able to teach us your statutes, give us understanding that we may learn to keep your laws and observe them with our whole heart. O God, we pray for our neighbor who lives in a world of broken promises. Help us to feel your urge and your message to "love our neighbor as ourselves." Help us to love those who hate us and hate the sting of sin that defuses our path of love.

Lead us in the path of your commandments, so we will take delight in them. Allow the flame of your love to burn in our world, not forgetting those who live next door. As we assemble in the Council chambers and corridors of our places of worship help us to allow the fire of your love to burn in our midst as a sign of your presence.

Let us pray for the church.

O God, you built your church upon love, help us to rekindle the flame of love. As the church moves into the world, remind us that a church aflame with love is a church with vision and purpose. For the unity of the church we pray, and for her fellowship across the embittered lines of race and nation; and to her growth in grace, her building in love, her enlargement in service, her increase in wisdom, faith, charity and power, we dedicate our lives.

Too often we assemble in our local places of worship forgetting about our neighbor's church in other places in the world. Forgive us for seeking the log that is in our neighbor's eye and refusing to remove the plank from our own. "Before we judge our friends, O let us wear their moccasins and share the path that they would take in wearing them; Then, we shall understand and not condemn." For we pray in Jesus' name. Amen.

November 10

□

Twenty-fifth Sunday After Pentecost

Two widows who offered their gifts and themselves to God are remembered in these lessons.

The Sunday Lessons

The Psalm: Psalm 146.

I Kings 17:8-16: The widow of Zarephath lived in a pagan land where the fertility god, Baal, was worshiped. In the midst of famine she gave her last bit of meal to Elijah. "The jar of meal was not spent, neither did the cruse of oil fail" (v. 16). God's power was revealed.

Hebrews 9:24-28: Hebrews explains how Christ has been made perfect. The obedient sacrifice of himself enabled him to enter, not a sanctuary made with hands, but into the very presence of God. Christ, who is both our priest and our sacrifice, intercedes for us before God.

Mark 12:38-44: Jesus rebuked the scribes, "who devour widow's houses" (v. 40) and pretend to pray. He noticed the gifts given to the Temple, even a very small coin, the widow's mite. Then he noted that in giving her last penny she gave more than those who, in showy and shallow ways, gave gifts that cost them little. She gave everything she had.

Interpretation and Imagination

In any pilgrimage the next step is obedience. We all know more good to do than we do. We have goals greater than our personal disciplines achieve. The great commandment surpasses our conduct. The next step in matters of faith is obedience.

From time to time there arises among us one whose love and

devotion is so compelling that he or she will give everything to God. Faith is not merely professed; love is not simply declared; they are lived out in simple, yet costly, ways.

Two widows, both poor and acquainted with hunger, suffering and tears, took all they had, put it in one heap and store, and gave it to the One they believed had it right. That kind of love is its own reward. Any mother who would gladly go hungry so that her children can eat and even longs to take the place of her suffering and dying child knows that.

The lessons suggest two reasons for giving. One is the hope of blessing. Give and it shall be given to you. Your jar of meal will never be empty, and your cruse of oil will never be dry. There is a more excellent way.

The other, not so much concerned about tomorrow but committed to forever, invests everything in the one that will last. It seeks no immediate reward. The story of the widow's mite is followed by signs of the end and then the story of Christ's arrest and crucifixion. Greater love has no one than to lay down one's life for one's friends.

A WIDOW'S TRUST ACCOUNT

Mark 12:44

A SERMON BY PETER D. WEAVER

You did what? You put in everything you had! Imagine the frustration and consternation in the minds of the friends and family of the widow we read about in the Gospel of Mark as she returned home—that is, if she had a home. *You did what?*

Poverty was the defining word of her life. The death of her husband had surely left her poor in spirit. Her emotions had been impoverished by grief. She knew a sense of loss far more profound than bankruptcy or stock crashes. She knew the depression of the heart—poverty.

Many here today understand that widow's loss and the "feeling poorly" that follows. Ira Nerken, Director of Widowed Persons Grieving Support Groups, writes: "Death's most frightening message is found in the griever's lament 'All is lost.' All that was once important and meaningful, all that made life valuable is gone" ("Making It Save to Grieve," *The Christian Century* [Nov. 30, 1988]:1092). When the valuable is gone, there is poverty. She was a widow. In that descriptive word we catch a glimpse of her heart.

Friends and family would be concerned that out of her grief, out of her poverty of the heart, she would not do anything hasty or seemingly irrational. *You did what?*

Poverty defined her financial condition as well. There was no trust account to see her through. There was no Social Security check in the mail or government program for the dependent children she may have had to feed and clothe. There was no "prudential rock" of mortgage insurance that assured her a place to continue to live.

But there were always the scribes, legal experts waiting in the wings to "grow fat on widows' property" (Mark 12:40 JBP). She would have understood the film *Places in the Heart.* She would have recognized that young widow who was visited, following the funeral, by the churchgoing banker who was accustomed to the best seats and places of honor. Dressed in the finest mourning black, he came to pay his respects to the widow and to remind her that she must pay the mortgage on the farm. Surely this would be an impossible task for a woman who didn't know the first thing about cotton farming. Therefore, being the religious man that he was, he and the bank would extend the generous gesture of taking the farm off her hands. Widows' hands were empty, impoverished hands. They rarely had as much as two coins to rub together.

You did what with those two coins?

Jesus saw what she did, even as he knows what we do. Sitting opposite the Jerusalem Temple alms box, he spotted her in the crowd. In her worn and simple clothing, she moved quietly along, brushing by those in elaborate long robes, who were proudly chattering their hearty salutations above her head. The Temple was a grand place to show off one's abundance of coins tumbling into the treasury—if they could give that much to God, just think how much more they must have for purchasing the latest robes and best tickets for the feasts.

Jesus alerted his disciples. Are you alert to see this? There, among those with princely life-styles, was a widow who undoubtedly knew the meaning of Psalm 146:3: "Put not your trust in princes." The bank trust accounts and elaborate robes and best seats are of no account when the "breath departs" (Ps. 146:4). Rather, "the Lord . . . upholds the widow" (Ps. 146:9). She was there, not to parade herself, but to praise God. She had a different trust account to tell about: the riches of trusting in God even in the times of the poverty of the heart. God had been with her, as God has been with us, through the valleys and the shadows and times of death and feeling poorly. Come to the Temple. Praise the Lord! Sing praises to God as long as we have being. This widow was a walking trust account.

Her whole living had been so enriched by God in her poverty of heart that when she saw the alms box as a way to give an account of her trust in and thanksgiving to God, she rubbed her two coins together, her only two coins, and "out of her poverty [she] put in everything she had, her whole living" (Mark 12:44).

You did what? She exercised radical trust that in her poverty God would provide. This was not the act of a deranged woman who did not know the critical value of her two coins, but rather an account of trust by a woman whose priorities in life had been rearranged because she knew the critical value of God's presence and promises in her life.

She understood the poverty and trust of the widow at Zarephath, who had "only a handful of meal in a jar, and a little oil [and] . . . a couple of sticks" (I Kings 17:12) for herself and her son. Yet, that widow heeded the call of God. According to the trust account in I Kings, she risked giving her bread, maybe her only bread, to Elijah first. "You did what?" you can imagine her hungry son asking her. Yet, as God promised, in that radical act of trust and giving "she, and he, and her household ate for many days. The jar of meal was not spent, neither did the cure of oil fail" (I Kings 17:15-16).

What about our trust? What account can we give? Do we give out of our abundance as these widows did out of their poverty? Do we trust God in the events that impoverish our spirits, when "all is lost?" Do we trust enough to come to worship with a genuine "Praise the Lord" as the offering of our heart? Does that spirit of praise and offering extend to our coins and checks in such a complete way that someone sitting across from the treasury might in astonishment blurt out, "You did what? You doubled your stewardship commitment of time, talents, and finances for God's work next year? Are you trusting God enough to tithe 10 percent of your income, including your jar of meal and cruse of oil? You did what—put everything in, your whole living?"

Betty had been homeless, sleeping on the streets of Pittsburgh, when she was welcomed into Smithfield Church and the Bethlehem Haven shelter for homeless women. She came to worship and then Sunday school. In Christian hospitality, she was welcomed by others in the congregation to eat with them after worship. Sometimes she would dig down into her bag and bring out tattered black and white photos of happier days with her family and the dog she dearly loved.

Now she was poor and lonely. Maybe she was a widow. She had no Social Security checks, fancy long robes, or places of honor in this world. But out of her poverty she came often to the "temple." Homeless and alone, she gave her accounts of trust in the loving God who was her "best Friend." One day she reached deep into her bag for something that she pressed quietly into the pastor's hand. "Use this," she whispered, "to share the love of Jesus, which I have experienced here." Opening his hand, the pastor discovered a carefully folded ten dollar bill, enough for Betty to buy coffee for a week or five meals at a fast-food restaurant or a warmer coat at Goodwill or a ticket for a good seat on a bus to a warmer climate. It was probably everything she had. But then, in her poverty she knew better than many of us that God is everything. Hers was the best trust account of all. Betty, you did what?

What kind of trust account is yours? A widow's trust? Have you ever been so moved to praise and trust God that you wanted to give God your all? But then someone might say, it might even be Jesus, You did what?

Suggestions for Worship

Call to Worship:

Minister: We brought nothing into the world!

People: **Yet, God has richly blessed us with gifts of love and bounty.**

Minister: We can take nothing out of this world!

People: **Thus God calls us to share our gifts with others now.**

Minister: Let us worship God, who is the giver.

People: **Let us dedicate ourselves to be giving.**

Suggested Hymns: "Awake, My Soul, and with the Sun"; "Take My Life, and Let It Be"; "We Give Thee but Thine Own"; "More Love to Thee, O Christ."

Pastoral Prayer: O Lord, your gifts surround us: loved ones, friends, creation, clothing, books, music, food, transportation, homes, freedom, the warmth of a smile. Your gifts are within us: joy, hope, confidence, peace, forgiveness, love, truth, faith, abundant life.

Having been given so much, we yearn for one more gift. God, grant us thankful hearts and sharing hands. Whether out of our abundance or out of poverty, may we trust you enough to offer you our all.

Hear our prayers in the name of Christ, who gave totally of himself for us and for our world. Amen.

NOVEMBER 17

□

Twenty-sixth Sunday After Pentecost

All time and the end of time are themes that mark the lessons of this next-to-last Sunday of the Christian year.

The Sunday Lessons

The Psalm: Psalm 145:8-13.

Daniel 7:9-14: In Daniel's vision, four beasts (four kingdoms) turned to see a throne above all thrones where the "ancient of days took his seat" (v. 9). The rule of all others was taken away and given to me "like a son of a man" (v. 13). His kingdom shall never be destroyed.

Hebrews 10:11-18: The perfect sacrifice made by Christ as the great high priest was not for today only, but "for all times." Seated at the right hand of God, sovereign grace waits, but the final victory is already won.

Mark 13:24-32: This apocalypse, like that in Daniel and Revelation, employs images and symbols that reach beyond the kind of time and space we have known and experienced: "the sun will be darkened, and the moon will not give its light, and the stars will be falling . . . the Son of man coming in clouds" (vv. 24-26). It teaches that the end is not yet here but that it is "at the very gate." Only God knows the hour.

Interpretation and Imagination

When I think of a kingdom that will last forever, I think in terms of time neverending. Forever is a very long time.

When I think of a day "when the trumpet of the Lord shall sound and time shall be no more," I think of the end of time, a final consummation of history.

304

Both ideas are present in these lessons, just as both ideas are present in our perceptions regarding time.

When you think of time, what is the first image that comes to your mind? A clock, a calendar, tomorrow, next year, time to kill? Or do you think of a season beginning and ending, a pregnancy that's run its term, a dying person whose time has come, no time to spare?

Sometimes we think of time as a circle, like a clock, it simply goes around and around without beginning or ending. Sometimes we think of time as a straight line, like a schedule, with a time to be born and a time to die, a time to laugh and a time to cry.

The texts teach that all time is God's time. God's rule will not end. Christ's salvation doesn't wear out. When we long for the day when righteousness will be more obviously in control, we can sense its nearness, but we can never know the hour of its arrival.

AROUND THE CORNER

Mark 13:24

A SERMON BY PETER D. WEAVER

"What's around the corner?" asked a curious little girl as she sat with her father in the doctor's waiting room. At the end of the room there was a fascinating hall that disappeared around a corner. Maybe beyond her view was a candy machine or a play room or toys around that corner. She eased out of her seat as if drawn to explore the alluring unknown around that corner. "Or maybe around that corner," her father ominously predicted, "is the examination room where you will get your shot!" The little girl quickly jumped securely into her chair.

We human beings are a curious lot. If we only knew what's ahead, then we could be prepared, or so we think. What was Jean Dixon's latest prediction? Just a glance at our horoscope couldn't hurt, even though I don't believe in such things, you understand. And what about the *Wall Street Journal* comments on where the economy is going? Please don't let me miss the five-day weather forecast. What was it the *Farmer's Almanac* said about the weather this winter? If we could only know what's around the corner. Lean forward, maybe it's something wonderful—or maybe it's a shot!

"In those days there will be . . ." reports the thirteenth chapter of the Gospel of Mark, which is called "the little apocalypse." Apocalyptic literature—like this chapter, the book of Daniel, and the Revelation to John—is often seen as revealing and unveiling the hidden and the future. Maybe finally we can see what's around the corner, but be prepared to sit back securely in your seat. "The sun will be darkened, and the moon will not give its light, and the stars will be falling from heaven, and the powers in the heaven will be shaken" (Mark 13:24-25). Read Daniel if you dare. Around the corner are burning wheels, streams of fire, and slain beasts (Dan. 7:9-11). Aren't you glad you now know what's around the corner?

There are those, even preachers, who will try to tell us they have figured out what all of this means, as indeed some have claimed periodically throughout Christian history. As if God had given them the inside tip or a personal periscope with which to see around the corner, they predicted and believed the world would end and Christ would come in 1893, revised to 1926, revised to 1968, revised to . . . well, you get the picture. These images from thousands of years ago remain cloaked in mystery for the twentieth-century mind.

But then mystery is part of the excitement of going around the corner. In his autobiography, *The Sacred Journey,* Frederick Buechner writes: "I choose to believe that, from beyond time, a saving mystery breaks into our time at odd and unforeseeable moments." The "what" of the mystery and the "time" of the odd moment are not ours to know as we prepare to turn the next corner of our lives. Jesus makes that much clear by saying: "Of that day or that hour no one knows" (Mark 13:32).

In one unforeseeable moment of surprise in that doctor's waiting room, out of the mystery and shadows around that fascinating corner, came the doctor himself. He was well-loved and trusted by the little girl. She eased forward in her chair again. She reached out her hand. She was ready and willing to go into the unknown because she knew who would be there with her, around the corner. And knowing who will be around the

corner with us is far more important than knowing what will be
around the corner.

> I know not what the future hath
>   Of marvel or surprise,
> Assured alone that life and death
>   His mercy underlies
>   . . .
> I know not where His islands lift
>   Their fronded palms in air;
> I only know that I cannot drift
>   Beyond His love and care.
> (John G. Whittier, from "The Eternal Goodness")

Whittier affirmed that God was the "who" in our future. Thus, by
faith, we dare to go with God into the mysteries of the unknown.
It is a "sacred journey."

That is the good news we can clearly understand in today's
reading of apocalyptic literature. God is who will always be with
us no matter what's around the corner. In his "night vision,"
Daniel sees the "one like a son of man" around the corner:

> His dominion is an everlasting
>   dominion,
>   which shall not pass away
> (Dan. 7:14)

Yes, affirms the psalmist:

> Thy kingdom is an everlasting
>   kingdom,
>   and thy dominion endures
>   throughout all generations.
> (Ps. 145:13)

Yes, affirms the writer of Hebrews: "Christ had offered for all
time . . . [and] has perfected for all time those who are
sanctified" (Heb. 10:12, 14). Yes, affirms Jesus: "In those
days . . . see the Son of man coming . . . know that he is near"
(Mark 13:24, 26, 29). Whatever comes, he is near for all time
throughout all generations. Ease to the edge of your seat. Reach
out your hand. He is here, ready to go with you around the
corner.

If illness is there, so will be the one who is the great physician. If grief is there, so will be the one who is our peace. If confusion and complexity are there, so will be the one who is the way, the truth, and the life. If joy is there, so will be the one from whom all blessings flow. If there are unexpected beginnings or endings there, so will be the one who is the alpha and the omega.

Some years ago, one of the first wrenching films about the war in Vietnam was produced with the title *Apocalypse Now*. In images as strangely frightening as stars falling from the heavens and streams of fire, the film sought to convey the chaos and anguish of the seeming end-time in the lives of those swept up in that time and place. The Wong family, who probably never saw that film, actually lived through the horror of that apocalypse and collapse swirling around them. From day to day, if not moment to moment, they had no idea what would be around the corner.

Mrs. Wong described being a few feet from her best friend as she was killed in an explosion in the streets of Saigon. Mrs. Wong gathered her three children and a few of their belongings and began to flee the city, not knowing where to go or what would be ahead. In desperation, she and her children boarded the "boat people" ships, launching out into the unknown. For days they sailed aimlessly. At times she was certain the boat and all on it would be lost to the high seas. She prayed regularly with a small group of other Christians who were also on board. "Even though we did not know what would happen, we feel God was with us," she reported to the congregation in America that had welcomed her as a refugee after she and her children had been rescued. Then, as she told the rest of the story of an incredible journey from one culture to another, never knowing what would be around the corner, she kept punctuating her recollections with "God was with us!" She thanked the congregation for all their generosity and love. "Can I sing a song I've learned from you which says it all for me?" she asked. With her beautiful Vietnamese accent, reminding all of the apocalypse she had experienced, she began to sing:

> Because he lives, I can face tomorrow;
> because he lives, all fear is gone.
> (Gloria and William J. Gaither, "Because He Lives")

You may not know what is around the corner, but do you know who is?

Suggestions for Worship

Call to Worship:

Minister: We have come together from different places.

People: **In all our places, God is with us.**

Minister: We have come together out of our different experiences.

People: **In every experience of life, God is there.**

Minister: We have gathered in this time and place because we are God's people.

People: **Let us worship the God of all times and all places.**

Prayer of Confession: Eternal God of mercy, hear us as we confess our sin. Daily we awaken to a new journey of life; yet, we fail to be thankful for the opportunities that lie before us. Moments await our decision to serve you; yet, time passes away as we think only of ourselves. Our routine gives us the chance to share your love with others; yet, we are absorbed with our own self-improvement. The day soon passes. It has been much the same as other days. Forgive us for casting aside the precious time you have given. Grant us the faith and excitement of walking with you into the future days, in the name of the Christ of all time. Amen.

Suggested Hymns: "O God, Our Help in Ages Past"; "Guide Me, O Thou Great Jehovah"; "God of Our Life, Through All the Circling Years"; "O Master, Let Me Walk with Thee"; "Because He Lives"

November 24

□

Last Sunday After Pentecost (Christ the King)

Stories of fallen kings and forgotten kingdoms litter history. Today we gather as part of a kingdom that is ruled by one who is alpha and omega, the beginning and the end.

The Sunday Lessons

The Psalm: Psalm 93.

Jeremiah 23:1-6: The prophet rebuked those shepherds (Israel's kings) who "scatter the sheep" (v. 1). He foresaw a new day and a new king who "shall execute justice and righteousness in the land" (v. 5).

Revelation 1:4b-8: From his prison island, the exiled John greeted the church in the name of one "who is and who was and who is to come" (v. 4). Christ had suffered and died at the hand of earthly rulers, but now, as firstborn of the dead, he rules all kingdoms.

John 18:23-27: Pilate asked, "Are you the King of the Jews?" (v. 33). Christ's mission cannot be understood in the power structure of an earthbound kingdom. "My kingship is not of this world," Christ answered (v. 36).

Interpretation and Imagination

Questions like Pilate's are too narrow. They only see the kingdoms of the world. Some questions of well-intentioned sermons are too narrow; for example: What are the ruling factors of your life—money, power, knowledge, relationship? To be sure, every priority is challenged, but one cannot assume that a mere mortal can take part in the coronation of this king. This ruler makes every worldly domination and every political kingdom a shadow.

Christ is king. His sovereignty was not decided by a vote of the people. His rule was not established with military conquest. His power does not rest upon economic stability. The royal line from which he came was without honor. Yet, he is king with all the dominion and power of eternal truth.

When King George III oppressed the colonies, the revolutionists declared their independence. They complained, "The king has plundered our seas, ravaged our coasts, burnt our towns, and destroyed our people." They separated themselves from his rule with words about inalienable rights endowed by the Creator. That same Creator, whose truth is revealed by Christ, had made Christ king before the world began. And he shall rule forever and ever. How can anyone escape his rule?

ONE OF OUR VERY BEST WORDS

Luke 17:11-19

A SERMON BY EUGENE BRICE

How much is a word worth? Back when Rudyard Kipling was England's most popular writer, the word went out that his publishers paid him a dollar a word for his work. Some Cambridge students, hearing of this, cabled Kipling one dollar, along with the instructions: "Please send us one of your very best words." Kipling replied with a one-word telegram: "Thanks."

The word *thanks* is indeed one of our very best words, worth much to the person who speaks it and to the person who hears it. The writer of Proverbs expressed it succinctly:

> A word fitly spoken
>   is like apples of gold in a setting
>   of silver.
> (Prov. 25:11).

Thanks is indeed a fitly spoken word. Why, then, do we not speak it and hear it more often than we do? It is not because we are not grateful. We remember well the story of the ten lepers in Luke 17, all of whom were healed of their disease, but only one of whom returned to thank Jesus. Sometimes that story is interpreted to mean that only one of them was grateful, but undoubtedly all of them were. The difference is that nine of them hurried home first, so as to greet their friends and attend to their business as soon as possible, intending, perhaps, to go to Jesus soon afterward and thank him. But, perhaps things did not turn out the way they expected. Maybe they were kept at home longer than they meant to be, and when they returned, Jesus was gone. Only one of them had a disposition that made him act in time to say "Thank you."

There is little doubt that we, today, are grateful for the blessings we have received. But the Thanksgiving season is a time for bringing gratitude to voice and for saying "Thank you"—so let's do that today.

"Thanks," to begin with, for our country. Undoubtedly we are appreciative for our country, but we seldom put our gratitude into words. Our instinct for self-criticism sometimes blinds us to what we do right in this country, and we neglect expressions of thanksgiving. To whom do we say thanks for our country? To patriots long since dead; to pioneers who displayed more courage, more endurance of hardship in a week than some of us do in a lifetime. There's a place off the highway a few miles west of Kansas City where a marker points out the old wagon tracks made by the people who first went westward. Stand there and imagine their hopes and dreams, their fears and hardships. Then say thanks for this country of ours.

We would say thanks as well to all those people who make our lives richer and more meaningful.

Thanks to our families, our parents, who sacrificed for us, our children for their patience, our spouses for their love and faithfulness.

Thanks to friends whose trust and whose laughter set a light in life that gives us both warmth and sight.

Thanks to people in public service—politicians, governors, senators, presidents—who endure unending criticism and little thanks.

Thanks to teachers and administrators in our schools for putting up with difficult children and unreasonable parents.

Thanks to nurses and doctors and custodians in hospitals. In every moment of need, day or night, they are always there.

Thanks to the safety officers who in good weather and bad help little children cross dangerous streets.

Thanks to public utility people, who are called out in storms and bad weather to keep our sources of power going. Thanks to those who are working right now in generating plants to give us power.

Thanks to police officers and fire fighters. We relax from our work occasionally, but they are always on call. They deal with all the tragedies of life and with some of our worst citizens, and they deserve our thanks.

Thanks to truck drivers who keep our stores supplied with food. Thanks to butchers and dairy workers and paper deliverers and garbage collectors.

All these people constitute the spokes of the wheels on which our lives turn. We need them, and to them we say one of our very best words: *thanks.*

We say thanks for things, the items and goods that enrich our lives. When I go home from church today, I am going to be well-fed. I have the good fortune of never having gone really hungry a day in my life, so I say thanks for food.

Thanks for good water to drink. Eddie Rickenbacker was once asked what was the biggest lesson he learned from drifting about with his companions in life rafts for twenty-one days in the Pacific. "The biggest lesson I learned," he said, "was that if you have all the fresh water you want to drink and all the food you need to eat, you ought never to complain about anything." Thanks then, for food and water.

Thanks for clothes to wear and for medicine that relieves pain and brings healing.

Thanks for the luxuries of life—for television and radio, for air conditioning and automatic furnaces, for telephones and refrigerators and good streets.

Thanks for the knowledge that seasons end for losing teams and that new ones begin again. Thanks for an endless stream of new days and new opportunities for beginning again.

And thanks for the church. Thanks for the building, this place of quiet beauty, given to us by a past generation.

Thanks to those who do the work of the church, who today in the steaming jungles of Zaire, in dangerous Thailand, in the isolated plains of Nigeria, are living out and sharing the gospel in our name.

Thanks to those here who keep the work of the church going,

who prepare the communion emblems on Saturday, who lead the Scout troop, who sponsor our youth groups and teach Sunday school classes. Thanks to the deacons and ushers and elders, to those who make calls on new people in this community. Thanks to the choir members, who give a night and a morning every week for the glory of God. Thanks to those who are faithful to the church, who can be counted on to be here in worship on Sunday. Thanks to those who give generously to the church, who give gifts worthy of what they have. Thanks for the church and those who make it up.

And bear down on this just for a moment: We have made a long list, but it is still incomplete. But how do we best say thank you for these things? Surely not by a tip of the hat and a binge of heavy eating on Thursday of this week.

We say thank you by committing ourselves to the best use of the things God has given us. How do you say thank you for a person who loves you and shares life with you? By commitment—utter commitment, without reservation. Singer Glen Campbell had a fascinating song a few years back that rose to number one on the charts by asserting in a fetching way that romantic love can survive only in the absence of permanent commitment. That song was called "Gentle on My Mind," and the singer explained why it was that he loved his girlfriend so much. With her, he wasn't "bound by any ink that's dried upon some line," and this knowledge has kept her:

> on the backroads by the rivers of my memory,
> and keeps you ever gentle on my mind.

You get that? I love you so much and am so thankful for you because I don't have to commit anything to you. I can abandon you at any moment. I am not committed, not obligated—and that's why I love you so much and am so thankful.

Now, while I enjoy this song, I would debate its sentiments all the way. Do we express gratitude for love by refusing to commit ourselves? We express gratitude by commitment. We express gratitude for our country not by reserving the right to desert it when it needs us, but by being willing to invest our best selves and our best thoughts in it.

We express gratitude for the church not by reserving the right to check out the first time it asks something of us, but by commitment. One of our best words, the word most fitly spoken, is *thanks*, and one of our best actions is commitment that rises out of gratitude.

Go one step further, then, and say thanks most of all to God for his gift of Jesus Christ, who gives us meaning to life now and life eternal to come. Thanks to God for knowing that nothing can ever happen to us that can take us away from his loving care.

This is the glory of Thanksgiving. It lets gratitude bubble up to the surface. As we drink from it, something of the radiance of life is recaptured. How much we have! Jan Struther's poem expresses it well:

> One day my life will end, and lest
>   some whim should prompt you to review it,
> Let one who knows the subject best show you
>   the proper way to do it.
> Just say, here lies doubly blest.
>   Say, she was happy. Say, she knew it.

The secret of the thankful life is to put that happiness, that blessedness, into words. One of our very best words is *thanks*, and one of our very best actions is giving. Put the two together, and it *is* Thanksgiving.

Then what we are after is not just being blessed, but feeling it, knowing it, responding to it, expressing it, coming to God and saying, "Lord, all this, so much, so much. How can I ever say thank you for it?"

The answer comes back clearly: ARE you thankful? Then let thanksgiving be lived. Let your gratitude find form; give it hands and feet. Give it voice and sound and sight. "Freely you have received," the scripture says, "now freely give." It's a way to put into action one of our very best words.

Suggestions for Worship

Call to Worship:

Minister: Lift up your heads, O you gates; be lifted up, you ancient doors,

People: **That the king of glory may come in.**

Minister: Who is the king of glory?

People: **The Lord Almighty, he is the king of glory.**

Prayer of Confession: We praise you Almighty King, for your sovereignty and for your sovereign grace. Gentleness and kindness have attended your rule. We have been blessed. Forgive us for seeking your blessings, but not your authority; for accepting your gifts with proud and disobedient hearts. Have mercy on us, O Christ. Amen.

Suggested Hymns: "Come, Thou Almighty King"; "Crown Him with Many Crowns"; "All People That on Earth Do Dwell"; "Come, Ye Thankful People, Come"; "Now Thank We All Our God."

Pastoral Prayer: Almighty God, Father of all mercies, we your unworthy servants give you humble thanks for all your goodness and lovingkindness to us and to all whom you have made. We bless you for our creation, preservation, and all the blessing of this life; but above all for your immeasurable love in the redemption of the world by our Lord Jesus Christ, for the means of grace, and for the hope of glory. And, we pray, give us such an awareness of your mercies that with truly thankful hearts we may show forth your praise, not only with our lips, but also in our lives, by giving up ourselves to your service and by walking before you in holiness and righteousness all our days, through Jesus Christ, our Lord, to whom, with you and the Holy Spirit, be honor and glory throughout all ages. Amen.

DECEMBER 1

□

First Sunday in Advent

A word for those who are worried or growing weary of the waiting.

The Sunday Lessons

The Psalm: Psalm 25:1-10.

Jeremiah 33:14-16: The exiles, about to give up on unfulfilled promises, are told afresh, "I will cause a righteous Branch to spring forth for David . . . Judah will be saved and Jerusalem will dwell securely" (vv. 15-16).

I Thessalonians 3:9-13: Paul prayed for his converts "that [God] may establish your hearts unblamable in holiness before our God and Father, at the coming of our Lord Jesus" (v. 13). Then he exhorted them to live in ways pleasing to God, following the teachings he had given them.

Luke 21:25-36: "Look up and raise your heads, because your redemption is drawing near" (v. 28). The apocalyptic discourse in Luke notes the "distress of nations" (v. 25) and "men fainting with fear" (v. 26) and then addresses the hopeless hearts that bend beneath the weight of "the cares of this life." He counsels the church (Luke expects it to last) to watch and pray, always ready "to stand before the Son of Man" (v. 36).

Interpretation and Imagination

The aircraft was cleaned. Baggage was loaded. The weather was clear. Passengers were on board, and the departure time had passed. One could sense the restlessness that began to build. We all hate to wait. The captain advised us that there was a small mechanical problem, and he forecast a delay of twenty minutes.

317

Thirty minutes later, the restlessness became impatience. An hour later, impatience became discontent. Personal plans and scheduled connections were now being upset. I complained that the airline was not dependable, knowing all the while that the preflight inspection and care for flight readiness were first-rate dependability.

If things don't happen when we expect them to happen, we are inclined to question God's faithfulness. When suffering and oppression try our patience and we've prayed and longed for some sign of relief or rescue, hope grows weary. Hearts get heavy. We conclude that the promises of God have failed. Our expectations are often unfulfilled, but God's promises never fail.

We ask, like those who waited for Christ's soon return, "Is God faithful?" Of course, God is faithful. The other side of the question is "Are you faithful?" Are you standing tall in faith and obedient in love?

Our discontent with delayed redemption should prompt us to consider divine discontent with our watching and waiting. If there is one hungry child who could be fed, one man enslaved who should be free, one woman devalued, one refugee camp gathering the dispossessed, one slum or ghetto breeding despair, one wandering soul without good news, there must be divine discontent.

"May he make your hearts firm, so that you may stand before our God and Father, holy and faultless, when our Lord Jesus comes."

SURVIVAL

Luke 21:5-19

A SERMON BY WILLIAM H. WILLIMON

Do not be terrified. . . . Nation will rise against nation, and kingdom against kingdom; there will be great earthquakes . . . famines and pestilences; and there will be terrors and great signs from heaven. . . . This will be a time for you to bear testimony. (Luke 21:9-11, 13)

They were walking by the Temple with Jesus, tourists admiring its massive beauty—so many stones, arches lined upon arches. And Jesus, the guide who led them on a tour to a land called Truth said, "The days will come when there shall not be left here one stone upon another that will not be thrown down" (Luke 21:6).

It must have been difficult for them to conceive of Herod's great Temple, one of the wonders of the world, being torn down, stone by stone, until it was nothing but a heap of rubble. Such a thing was unimaginable. The Temple, the very center of national life and pride, the very seat of God, destroyed? Unthinkable!

Close your eyes and think the unthinkable. Imagine the earth heaving, that one-ton boss shaking loose and crashing to the floor, arches falling, piers collapsing, glass shattering, leaded windows melting. It sends shivers down your spine. And yet, this is what Jesus predicted about the Temple. Barely forty years after Jesus spoke, his prophecy came true. The eternal Temple of God was in ruin. Jesus' words were true: "Nation will rise against nation, and kingdom against kingdom; there will be great earthquakes, and . . . famines and pestilences . . . terrors and great signs."

We are unaccustomed to hearing talk like that around places like this. Most mainline, liberal religion has had as its goal adjustment to and satisfaction with the present order rather than speculation or concern about the future. There was a time when talk about the end of the world and biblical passages like Luke 21 were the sole property of the late-night radio preachers and shouting Bible-pounders. But no more. Even United Methodist and Roman Catholic bishops speak of apocalypse now. The recent United Methodist bishops' pastoral, "In Defense of Creation," says that we live in a fearful time when all creation is threatened. We hold the powers of life and death within our hands. Our nuclear weapons could destroy every living thing on our earth. The end is near, the doomsday clock is ticking, if we don't take matters into our hands and work for peace.

Ironically, it is just that sort of thinking that may have gotten us into this nuclear madness in the first place. The people who believe that the bomb is our only hope and the people who believe that doing away with a bomb is our only hope have much in common. As Christopher Lasch said in a recent book, the modern world makes "survival artists" of us all. Fearful of the water we drink, the air we breathe, ecological disaster, the great mushroom cloud looming over us, we get by as best we can and grab hold of what we can.

What is our only hope? You tell me. What does it do to a generation of college students, the majority of whom believe (according to a recent poll) that we shall have a nuclear confrontation within their lifetime? Eat, drink, and be merry, for tomorrow—who knows? "We may be on the Titanic," said one student, "but at least I can go down in a first-class cabin."

The ancient words of Jesus—so foreign to our ears, so primitive with their prediction of wars and rumors of wars, of stones upturned, of pestilence and signs from heaven—isn't it strange that we may be the first generation in a long time to believe them?

Jesus said that the day would come when there would not be left one stone upon another of the Temple. And the students in the tour said, "Jesus, we believe you. Though there may be many who do not believe in you, we all believe you—nuclear winter, ecological disaster, thinning ozone, shrinking resources, exploding population—tell us about it."

Jesus, when asked about possibilities for the future, about prospects for tomorrow, was up front with his belief that for us there will be an end—stones cast down, famine, pestilence, terrors, signs from heaven. It's in the Bible. The end is near. And because of our bomb, and Shearon Harris, and Carl Sagan's bleak predictions for the future, it's in us. The nuclear threat has put us in the unique position of being the first generation in a long time to understand what Jesus meant on the subject of the end. There have been wars and rumors of wars, but still the world endures. The end has not come. Jesus said that the end was here, but it wasn't. Seedtime and harvest, summer, winter, spring—the world survives.

Quite the contrary. Christians believe that they have already seen "the end," that the world has come to a decisive crisis in the life and death of Jesus of Nazareth. In his death, we believe, the whole history of the universe reached a turning point. At that moment, when they nailed him to a cross, the conflict between life and death, good and evil, God and Caesar, was resolved in favor of God's lordship over existence. We have seen "the end" in his end. We got a glimpse of the last chapter. A new kingdom was established. This is a kingdom not dependent on whether or not we get a mutually verifiable arms freeze or the "right" person in the Kremlin or the White House. Here is a kingdom that is based on what God has done and is doing for us and the world rather than on what we do.

Jesus says, "When you hear of wars and tumults, do not be terrified" (Luke 21:9). How can he tell us not to be afraid? How is it possible to think of the future and not be terrified? Robert J. Lifton called it "nuclear numbness"—paralysis brought on by terror of the future. How is it possible not to be terrified? It is possible only for those who are convinced that something decisive has happened for the world in the life and death of Christ, that God has entered our world and—despite what we do with the world—God will not desert us. I believe that there is no way for us to think about the future realistically without faith in the fact of God's loving grasp on the future.

Much of our thought about war and peace arises from our terror rather than from our faith. You may criticize the Dr. Strangelove Generals in the Pentagon, but are they so different from our peace activists? If we don't get peace, what might happen to us? We might not survive, the end might come, and then where would we be? When you feel very alone, very terrified, you hold on very tight.

Jesus, when questioned about peace, was up front: You will have no peace. There will be wars and rumors of wars, tumults, signs from above—do not be terrified. God's purposes do not utterly depend on the success, nor are they utterly defeated by the failure, of Salt II. Peace based on a desire for mere survival can be idolatrous, unjust, as we swallow some lesser evil—the enslavement of Eastern Europe, totalitarian governments, a monolithic national defense establishment, the bomb—in the name of security and order. A peace movement arising out of terror is as idolatrous as peace based on the bomb.

As that great theologian General Alexander Haig said, "There are worse things than a nuclear war." That's a stupid statement. But in a way, that's what Christians believe. We fear not only war, but also peace based on idolatrous self-love and based on the lie that it is up to us to make history come out right. Pontius Pilate conspired with the religious leaders to give Jesus over to die because he wanted peace.

"My peace I give to you; not as the world gives do I give [peace] to you" (John 14:27). The peace we should desire is *that* peace, his peace. The peace we desire is only God's to give, for it is peace based on the recognition that it is not our task to make history come out right or to save the world—either through our bombs or our peace—because in Jesus Christ history has already come out right. We have already seen the end, the last chapter, the final scene. Jesus has already shown us a picture of the end, and he has told us not to be terrified.

During the dark days of World War II, a man emerged from a bomb shelter in London and saw an old newspaper vendor selling his papers amid the rubble. "Who won the battle last night?" he asked the old man, half in jest.

"I don't know," replied the old man. "I don't read the papers. I don't have to worry about who wins battles because I already know who has won the war."

We do not have to construct a world out of fear. Christians can work for peace, and should. But we work as those who know something about the end, which the world does not know. We are free to be peaceful because though we may not know what the future holds, we know who holds the future. What can we do? As Jesus says, such frightening times are for us a "time for you to bear testimony."

There can be no better work for us than—each in our own way, each in our own place—to testify that God, not nations, rules the world. History has already come out right in the establishment of the lordship of Christ. Cling to that. Only one thing survives in this world. Only one name lasts. Only one truth is sure.

Suggestions for Worship

Call to Worship:

Minister: How beautiful upon the mountains are the feet of him who brings good tidings.

People: **Who publishes peace, who brings good tidings of good.**

Minister: Who publishes salvation,

People: **Who says to Zion, "Your God reigns."**

Prayer of Confession: Almighty God, who taught us that the night is far spent and the day is at hand: Save us from our complacency and contentment, which blind us to your Advent. Save us from undue love of the world, that we might wait with patient hope for the day of the Lord, so that when he appears, we shall not be ashamed. Teach us to look for your Advent in all things, to forsake our dependence on our possessions, our achievements, and our securities so that we might put our trust only in you and your peace. Amen.

Suggested Hymns: "O Come, O Come, Emmanuel"; "Come, Thou Long-Expected Jesus"; "Jesus Shall Reign."

Pastoral Prayer: Gracious God, we come before you in prayer because, in the Christ, you have come to us. Because you came to us, took upon yourself our frail human frame, and fully participated in our humanity, we know that you not only care about us, but that you also fully understand us and want the best for all your human family.

Therefore we pray for all our brothers and sisters who live in circumstances of war or civil unrest. O Prince of peace, silence the guns of war and make us to love your peace above all else.

We pray for all those who suffer from poor housing, inadequate nourishment, or other misery. O suffering Servant, be among your poor and impoverished, standing beside them, as you always have, their helper and advocate.

We pray for all those who suffer bereavement through the loss of someone they love. O Comforter, stand beside those who grieve, particularly at this time of year, when their loss seems all the greater.

We pray for all those who have lost their faith. O Teacher, during this Advent, may our faith be strengthened by your presence among us even as you healed the doubts of your frail disciples.

We pray for all who seek to follow your way but are troubled by temptations and distractions. O Lord and Master, strengthen us in our attempts to do your will and to be faithful disciples, even as you prayed for and encouraged your first disciples.

For all these needs and the other unspoken needs of our hearts, come, O come, Emmanuel. Amen.

December 8

□

Second Sunday in Advent

We are people with broken promises and wilderness conflicts. These lessons tell of the God who comes to save us.

The Sunday Lessons

The Psalm: Psalm 126.

Malachi 3:1-4: Malachi, whose name means "my messenger," rebuked the priests for their faithless teaching and announced that "the Lord whom you seek will suddenly come to his temple" (v. 1) and make the worship of the people "pleasing to the Lord" (v. 4).

Philippians 1:3-11: Paul, writing from prison, prays for "knowledge and all discernment, so that you may approve what is excellent, and may be pure and blameless for the day of Christ" (vv. 9-10).

Luke 3:1-6: John, the son of Zechariah, preached a baptism of repentance. For Luke, he was "the voice of one crying in the wilderness" (v. 4) that Isaiah 40 had promised. Noting the time in secular history, "the fifteenth year of the reign of Tiberius Caesar" (v. 1), the Gospel writer points to a new happening in salvation history.

Interpretation and Imagination

Some gifts received are only appreciated and admired. Displayed on a shelf or stored in a box, they don't make much difference in our lives. Other gifts literally change us. A ten-year-old's first bicycle, a great book, a television set—some truths grasped and achievements attained have transforming power. Like a child learning to walk, we get a new earth beneath us and new horizons around us. We need not creep again. When Christ comes into our lives, everything we do, every thought we frame, every word we speak is changed.

To be sure, there is always a givenness that precedes every arrival. The moon was there before the first astronauts landed on it. The Americas were here before the first colonists settled. The law and the prophets, the high priests, the empire, and Tiberius Caesar were all in place before the first advent. These givens set the scene. They did not describe completion.

Luke was acquainted with the powers that be. He understood well the sovereignty of Rome and the position of the high priests, but that situation was not a prison. It did not hold him. Neither was it a finality that he feared. Secular history is temporal and cannot provide the formulations of hope or lock the shackles of hopelessness.

Direction, fulfillment, ultimate value, completion—these belong to the day of Christ. Salvation belongs to our God.

Why, then, do we view our times with anxious and busy schemes? Surely, we know by now that a little more insight, a few more programs, a bit better management and finer technology will not complete our salvation. The way has come with the coming of Christ. Completion will come in the day of Christ.

A VOICE IN THE WILDERNESS

Luke 3:1-6

A SERMON BY WILLIAM H. WILLIMON

Well, it's wonderful poetry—the passages that Handel set to music in *Messiah*. But it's only poetry. And what match is poetry, even that of Isaiah or Luke, when set next to the facts of life?

> The voice of one crying in the
>   wilderness:
> Prepare the way of the Lord,
> make his paths straight. . . .
> and all flesh shall see the salvation
>   of God.
> (Luke 3:4, 6)

To hear the poetry you need to know the context. Today's Gospel lesson is John the Baptist's quote from Isaiah—Handel's (and Jesus') favorite poet. This is poetry addressed to Jews in exile in Babylon. Out in Babylon, the captors try to talk the Jews out of believing their Jewish perceptions of reality, to define life exclusively by imperial Babylonian definitions of what's what, Babylonian hopes, Babylonian fears.

God's people, out in Babylon, were told that they were privileged to live within one of the greatest, most noble, most beautiful civilizations ever devised. Babylonia had some beautiful poetry of its own, you know. On the other hand, God's people, out in Babylon, had poetry that asserted that they were really in the wilderness. They made a covenant not to forget, not to be seduced by Babylonian poets. "Sing us one of your gospel songs from the old country," the Babylonians tempted them. But the exiles replied: "How shall we sing the Lord's song in a foreign land?" (Ps. 137:4).

Just to sing God's song was to be reminded that they were out of place, in exile. There must have been Jews in sixth-century Babylon who did not perceive themselves as exiles. They settled in, made it home, assimilated, learned Babylonian songs to replace songs of Zion.

Others, of a more revolutionary bent, reached into their memories for an adequate metaphor to describe their situation as aliens, strangers in a strange land. Like Luke's John the Baptist, they remembered Israel's experience in the wilderness—*midbar*, a desolate, lonely place, disorderly, dangerous, home of wild beast, barbarians more savage than fraternity row on Saturday night. When the Israelites thought of wilderness, they recalled Sinai, the pathless place where the Hebrew slaves, once freed, lost their way: "the great and terrible wilderness, with its fiery serpents and scorpions and thirsty ground" (Deut. 8:15). Wilderness means wild, where people get "bewildered." It was in the wilderness that Zion said, "My Lord has forgotten me" (Isa. 49:14).

Forget your modern, ecological romanticism. Wilderness is not the place for Boy Scouts, John Denver, and A-frame condominiums. Biblical wilderness is a place where Israel lost its way, couldn't find home, bowed before alien gods. In the wilderness, Jesus was tempted by Satan to abandon God's will (see Luke 4:1-13).

Wilderness is not a place; it's a state of mind, a metaphor to describe a terrifying situation where wild beasts lurk. There are no clear paths; chaos, temptation, and bewilderment reign.

Wilderness is a metaphor for the address of many of us. Some, of course, deny it. Just as some Jews tried to assimilate themselves into the values of the Babylonian Empire, so also some today look upon our culture and sense no conflict between cultural values and gospel values.

Vast numbers of us are self-destructive—booze, drugs, cholesterol. The dogs of war are ready to jump at the push of a button. The threat of AIDS has transformed what used to be called casual sex into a loaded gun. More than one thousand New Yorkers were murdered by their fellow citizens last year, in a city with a police department larger than the standing armies of most nations. Is this home, or is it a wilderness? It is no accident that T. S. Eliot entitled his great poem about the modern world "The Wasteland."

John the Baptist's poetry from Isaiah makes sense only to those who read their context as wilderness, a place of crooked, treacherous paths and high, unscalable mountains and dark, unreachable valleys. Here is poetry that liberates because it enables us to be honest about our situation and name it as wilderness. Here is poetry that liberates because it proclaims a way out of wilderness. In a wild place where only the shrieks of beasts are heard, there is a voice announcing: "Prepare the way of the Lord." Because we can't find our way out to him, he finds his way in to us. *The Lord comes.*

Such speech, spoken by a crazy person like John or sung by a tenor in *Messiah*, is an imaginative revolt against the status quo. It is speech that intends to evoke new reality in order to lead us out of our present situation.

People in exile, people in the wilderness, are usually either serenely secure or despondently depressed. They can imagine no other status. They have lived in this remote, wild valley for so long that they think this is normal, or they are depressed and powerless because they can imagine no alternative. There were Jews in Babylon who came to believe that Nebuchadnezzar was stronger than Israel's God. Zion said, "My Lord has forgotten me" (Isa. 49:14).

It was the vocation of Isaiah the poet and John the messianic tenor to announce an alternative reality to wilderness, to subvert the tightfisted grip of the empire through a song—poetry that disengages us from the dominant mode of thought.

Prepare the way of the Lord. We've heard the words so often that we sometimes miss the way in which the poet hopes to jar our perceptual field and to evoke a totally new reality: This God bulldozes a way through the jungle to get to us because we couldn't get to him. Jesus' parables are similar literary attempts to jar us loose from our conventional modes of looking at life, to remind us of home and thereby name this wilderness for what it is. The prodigal son remembered home from his stay in the "far country."

"I have a dream," said Martin Luther King, Jr. People who don't dream, who don't sing songs or preach poetry become trapped in whatever mire politicians or news reporters or other imperial managers of metaphor give us. Most of us are good soldiers, docile and obedient clerks who have deceived ourselves into believing that this is home. In such a situation, all language is flattened to prose, descriptive of what *is* rather than evocative of what *will be*. Church talk becomes as dull and tame as the *Congressional Record.* We are all heirs of modernism—that is, we take things as we see them and think poetry is no match for the facts.

John the Baptist spoke to those in wilderness in first-century Roman-occupied Judea by quoting poetry of sixth-century Babylonian-exiled Israel. Just as Israel was summoned home from the wilderness by a voice, so also are we: *Prepare the way of the Lord.*

"In the fifteenth year of the reign of Tiberius Caesar, Pontius Pilate being governor of Judea, and Herod being tetrarch of Galilee, and his brother Philip tetrarch . . . and Lysanias tetrarch of Abilene, in the high-priesthood of Annas and Caiaphas . . ." (Luke 1:1-2). This is how we tell the facts of life—who is in power in Moscow or Washington, who is Chief of Staff and controls the state police in Johannesburg. Wait for another administration, some new government program, tax break, entitlement, or handout. Wait. Adapt. Keep your head down.

The word of God came to John the son of Zechariah in the wilderness; and he went into all the region about the Jordan, preaching. . . . As it is written in the book of the words of Isaiah the prophet,
"The voice of one crying in the
    wilderness:
Prepare the way of the Lord."
(Luke 3:2-4)

You don't have to call the wilderness home or stumble bewildered in the dark. Hear the announcement: God comes. The multitudes of angels sing their songs to shepherds (Luke 2:8), keeping watch over their flocks *in the wilderness*. Will you let them sing to you? I know, it's only poetry, but. . . .

Suggestions for Worship

Call to Worship:

> Lift up your heads, O gates!
>   and be lifted up, O ancient doors!
>   that the King of glory may come
>   in.
> (Ps. 24:7)

It will be said on that day, "Lo, this is our God; we have waited for him, that he might save us. This is the Lord; we have waited for him; let us be glad and rejoice in his salvation. (Isa. 25:9)

Prayer of Confession: Gracious God, we confess that we content ourselves with things as they are, rather than look forward to things as they might be. We make peace with injustice and assist in oppression, rather than pray and work for your kingdom. Disturb, by your word, our tranquility. Inspire, through your prophets, our deadened spirits. Forgive, by your grace, our lethargy, so that we might be better prepared to see you and to welcome you on this Advent. Amen.

Suggested Hymns: "Angels from the Realms of Glory"; "Hail to the Lord's Anointed"; "Gentle Mary Laid Her Child."

Pastoral Prayer: Gracious God, whose love for us is revealed so beautifully in the Christ-child of Bethlehem, come among us again, we pray, as we prayerfully, expectantly await your Advent.

In a world constantly at war, where the innocent suffer, the powerful are arrogant, and the poor are victimized, come and stand among us in compassion and power.

Into lives that are often filled with despair and misery due to hunger, lack of shelter, injustice, racism, tyranny, and inhumanity, come and let us see our humanity ennobled in your incarnation among us.

In a time when there is much uncertainty among us, when we are fearful for the future and are unsure of which way to turn, come and make straight our crooked paths and guide us by the light of your love.

In a church that is often discouraged by a lack of results, that often seems to be ignored by the world, come and remind us of the ways the world ignored you, even though you were the world's Savior, and encourage us to continue the course you set before us.

In hearts that feel yearning and need, even though they are unable to express their need, come and let us feel the warmth of your compassion for us, our Lord and our Savior, our hope and our friend. Amen.

DECEMBER 15

□

Third Sunday in Advent

Repentance is a part of Advent preparations, but it is repentance prompted by expectancy. New life is embraced with joy.

The Sunday Lessons

The Psalm: Isaiah 12:2-6

Zephaniah 3:14-20: The judgments of Zephaniah are followed by a psalm of joy. God is in the midst of his people, saying, "I will change their shame into praise" (v. 19).

Philippians 4:4-9: "The Lord is at hand" (v. 5). With his truth lifted up, Paul encourages joy: "The God of peace will be with you" (v. 9).

Luke 3:7-18: John preached judgment and repentance. His hearers wondered whether John was the messiah, but John said: "He who is mightier than I is coming, the thong of whose sandals I am not worthy to untie" (v. 16). Luke, contending for faith, contrasts the baptism of repentance with the baptism of the Holy Spirit.

Interpretation and Imagination

The bishop was coming to our church in a little out-of-the-way town in Montana. He, who was clearly the most important visitor ever to come our way, would stay at the parsonage. Things had to be made ready. The guest room was painted, closets were cleaned, the yard was raked. We even had new sheets for the bed, and the very best towels were set out. Our ordinary behavior was of some concern to Mother, who reminded us of proper etiquette and politeness.

331

None of it was of final importance. The bishop proved to be a warm and gracious servant of Christ, quite human and genuinely kind. His stay was a benediction. His visit was a bit like Christmas. Preparation for his coming was demanding, but it was never a burden, and it became a joy. The changes that needed to be made were done with gladness. Repentance in Advent is like that. It's not heavy with remorse, but expectant, glad-hearted, and free.

When heaven's very best, God's own Son, enters our world, our communities, our homes, indeed our very lives, some changes need to be made. When Tiberius Caesar visited Judea, Herod and his lieutenants would have had all things ready. If you were the chair for the hospitality committee to welcome President Bush to your town, the task of getting ready would be both clear and compelling to you.

The coming of Christ (he is in the midst of us) and the second coming of Christ (Christ has come; Christ will come again) prompt the preaching of the church to call for repentance that will turn us from false loyalties and self-centered indulgence.

THE GIFTED

Luke 3:1-7; Philippians 4:4-9; Isaiah 12:1-6

A SERMON BY WILLIAM H. WILLIMON

Have any of you had the experience of receiving a gift from someone you really don't know very well? You casually know this person, but certainly do not consider him or her to be one of your good friends. And here this person gives you a gift. To your consternation, it turns out to be a really nice gift—one that you didn't ask for, but a really good gift from someone who is not a really good friend. Now, what is the first thing you want to do?

Right. You try to come up with a gift to give this person in return, not out of gratitude—after all, you didn't ask for it—or out of friendship—after all, you hardly even know the person—but because you don't want to feel guilty. Right?

You don't want to be indebted to that person. That gift lays a claim on you, and you don't like that. It's hard to look the person in the face until you have somehow reciprocated because suddenly, where there had been absolutely nothing linking you together before, now you are indebted to this virtual stranger. This person, in giving you a gift, has power over you now that you are indebted to that person.

It may well be, in Jesus' mind, more blessed to give than to receive. But I'll tell you that it is more difficult to receive. Watch how people blush when they are given a compliment. And watch what we do to Christmas, the so-called season of giving. We enjoy thinking of ourselves as basically generous, beneficent, giving people. That's one reason why everyone, even the nominally religious, loves Christmas. Christmas has become a season to celebrate our alleged generosity. The newspaper keeps us posted on how many needy families we have adopted this December. The Salvation Army kettles enable us to be generous while buying groceries for ourselves at the supermarket or gifts for our families at the shopping malls. The people at the office, who usually balk at taking up a collection to pay for the morning coffee break, fall all over themselves to collect funds to provide Christmas joy for some family who otherwise would have none.

We love Christmas because, as we say, Christmas brings out the best in us. Everyone becomes a giver at Christmas, even the stingiest among us, even the Ebenezer Scrooges. Charles Dickens' story of the transformation of Scrooge has probably done more to form our notions of Christmas than has Luke's story of the manger. Whereas Luke tells the tale of God's gift to us, Dickens told us a story of how we can give to others. Dickens' *A Christmas Carol* is more congenial to our images of ourselves, suggesting that down deep even the worst of us is capable of becoming a generous, giving person, just like Ebenezer Scrooge.

Yet, we are better givers than we are getters, not because we are generous people, but because we are also proud, arrogant people for whom it is easier to give than to receive.

The Christmas story, according to the Gospel of Luke rather than to Charles Dickens, is not about how blessed it is for us to be *givers*, but how essential it is for us to see ourselves as *receivers*. If you have ever been given a gift, a really good gift, by someone who is a virtual stranger, you know what I mean.

Oh, we like to think of ourselves as givers, powerful, competent, self-sufficient, capable people for whom goodness consists of being motivated to employ a little of our power, competence, and gifts for the benefit of the less fortunate among us. So, every Christmas, most newspapers set aside a few weeks to focus its readers' attention on "the less fortunate" among us. In so doing, the poor perform a valuable function in our society—namely, to remind us of how fortunate we are, how powerful, competent, capable and self-sufficient we are, unlike the poor, who are powerless and often considered incompetent, incapable, and dependent upon the gifts of someone else to have a merry Christmas.

This is a direct contradiction of the biblical account of the first Christmas. There, I think I could argue, the story is not about us as givers but our nature as receivers. Read again the accounts of the nativity in the Gospels of Luke or Matthew, and you will be struck with how the stories of Jesus' birth go to great lengths to demonstrate that we—our power, generosity, competence, capabilities—had little to do with God's work in Jesus. God wanted to do something for us that would be so strange, so utterly beyond the bounds of human imagination, that God had to resort to angels, pregnant virgins, and stars in the sky. We didn't think of it, understand it, or approve it. All we could do at Bethlehem was receive it—a gift from a God we hardly even knew.

The faith that arises from this strange story of birth in Bethlehem trains us to be good receivers. The first word of the church, a people born out of so strange a nativity, is that the most important thing about us is that we are getters rather than givers. Discipleship is training in the art of seeing our lives as gifts. That's tough because we would rather see ourselves as givers. We want power to stand on our own. We don't like to see ourselves as being dependent, needy, empty-handed.

It's tough to be on the receiving end of God's love. It requires that we see our lives not as our possessions, but as gifts. It's tough to admit that the things we need most come not as the result of our programs, projects, and striving, but as a result of God's gracious giving. "Nothing is more repugnant to capable, modern people than grace," wrote John Wesley a long time ago.

One of the most familiar Christmas texts is in Isaiah: "Therefore the Lord himself will give you a sign. Behold, a young woman shall conceive and bear a son, and shall call his name Immanuel" (7:14). Less familiar is the context in which this was written. Isaiah had been pleading with King Ahaz to put his trust in God's promise to Israel rather than in alliances with stronger military powers. "If you will not believe, surely you shall not be established" (7:9), Isaiah warned King Ahaz. Then Isaiah told the fearful king that God was going to give him a baby as a sign. "Isn't that just like God?" Ahaz must have thought. What Ahaz needed, with Assyria breathing down his neck, was a good army, not a baby.

This is often the way God loves us—with gifts we thought we didn't need that transform us into people we don't necessarily like to be. With our advanced degrees and armies and government programs and material comforts and self-fulfillment techniques, we assume that religion is about giving a little of ourselves to confirm that we are indeed as powerful and self-sufficient as we claim.

Then this stranger comes to us and blesses us with a baby, thus calling us to see ourselves for who we really are: empty-handed recipients of a gracious God who, rather than leave us to our own devices, gave us a gift.

Suggestions for Worship

Call to Worship:

Minister: O wisdom from the mouth of the highest, reaching from eternity to eternity,

People: Come, teach us the way of knowledge.

Minister: O Dayspring, splendor of eternal light and sun of righteousness:

People: Come and enlighten those that sit in darkness and in the shadow of death.

Minister: O King of nations, their desire and the cornerstone that binds them in one:

People: Come and save humanity.

Minister: O Emmanuel, our King, the expectation and Savior of all the nations:

People: Come and save us, O Lord and God.

Prayer of Confession: Almighty and eternal God, whose eternal love searches our hearts, we acknowledge and confess that we sin against your love in thought, word, and deed. Here in church, we feel full of faith, committed and caring. Yet, we know that when we leave here and go forth, our commitment wavers and we are too easily distracted and captured by the cares of the world. Forgive us, we pray, and strengthen us that, even as Mary, mother of our Lord, we might be willing and obedient disciples. Amen.

Suggested Hymns: "Love Divine, All Loves Excelling"; "There's a Song in the Air"; "Joy to the World."

Pastoral Prayer: We have been awaiting your advent, Lord. We know that there is much wrong with us and our world that can only be set right by your powerful work among us. Therefore, we pray for the sick and suffering; for the bereaved and the mourning; for the lonely and the friendless; for the oppressed and their oppressors; for the unfulfilled poor and the unfulfilled rich; for the courageous prophets who want change and the timid and fearful who are content with things as they are; for the youth who are uncertain about their future, and for the old who do not like the present; for this congregation and its people; for all our brothers and sisters who have not heard your good news in such a way as to realize that it is meant for them; and for all the silent, unspoken needs among us today, yearning that can be assuaged only by your presence.

Come, Lord Jesus. Come quickly and be born among us, we pray. Amen.

DECEMBER 22

□

Fourth Sunday in Advent

Our expectations are focused now on the meeting of two expectant mothers: Mary, mother of Christ, and Elizabeth, mother of John the Baptist.

The Sunday Lessons

The Psalm: Psalm 80:1-7.

Micah 5:2-5a: The promised son of David, ruler of Israel and Messiah, would come forth from Bethlehem Ephrathah, "little to be among the clans of Judah" (v. 2). The exile had ended, and Micah expected the Davidic rule to be established again.

Hebrews 10:5-10: The passage speaks of the perfect obedience and perfect sacrifice of Christ. When Christ came into the world, he said, "Lo, I have come to do thy will" (v. 9). The Son accepts human birth, the incarnation, so that the offering of that body may manifest obedience to the will of God.

Luke 1:39-55: When Mary, too young to be a mother, visited Elizabeth, too old to be a mother, they were filled with the Holy Spirit. Elizabeth exclaimed, "Blessed are you among women and blessed is the fruit of your womb!" (v. 42). Mary's praise (the Magnificat) begins: "My soul magnifies the Lord, and my spirit rejoices in God my Savior" (vv. 46-47). Mary is blessed because God, in Christ, "has put down the mighty from their thrones, and exalted those of low degree" (v. 52). Two babes in two wombs are the prelude to a new age in salvation history.

Interpretation and Imagination

There is a gentle humility in the Magnificat, which describes the worship and obedience of Mary, handmaiden of the Lord.

337

Responsive, responsible, and not claiming too much, Mary honors God. She has been called blessed by the church because the church first honored Christ.

The birth of a child reflects a union, not simply of man and a woman, but of creature and Creator. Live and growing things have such beginnings. A farmer plants the corn and then soil, sunshine, and rain make it grow. Babies begin with deliberate human action, but nature carries the pregnancy to delivery. In his sermon "The Planter and the Rain," Phillips Brooks reflected on the relationship of human will and natural force and spoke of "man the deviser, the conceiver and the great system of the universe taking his device or conception at his hands and carrying it forward to its fulfillment."

The birth stories of John and Jesus accent divine authority. Women are the primary players, but clearly God is the chief actor. Luke lets us listen in on the conversation between the two expecting mothers. More is said than "The baby moved." Mary's song says it right: "He who is mighty has done great things for me . . . his mercy is on those who fear him" (Luke 1:49-50).

Christmas will soon be upon us. Already we sense its crowded and compelling ways. But we cannot postpone the time. We cannot stop the clock or turn back the calendar. Even kings and presidents have no rule over this. "He has shown strength with his arm," and that primarily through the gift of the Christ child.

MARY'S SONG

Luke 1:39-55

A SERMON BY WILLIAM H. WILLIMON

I suspect that many of you are anxious for me to get off my chest quickly whatever it is that I want to say and get out of the pulpit so that you can hear the beautiful music of Christmas. We have restrained ourselves throughout the Sundays of Advent, confined ourselves to slow-moving, somewhat somber hymns of hope, anticipation, and expectancy: "O come, O come, Emmanuel, and ransom captive Israel." Anticipation has become fulfillment. Now we are at last ready to sing of

Christmas. There are Sundays when you can come to this place and not know half of the hymns. Today is different. Even the Easter Sunday-Christmas Eve crowd knows all the hymns today. Christmas is the season of singing.

This is one of those Sundays when the words of a prosaic preacher inevitably fail to match the event that unfolds before us. I once thought that Billy Graham couldn't fail after George Beverly Shea and the five-hundred-voice Crusade Choir had sung. What a warm up for a sermon! Now, after being here, I know differently. A good choir, a great organ, and beautiful music can sometimes say so much that there's nothing left for the preacher. I know that these songs of Christmas will move you more than my sermon will. Christmas is the season of singing.

No gospel does this better than Luke. Luke tells of the birth of Jesus with song and poetry rather than with prose. Zechariah hears that he is going to be a daddy, and he sings. Mary hears that she is going to be a mama, and she sings. The angels sing, Elizabeth sings, Simeon sings—everybody is singing.

In your own life, you know what this is like. You are moving through your ordinary, prosaic day—washing to be done, letters to be written, dusting to be done. Then there is a telephone call, a knock at the door. Some good news meets you, and what is your immediate, unconscious, innate response? You *sing*. Suddenly, quite without conscious effort, you go about the rest of your day with a song. Mary's good news evoked exactly the same response.

Would you sing if you were Mary? After all, Mary's being "great with child" is not something she could explain or understand, not something she had chosen or planned. It put her in a bad way with her fiancé. The angel told Mary to "fear not," but old Simeon told Mary the truth of what it meant for her to be "blessed among women" when he predicted that "a sword will also pierce your side." Motherhood would not be easy for Mary. Yet, Mary sang:

> My soul magnifies the Lord,
> and my spirit rejoices in God my
>   Savior
> (Luke 1:46-47)

This is no lullaby Mary sings. The words thunder forth like a battle chant:

> He has shown strength with his arm,
> he has scattered the proud in the
> imagination of their hearts,
> he has put down the mighty from
> their thrones . . .
> and the rich he has sent empty away.
> (Luke 1:51-53)

That's not too sweet a Christmas carol, I think. It's a song about someone low going up, someone up high being brought low. You won't hear women singing like this except in Soweto, Warsaw, Harlem, South Chicago, or such places.

A few years ago, the government of South Africa banned the lighting of candles or the singing of Christmas carols in Soweto. When asked by the press why these restrictions were made, the government replied, "You know how emotional black women are. Christmas carols have an emotional effect upon them." (see St. Louis *Post-Dispatch*, Dec. 27, 1985). If you let a poor Jewish woman like Mary or a black mother in Soweto sing, you don't know where it might lead.

I'm a child of the 1960s. The German magazine *Der Speigel* did a special issue this summer on my student years, "Der Wilden Sechstige" ("The Wild Sixties"), most of which was about the music of the sixties. It is difficult for you to understand what drove rebelling, protesting, out-of-control students into the streets of Detroit, Berlin, Paris, Chicago, or Kent State if you never heard Janis Joplin, if you never heard Dylan whine "the times they are a 'changin'," if you never sat at a Jimi Hendrix concert and felt a solid wave of piercing sound rush past you with such force that it would part your hair. If you never heard them, then you missed it. The sixties—times of violence, peace, protest, civil rights, and a changing world order—began as a nearly spontaneous street outburst of boogie. It was a world torn loose with a solid wall of hard rock sound or a group of peace marchers, hands joined, singing "We Shall Overcome."

"Music hath charms to soothe a savage breast," said William Congreve. That is true, but it also has power to release, cut loose, pull down, raise up. Imagine Mary's *Magnificat* sung, not by an operatic soprano accompanied by a full choir, but belted out by Janis Joplin, backed up by the Rolling Stones, and you'll get my point.

Think, this December, of all those brothers and sisters, near and far, who have lost the ability to sing. A missionary once told me that when a child is starving, when a child is that utterly emaciated and near death, that child no longer cries. Tears dry up, and the child is silent. The hunger is so deep that it has moved beyond pain, beyond feeling, to utter, empty silence. If you are hurt, disappointed, defeated, and pushed down enough, before long you become withdrawn, quiet, and silent.

The government is proud to report that Soweto is silent this Christmas. The world has its brand of "Silent Night," but there is nothing holy or bright about it. I can't remember a Christmas when there were not enough starving children, enough grieving mothers, enough newly opened graves or raging King Herods to mock our happy yuletide music and to silence our singing.

In first-century Judea, in the December darkness, without a star in the sky, people were shut up in the darkened houses for fear of Roman soldiers. The streets were deserted and fearfully quiet. (One way to handle an oppressive situation in a place like Nazareth is to keep your head down, your mouth buttoned shut.) There, in the dark silence, a pure, clear, feminine voice cut through the night: "My soul magnifies the Lord . . . He has put down the mighty from their thrones, and exalted those of low degree."

Before the Herods know what's happening, the streets are full of chanting, restless people on the move, and the Herods regret that they gave their troops time off for Christmas.

In her singing, Mary became the premier disciple, a model for us all. She was the first person to hear the announcement that God is with us and the very first to believe. As Martin Luther once said in a Christmas sermon, three miracles occurred at Christ's nativity: God became human, a virgin conceived, and Mary believed. For Luther, the greatest miracle that first Christmas was the last: Mary believed. Despite all the oppression, closed doors, brick walls, blind alleys, and dark, silent death, she believed. She sang.

In chapter 11 of Luke's Gospel, when a well-meaning woman pronounces blessings on Jesus' mother, Jesus responds that the blessed are not those who claim biological kinship with him. The blessed are those who hear and do God's word. Mary is called "blessed among women" because she heard and responded. She sang. Thus she is a model for us.

Sure, there were dark days ahead for Mary. Her joy as a mother was mixed with much pain, as it is for any mother. Just down the road in Ramah, mother Rachel weeps for her slaughtered babies, as others will weep for Mary's son. But for now, her faith enables Mary to sing.

And your life, too, is not all Christmas carols and joy. Dark, cold January days lie just beyond our yuletide gladness. The days grow short, the nights long. But for now, our faith enables us to sing. We sing because we believe; we believe as we sing. *My sound magnifies the Lord, and my spirit rejoices in God my Savior.*

Suggestions for Worship

Call to Worship:

Minister: O Lord, thou art very near to all who call upon you.

People: O Lord, thou art our help and our deliverer.

Minister: Come, let us worship and bow down.

People: Blessed be the name of the Lord.

Prayer of Confession: O Lord, holy and righteous God, it is not easy for us to be honest with ourselves or with you. Yet, because of your love and grace, we are free from our defensiveness long enough to confess that we have not loved you above all things; that we do not take pleasure in your truthful word; that we have not loved our neighbors as ourselves; that we lack the conscience that should accompany our creed; that our hearts are divided, in conflict over doubts and desires.

O God, whose nature is to forgive and to love, forgive us we pray and, in forgiving, heal us, so that our lives might be changed and that we might be better able to receive our Savior. Amen.

Suggested Hymns: "O Come, All Ye Faithful"; "Hark! the Herald Angels Sing"; "While Shepherds Watched Their Flocks."

Pastoral Prayer: Eternal God, Alpha and Omega, who stands at the end and the beginning of our lives, we worship you. In this season when your people prepare again for the Advent of our Savior, we do especially recall how you took our hate and met it with your love, took our death and deadliness and transformed it into new life, took our tiredness and met it with a baby in a manger.

Having witnessed your solidarity with the human race and all our cares in your incarnation, we are therefore bold to pray for all brothers and sisters caught in entanglements of hate, death, or evil.

We pray for all those who feel trapped in habits they are unable, by themselves, to overcome. O God of triumph, help them to overcome.

We pray for those present here today who find it difficult to believe. O God, whose angels confronted the doubts of Zechariah and Mary, assuage our doubts and bring us to sure faith.

We pray for those who, in this season of joy, suffer from great sadness—the terminally ill, the severely injured, the victims of war or civil unrest. O God of life, who disarmed arrogant King Herod and came to earth among the poor and the lowly, come among us and stand beside those who hurt.

We pray for those we regard as strangers—people of other nations whom our nation regards as enemies; people with religions other than our own; people who, by life-style, ideology, or some other label, seem strange to us. O God, who came to us as a stranger, receiving us as strangers, teach us Christian hospitality toward others, remembering the hospitality you have shown toward each of us.

We pray for people and needs that lay heavy on our hearts this day, which we now name before you in the silence of our hearts (*silence*). Teach us to hurt with and to act for others. Because you did not leave us to our own devices, but came and stood beside us, became one of us, our Brother, our Savior, our Friend, we know that we can turn to you in prayer, asking things that we once regarded as impossible, knowing that now, by your grace, all is possible. Amen.

DECEMBER 29

☐

First Sunday After Christmas

Family loyalty, like national loyalty, is a good thing. Yet, its potential for conflict is diminished only by our higher devotion to the Father of us all.

The Sunday Lessons

The Psalm: Psalm 111.

I Samuel 2:18-20, 26: The boy Samuel had been given to the Lord to serve in the Temple. Each year his mother made him a robe and brought it to him. He grew "in stature and in favor with the Lord and with men" (v. 26).

Colossians 3:12-17: The Colossian letter offers Christ as all in all. In relationships, that means that God's chosen ones shall evidence compassion, gentleness, and patience. The peace of Christ will rule in our hearts. The word of Christ will inform our teaching and admonitions.

Luke 2:41-52: In Nazareth, among family and kinsfolk, Jesus grew in favor with God and humankind. In Jerusalem, Jesus displayed his loyalty to a sacred place and to holy teachings. When his parents found him in the Temple among the teachers, they asked, "Son, why have you treated us so?" (v. 48). He answered, "I must be in my Father's house" (v. 49).

Interpretation and Imagination

The Christmas card was bright blue with only one image: a white dove carrying an olive branch in its beak. The message inside gathered sincerity through its brevity and directness: "Wishing You Christmas Peace." The card remains one of my favorites. I like the color, the image, the style, but most of all I like the greeting, "Peace."

Another Christmas has come and gone. Once again, we've sung of "peace on earth! Good will!" But there has not yet been a Christmas without conflict. There is still fighting among enemy armies, and also among brothers and sisters, and there is conflict in our families. The age-old question is our question: "Will the sword devour forever?"

The article entitled "Kinship and Family" in *The Interpreter's Dictionary of the Bible* (supplement) notes that "in most human societies kinship ties are the most important ties between persons, and the obligations they entail override all others." When recalling religious war as some of the bloodiest, it seems foolhardy to suggest that all who long to be in the "Father's house" will dwell together in peace. Samuel Stone speaks of the church's one foundation and proclaims: "Mid toil and tribulation, and tumult of her war,/ She waits the consummation of peace for evermore."

CHRISTMAS IN A CUP

I Corinthians 10:16-17

A SERMON BY RICHARD ANDERSEN

The cup of blessing which we bless, is it not a participation in the blood of Christ? The bread which we break, is it not a participation in the body of Christ? Because there is one bread, we who are many are one body, for we all partake of the one bread. (I Cor. 10:16-17)

For Mary and Joseph, Christmas was spent in a barn. For the angels who sang so gaily against the starry midnight sky to wary shepherds attending their flocks, Christmas was in a manger. To the wise men traveling from Persia to Bethlehem, Christmas was seen in a gigantic star that was so radiant and so splendid that they could not ignore it or the King it proclaimed.

But for you and me, coming together in the stillness of this wondrous Christmas season, Christmas is in a cup. Christ is here as he once was there in Bethlehem's cave. And everywhere men and women and youth kneel before alters or sit in pews, sharing the wine of communion and the bread of the sacrament, Jesus is born. There may not be the rich, nostalgic scene of the night that is remembered above all others in the chalice, but there is something more. He who was in a manger born, is nestled mysteriously within the rim of every chalice that conveys his presence in tasty wine.

Together, we celebrate Christmas in a cup. It should be no more difficult to accept this fact than to reminisce about our Lord's birth two thousand years ago in David's city.

For thousands of years before, God was first readying the world for the advent of his Son. In Abraham, the promise was first given and then shared with Isaac and Jacob and the whole nation of Israel. They were blessed to be a blessing, blessed to convey to the world humanity's Redeemer, its Savior, our Lord. All of that history is present within the savor of wine tonight, the taste of bread. Christmas in a cup.

You may not see an angel choir in the rippling wine or behold the shepherds in their winter's garb, climbing that steep, rocky incline to Bethlehem's table in the wafer of bread, but you are nevertheless celebrating Christmas in a cup. To you is born this day in this city a Savior who is Christ the Lord. You will find that babe wrapped in swaddling bands of Holy Communion, lying in the manger that is the sacrament's chalice.

None of the shepherds, not the innkeeper, not the town crier, not the guards at the city gate, not the rabbi of Bethlehem, nor the other guests in that caravansary knew that in that manger was a Lamb who would atone for the sins of the world. They saw a baby, a beautiful baby, God's own child, and they knew what the angels had said, but it was beyond them. It is beyond us, too, to comprehend how Christ can convey himself, his body and blood, in this holy sacrament. We are like the shepherds, awed, but incapable of grasping the whole wondrous Word of God incarnate, but God is still God. He can and does stretch beyond our understanding to fulfill his promises.

When we celebrate Christmas in a cup, it is because we know that beyond Bethlehem there was a hill called Calvary and a day known as Easter. Wrapped up in the sinews of those tiny arms of the manger's child was the carpenter's strength and the Savior's nail-pierced limbs—God was in a human body reconciling the world to himself. When we sip the wine and receive the bread, we know that baby became the Christ of the cross, the Lord of life, the resurrected Son of God, our Lord, our Savior, our Redeemer.

Thus it is more than Christmas in a cup, but Christ himself and all that he did and continues to do, for that cup is ours to share because of our common need. We have sinned. *Sin* is an old fashioned word that some want to avoid. They call it the "s" word. They would prefer to say that we say we have "erred" or "made mistakes" or "messed up." They have a gentler sound, these words, but it was not a gentle reason that thrust Jesus upon Golgotha's tree. It was sin—our sin!

But the Christmas that comes in the cup we share says that sin of the past is gone, forgiven, atoned for. Therefore, we have as much right to be excited about our Christmas in a cup as the shepherds were in plodding hurriedly up the steep ascent of Bethlehem's shepherds' field to "see this thing that has happened, which the Lord has made known to [them]" (Luke 2:15).

It is said that Henry V was attending Christmas worship in Westminster Abbey. A famous preacher was expounding in the pulpit of the choir, and hundreds of worshipers were attentive to every word, but the king himself was nowhere to be seen. One of his courtiers found him kneeling at a small altar in one of the abbey's side chapels, receiving the Sacrament of the Altar with but a few persons. When asked by the courtier later why he was not with the larger crowd, Henry V responded, "I would rather meet with my Friend than merely hear him talked about." He wanted his Christmas in a cup also, rather than just in the pulpit. That was more than five centuries ago, and still the sentiment is true. Christmas in a cup conveyed in the same mysterious way Christ first entered this world surpasses anything that can be said, no matter the preacher's fame or lack thereof. In that cup you meet the One who is friend to every repentant soul.

He breaks down the barriers that arise between people and draws us together as one family, one body, just as he offered but one cup on that Maundy Thursday when he instituted the sacrament, instead of the four cups Passover required. To the Twelve, unity came about in that one, solitary cup. To us, we are joined with the saints of all time, with those next door in the little churches north and south of us as well as those in vast cathedrals and village chapels across the globe for all time. Christmas in a cup makes for unity, oneness, and solidarity.

Tom, in *Tom Brown's School Days*, a Victorian epic by Thomas Hughes that changed the English school system, inquired of his closest friend, "Do you remember how we both hated Flashman?" (He was the tyrannical bully of the school's faculty.)

"Of course, I do," answered East.

"Well, when I came to take the Sacrament," said Tom, "I had a great struggle about that. I tried to think of him as evil, as something the Lord hated and I might hate, too. But it wouldn't go. I broke down; I believe that Christ himself broke me down, and when the [priest] gave me the bread and wine and leant over me praying, I prayed for poor Flashman as if he had been you"—his best friend.

One can imagine that the shepherds were changed after the angelic visitation. The Magi, too, were totally different. We know that Mary and Joseph were different after Gabriel's visits. And the Twelve, and hundreds of thousands, millions, and billions of Christians since have been changed by meeting the Christ of Christmas, the King of Calvary. Their lives have been made drastically different. But can it be that you and I will find within this Christmas cup not only a forgiveness that changes us from inside out, but also a forgiveness that we gladly extend to everyone who has ever offended us? If we drink deeply enough of this heady wine, you and I will find that Christmas means love and that Christ means forgiveness, and there cannot be one without the other.

So, come to the table—or, if you prefer, the stable—and find Christ, wrapped in the swaddling bands of bread and wine. He was born to set us free, to unite us as his family, to give us joy that stretches beyond the last carol of the season into the eternal chambers of heaven itself.

Recently, three dozen of us made our way to David's city and entered the ancient Church of the Nativity off Manger Square, where, under the high altar, is the cave in which tradition says Jesus was born. We were a few weeks late for Christmas, shepherds who were delayed in our journey, where thousands before us had gathered for his birthday on December 24. The decorations were still up. The priest still greeted us with a

Christmas salutation, and so we felt something like what the first shepherds may have felt two thousand years ago. That year, the people of Bethlehem, because of the strife between Palestinians and Israelis, had cancelled Christmas services. But they could not cancel Christmas. Wherever the sacrament is celebrated, there Christ is born all over again—in Bethlehem, in San Jose, throughout the world.

During the Sunday school Christmas program this year, someone had forgotten the manger. They were attempting to cancel Christmas. Simply, there was no baby Jesus, no plastic doll in a wooden manger. All the rest of the retinue of that night—Mary and Joseph, angels and shepherds, sheep and magi—made it. But there were no styrene Jesus and no feed-box birthing place. The meaning was obvious: Jesus is not a doll to be hauled out once every year, but our Lord, who needs no manger made of wood, but one that is as personal as our hearts. He needs you and me as his stables of today. That's why he left us the gift of communion. He brings the nativity to each of us.

Christmas in a cup. It's all here: Bethlehem, the manger, the virgin and the carpenter, the star, the angelic choirs, the shepherds, and the wise men. But more than any of these, Christ is here. Yes, in a cup, and beyond it in the hearts of all his disciples for all time. The chalice has been his manger bed of unending centuries, and it is so once again this Christmas Eve. And so we sing with the angels, "Glory to God in the highest, and on earth peace among men with whom he is pleased." Come and see this thing that happened and is happening and will continue to happen as long as humanity has hearts and people possess faith. Christmas in a cup—your cup. Amen.

Suggestions for Worship

Call to Worship: "Behold, I bring you good news of a great joy which will come to all the people; for to you is born this day in the city of David a Savior, who is Christ the Lord." (Luke 2:10)

Prayer of Confession: O God, who makes us glad with the yearly remembrance of the birth of your only Son, Jesus Christ, grant that just as we joyfully receive him as our Redeemer, so also may we with sure confidence behold him when he comes to be our judge, who lives and reigns with you and the Holy Ghost, one God, world without end. Amen.

Suggested Hymns: "Angels We Have Heard on High"; "Angels from the Realms of Glory"; "What Child Is This"; "Away in a Manger."

Pastoral Prayer: Almighty God, our heavenly Father, we thank you for your gifts of Christ and Christmas. Today we remember stardust and stable straw, the manger and the mother, shepherds and angels, and the Child of Bethlehem. Tremendous is your mystery, O God. You are immortal, eternal, invisible to our eyes and beyond our reach. You are infinitely greater than our highest thought of you and much more than our best prophets can tell of you. Yet, you chose to come to us in a lowly place as a baby. Make this holy birth so real to us that we may forever cherish the ordinary gifts of life: a child's laughter, the warmth of home, good music and quiet prayer, the peaceful night and the awakening dawn, human friendship and common charity, and hearts that long for God. We bow before your glory, which came among us as a child. Amen.

SECTION II

□

SERMON RESOURCES

LESSON GUIDE
BASED ON *THE NEW COMMON LECTIONARY*

	PSALM	1st LESSON	2nd LESSON	3rd LESSON
January 6, 1991 Epiphany (white)	72:1-14	**Isa. 60:1-6** A new light shines on Zion.	**Eph. 3:1-12** Paul—servant of the gospel and preacher to the Gentiles.	**Matt. 2:1-12** Visit of the Magi.
January 13, 1991 1st Sunday After Epiphany *Baptism of the Lord* (white)	29	**Gen. 1:1-5** The first day of creation.	**Acts 19:1-7** Paul baptizes in Jesus' name in the city of Ephesus.	**Mark 1:4-11** John the Baptist foretells the coming of Jesus and baptizes Jesus in the Jordan.
January 20, 1991 2nd Sunday After Epiphany (green)	63:1-8	**I Sam. 3:1-10 (*or* 20)** The Lord calls Samuel.	**I Cor. 6:12-20** The body is the temple of the Holy Spirit. Paul writes concerning sexual immorality.	**John 1:35-42** Jesus calls the first disciples.
January 27, 1991 3rd Sunday After Epiphany (green)	62:5-12	**Jon. 3:1-5, 10** Jonah preaches to the people of Nineveh, and they turn from their evil ways.	**I Cor. 7:29-31 (32-35)** Concerning marriage.	**Mark 1:14-20** "I will make you fishers of men."

	PSALM	1st LESSON	2nd LESSON	3rd LESSON
February 3, 1991 4th Sunday After Epiphany (green)	111	**Deut. 18:15-20** The Lord will raise up a prophet from among the people.	**I Cor. 8:1-13** A stumbling block: food sacrificed to idols.	**Mark 1:21-28** Jesus has authority over an evil spirit in Capernaum.
February 10, 1991 Last Sunday After Epiphany *Transfiguration Sunday* (white)	50:1-6	**II Kings 2:1-12a** Elijah passes his mantle to Elisha.	**II Cor. 4:3-6** The light of the gospel shines in the darkness.	**Mark 9:2-9** Jesus is transfigured on the mountain.
February 13, 1991 Ash Wednesday (purple)	51:1-12	**Joel 2:1-2, 12-17a** A rending of hearts, not garments.	**II Cor. 5:20b–6:2 (3-10)** "Now is the acceptable time; Now is the day of salvation."	**Matt. 6:1-6, 16** Jesus' teaching on giving alms, prayer, and fasting.
February 17, 1991 1st Sunday of Lent (purple)	25:1-10	**Gen. 9:8-17** God established his covenant (rainbow) with Noah.	**I Pet. 3:18-22** Jesus Christ, the righteous for the unrighteous.	**Mark 1:9-15** Jesus is baptized and immediately driven into the wilderness.
February 24, 1991 2nd Sunday of Lent (purple)	105:1-11	**Gen. 17:1-10, 15-19** A covenant between God and Abraham. Old Sarah laughs at the promise of a child.	**Rom. 4:16-25** Abraham remained faithful even when all seemed hopeless. His faith was "reckoned to him as righteousness." Justification by faith.	**Mark 8:31-38** Deny yourself, take up your cross and follow me. *or* **Mark 9:1-9** The Transfiguration of Jesus.

	PSALM	1st LESSON	2nd LESSON	3rd LESSON
March 3, 1991 3rd Sunday of Lent (purple)	19:7-14	**Exodus 20:1-17** The Ten Commandments.	**I Cor. 1:22-25** Not signs or wisdom, but Christ crucified.	**John 2:13-22** Jesus cleans the Temple and foretells his resurrection.
March 10, 1991 4th Sunday of Lent (purple)	137:1-6	**II Cor. 36:14-23** Jerusalem destroyed and the Hebrews taken into exile in Babylon.	**Eph. 2:4-10** By grace we are saved through faith.	**John 3:14-21** "For God so loved the world. . . ."
March 17, 1991 5th Sunday of Lent (purple)	51:10-17	**Jer. 31:31-34** A new covenant written upon their hearts.	**Heb. 5:7-10** Jesus Christ—the source of eternal salvation.	**John 12:20-33** "The hour has come for the Son to be glorified."
March 24, 1991 *When Observed as Palm Sunday* (purple)	118:19-29	**Isa. 50:4-9a** God's steadfastness and the servant's obedience.	**Phil. 2:5-11** Love in the form of a suffering servant.	**Mark 11:1-11** Triumphal entry into Jerusalem. *or* **John 12:12-16** Jesus enters Jerusalem.
March 24, 1991 *When Observed as Passion Sunday* (purple)	31:9-16	**Isa. 50:4-9a** (Same as above.)	**Phil. 2:5-11** (Same as above.)	**Mark 14:1–15:47** Long Passion narrative. *or* **Mark 15:1-39** Short Passion narrative.
March 28, 1991 Holy Thursday *Maundy Thursday* (purple)	116:12-19	**Exod. 24:3-8** The children of Israel make covenant with God through blood.	**I Cor. 10:16-17** One loaf, one body in Christ.	**Mark 14:12-26** The Last Supper.

	PSALM	1st LESSON	2nd LESSON	3rd LESSON
March 29, 1991 Good Friday (no color or black)	22:1-18	**Isa. 52:13–53:12** The suffering servant.	**Heb. 4:14-16; 5:7-9** Jesus Christ: a great High Priest.	**John 18:1–19:42** Long Passion and Crucifixion narrative. *or* **John 19:17-30** Short narrative of Crucifixion of Jesus.
March 31, 1991 Easter Sunday (white)	118:14-24	**Isa. 25:6-9** The Lord will swallow up death forever. Let us be glad and rejoice. *or* **Acts 10:34-43** Peter preaches Christ crucified, dead, and risen for our salvation.	**I Cor. 15:1-11** A risen Jesus—so we preach and so you believe. *or* **Acts 10:34-43** (Same as 1st lesson above.)	**Mark 16:1-8** "He has risen, he is not here." *or* **John 20:1-18** The resurrection of Jesus. "Woman, why are you weeping?"
April 7, 1991 2nd Sunday of Easter (white)	133	**Acts 4:32-35** Those who believed were of one heart and soul, and they held all things in common.	**I John 1:1-2–2:2** "God is light and in him is no darkness at all."	**John 20:19-31** A doubting Thomas meets the risen Lord.
April 14, 1991 3rd Sunday of Easter (white)	4	**Acts 3:12-19** Peter calls to repentance those who saw the healing of a lame man at the Temple.	**I John 3:1-7** "We are God's children now!"	**Luke 24:35-48** The risen Jesus touches, eats with, and teaches his followers.

	PSALM	1st LESSON	2nd LESSON	3rd LESSON
April 21, 1991 4th Sunday of Easter *Good Shepherd Sunday* (white)	23	**Acts 4:8-12** "The stone which was re- jected by the builders has become the head of the corner."	**I John 3:18-24** "Love in deed and in truth."	**John 10:11-18** "I am the good shepherd."
April 28, 1991 5th Sunday of Easter (white)	22:25-31	**Acts 8:26-40** Philip and the Ethiopian eunuch.	**I John 4:7-12** Love born of God.	**John 15:1-8** "I am the vine, you are the branches."
May 5, 1991 6th Sunday of Easter (white)	98	**Acts 10:44-48** Gentiles receive the gift of the Holy Spirit.	**I John 5:1-6** Faith—the victory that overcomes the world.	**John 15:9-17** A new commandment: "Love one another even as I have loved you."
May 9, 1991 Ascension Day (white)	47	**Acts 1:1-11** "You shall receive power to be my witnesses."	**Eph. 1:15-23** Christ is head over all things for the church.	**Luke 24:46-53** Witnesses to the power and victory of Jesus. *or* **Mark 16:9-16, 19-20** "Go into all the world."
May 12, 1991 7th Sunday of Easter (white)	1	**Acts 1:15-17, 21-26** Matthias enrolled as one of the apostles to take Judas' place.	**I John 5:9-13** Eternal life through the Son, Jesus Christ.	**John 17:11b-19** The high priestly prayer: "I am praying for them."

	PSALM	1st LESSON	2nd LESSON	3rd LESSON
May 19, 1991 Day of Pentecost (red)	104:24-34	**Acts 2:1-21** The coming of the Holy Spirit—"wind and fire." *or* **Ezek. 37:1-14** "Can these bones live?"	**Rom. 8:22-27** The Spirit intercedes for us. *or* **Acts 2:1-21** (Same as 1st lesson above.)	**John 15:26-27; 16:4b-15** "When the Spirit comes, he will guide you into all truth."
May 26, 1991 Trinity Sunday (white)	29	**Isa. 6:1-8** Isaiah's vision. "Woe is me! For I am lost; for I am a man of unclean lips."	**Rom. 8:12-17** "We are children of God . . . heirs with Christ."	**John 3:1-17** Jesus and Nicodemus. "You must be born anew."
June 2, 1991 2nd Sunday After Pentecost (green)	20	**I Sam. 16:1-13** The anointing of David.	**II Cor. 4:5-12** A treasure in earthen vessels.	**Mark 2:23-3:6** "Sabbath was made for man, not man for the Sabbath."
June 9, 1991 3rd Sunday After Pentecost (green)	57	**I Sam. 16:14-23** David finds favor in the sight of Saul.	**II Cor. 4:13-5:1** "We do not lose heart . . . because we look to . . . the things that are unseen [and] eternal."	**Mark 3:20-35** "Who are my mother and brothers?"
June 16, 1991 4th Sunday After Pentecost (green)	46	**II Sam. 1:1, 17-27** David's lament over Saul and Jonathan.	**II Cor. 5:6-10, 14-17** "The love of Christ controls us."	**Mark 4:26-34** The parable of the mustard seed.

	PSALM	1st LESSON	2nd LESSON	3rd LESSON
June 23, 1991 5th Sunday After Pentecost (green)	48	**II Sam. 5:1-12** David becomes king.	**II Cor. 5:18-6:2** Ambassadors for Christ.	**Mark 4:35-41** Jesus calms the storm at sea.
June 30, 1991 6th Sunday After Pentecost (green)	24	**II Sam. 6:1-15** David brings the ark of God to the city of David.	**II Cor. 8:7-15** The sharing of one's abundance with the poor.	**Mark 5:21-43** Jesus heals the woman with the flow of blood and raises Jairus' daughter.
July 7, 1991 7th Sunday After Pentecost (green)	89:20-37	**II Sam. 7:1-17** The Lord promises to establish David's kingdom forever.	**II Cor. 12:1-10** Paul's thorn in the flesh.	**Mark 6:1-6** Jesus rejected in his own town.
July 14, 1991 8th Sunday After Pentecost (green)	132:11-18	**II Sam. 7:18-29** David praises God for God's promise to him.	**Eph. 1:1-10** We have been blessed by God through Christ with every spiritual blessing.	**Mark 6:7-13** Jesus sends out the Twelve with no bread, no bag, and no money.
July 21, 1991 9th Sunday After Pentecost (green)	53	**II Sam. 11:1-15** David and Bathsheba.	**Eph. 2:11-22** "No longer strangers and sojourners."	**Mark 6:30-34** Miraculous feeding of five thousand.
July 28, 1991 10th Sunday After Pentecost (green)	32	**II Sam. 12:1-14** Nathan confronts David and his sin.	**Eph. 3:14-21** "Rooted and grounded in love."	**John 6:1-15** Jesus feeds the multitude with five barley loaves and two fish.

	PSALM	1st LESSON	2nd LESSON	3rd LESSON
August 4, 1991 11th Sunday After Pentecost (green)	34:11-22	**II Sam. 12:15b-24** David mourns the death of his son by Bathsheba.	**Eph. 4:1-6** One body and one spirit.	**John 6:24-35** "I am the bread of life."
August 11, 1991 12th Sunday After Pentecost (green)	143:1-8	**II Sam. 18:1, 5, 9-15** The death of Absalom.	**Eph. 4:25–5:2** "Be imitators of God, as beloved children."	**John 6:35, 41-51** "Jesus is the living bread."
August 18, 1991 13th Sunday After Pentecost (green)	102:1-12	**II Sam. 18:24-33** David mourns the death of Absalom. "Death of a son."	**Eph. 5:15-20** Paul teaches the way to live in these days of evil.	**John 6:51-58** A hard saying: "My flesh is food indeed and my blood is drink indeed. He who eats this bread will live for ever."
August 25, 1991 14th Sunday After Pentecost (green)	67	**II Sam. 23:1-7** The last words of David.	**Eph. 5:21-33** A profound mystery. "Be subject to one another."	**John 6:55-69** The Spirit gives life.
September 1, 1991 15th Sunday After Pentecost (green)	121	**I Kings 2:1-4, 10-12** The enthronement of Solomon.	**Eph. 6:10-20** The whole armor of God.	**Mark 7:1-8, 14-15, 21-23** The real defilement.
September 8, 1991 16th Sunday After Pentecost (green)	119:129-136	**Ecclus. 5:8-15** Teachings for a godly life. *or* **Prov. 2:1-8** The way to true wisdom and knowledge.	**James 1:17-27** "Be doers of the word and not hearers only."	**Mark 7:31-37** Jesus heals the deaf man.

	PSALM	1st LESSON	2nd LESSON	3rd LESSON
September 15, 1991 17th Sunday After Pentecost (green)	125	**Prov. 22:1-2, 8-9** "He who sows injustice will reap calamity."	**James 2:1-5, 8-10, 14-17** "Faith without works is dead." "Show no partiality to anyone."	**Mark 8:27-38** "Who do you say that I am?"
September 22, 1991 18th Sunday After Pentecost (green)	27:1-6	**Job 28:20-28** "Whence then comes wisdom?" Discourse by Job.	**James 3:13-18** True wisdom from above. "The harvest of righteousness is planted in peace by peacemakers."	**Mark 9:30-37** "Who is the greatest?" "The one who would be first must be last and servant of all."
September 29, 1991 19th Sunday After Pentecost (green)	27:7-14	**Job 42:1-6** Job repents for questioning God.	**James 4:13-17; 5:7-11** "Be patient, and establish your hearts for the coming of the Lord."	**Mark 9:38-50** Jesus teaches four lessons: exclusion, hospitality, special care of new believers, and self-discipline.
October 6, 1991 20th Sunday After Pentecost (green)	128	**Gen. 2:18-24** God creates woman from man.	**Heb. 1:1-4; 2:9-11** Jesus Christ, the pioneer of our salvation.	**Mark 10:2-16** Jesus teaches about divorce. Jesus blesses the children.
October 13, 1991 21st Sunday After Pentecost (green)	90:1-12	**Gen. 3:8-19** God drives Adam and Eve from the garden.	**Heb. 4:1-3, 9-13** Striving to enter the "rest" of salvation.	**Mark 10:17-30** The rich young ruler.

	PSALM	1st LESSON	2nd LESSON	3rd LESSON
October 20, 1991 22nd Sunday After Pentecost (green)	35:17-28	**Isa. 53:7-12** The Servant's Song; the suffering of the servant.	**Heb. 4:14-16** Jesus Christ, the great high priest who knows our weaknesses.	**Mark 10:35-45** "Are ye able to drink the cup that I drink?" A dangerous question.
October 27, 1991 23rd Sunday After Pentecost (green)	126	**Jer. 31:7-9** The Lord will redeem the remnant of Israel.	**Heb. 5:1-6** Christ appointed high priest by God. "Thou art my Son, today I have begotten thee."	**Mark 10:46-52** "Jesus, Son of David, have mercy on me!" Jesus heals the blind beggar.
November 3, 1991 24th Sunday After Pentecost *All Saints Day* (white)	119:33-48	**Deut. 6:1-9** "You shall love the Lord your God with all your heart, and with all your soul, and with all your might."	**Heb. 7:23-28** An eternal high priest who intercedes for us.	**Mark 12:28-34** The greatest commandment: "Love your neighbor as yourself."
November 10, 1991 25th Sunday After Pentecost (white)	146	**I Kings 17:8-16** The widow's jar of meal.	**Heb. 9:24-28** Christ sacrificed for sin once and for all.	**Mark 12:38-44** The widow's mite and two copper coins.
November 17, 1991 26th Sunday After Pentecost (white)	145:8-13	**Dan. 7:9-14** Daniel dreams of the destruction of the four beasts and an eternal kingdom.	**Heb. 10:11-18** Because of forgiveness of sin, we no longer need any offering for sin.	**Mark 13:24-32** Jesus foretells the end of time.

Date	PSALM	1st LESSON	2nd LESSON	3rd LESSON
November 24, 1991 Last Sunday After Pentecost *Christ the King* (white)	93	**Jer. 23:1-6** A righteous branch from David shall be raised up.	**Rev. 1:4b-8** "I am the Alpha and the Omega."	**John 18:33-37** A kingship not of this world.
December 1, 1991 1st Sunday in Advent (purple)	25:1-10	**Jer. 33:14-16** The coming of the promise of the Lord of a righteous branch for David.	**I Thess. 3:9-13** Establishing our hearts in holiness. Paul gives thanks for the faithfulness of the Thessalonians.	**Luke 21:25-36** Signs of our redemption drawing near.
December 8, 1991 2nd Sunday in Advent (purple)	126	**Mal. 3:1-4** The sending of the Lord's messenger to prepare his way.	**Phil. 1:3-11** Paul prays that love may abound.	**Luke 3:1-6** "Prepare the way of the Lord!" The appearance of John the baptizer.
December 15, 1991 3rd Sunday in Advent (purple)	**Zeph. 3:14-20** The Lord restores Israel.	**Isa. 12:2-6** God is my salvation. Sing praises to the Lord!	**Phil. 4:4-9** "Rejoice in the Lord always!" The example of Paul.	**Luke 3:7-18** John foretells the coming of the One who will baptize with the Holy Spirit and with fire.
December 22, 1991 4th Sunday in Advent (purple)	80:1-7	**Mic. 5:2-5a** From Bethlehem will come a Savior.	**Heb. 10:5-10** The one offering of Jesus Christ.	**Luke 1:39-55** The Magnificat.
December 29, 1991 1st Sunday After Christmas (white)	111	**I Sam. 2:18-20, 26** Samuel dedicated to the Lord.	**Ecclus. 3:3-7, 14-17** "For everything there is a time." *or* **Col. 3:12-17** "Put on the love of Christ"	**Luke 2:41-52** Jesus is twelve and at the Temple in Jerusalem: "I must be in my Father's house."

OFFERTORY SCRIPTURE

□

1. Therefore, I command you, You shall open wide your hand to your brother, to the needy and to the poor, in the land. (Deut. 15:11)
2. Every man shall give as he is able, according to the blessing of the Lord your God which he has given you. (Deut. 16:17)
3. Thine, O Lord, is the greatness, and the power, and the glory, and the victory, and the majesty; for all that is in the heavens and in the earth is thine; thine is the kingdom, O Lord, and thou art exalted as head above all. (I Chron. 29:11)
4. Blessed is he who considers the poor! The Lord delivers him in the day of trouble. (Ps. 41:1)
5. Offer to God a sacrifice of thanksgiving, and pay your vows to the Most High. (Ps. 50:14)
6. He who is kind to the poor lends to the Lord, and he will repay him for his deed. (Prov. 19:17)
7. Let your light so shine before men, that they may see your good works and give glory to your Father who is in heaven. (Matt. 5:16)
8. Do not lay up for yourselves treasures on earth, where moth and rust consume and where thieves break in and steal, but lay up for yourselves treasures in heaven, where neither moth nor rust consumes and where thieves do not break in and steal. For where your treasure is, there will your heart be also. (Matt. 6:19-21)
9. So whatever you wish that men would do to you, do so to them; for this is the law and the prophets. (Matt. 7:12)
10. Not everyone who says to me, "Lord, Lord," shall enter the kingdom of heaven, but he who does the will of my Father who is in heaven. (Matt. 7:21)
11. [Remember] the words of the Lord Jesus, how he said, "It is more blessed to give than to receive." (Acts 20:35)
12. He who sows sparingly will also reap sparingly, and he who sows bountifully will also reap bountifully. Each one must do as he has made up his mind, not reluctantly or under compulsion, for God loves a cheerful giver. (II Cor. 9:6-7)
13. So then, as we have opportunity, let us do good to all men, and especially to those who are of the household of faith. (Gal. 6:10)
14. There is great gain in godliness with contentment; for we brought nothing into the world, and we cannot take anything out of the world. (I Tim. 6:6-7)

FUNERAL RESOURCES

□

Scripture Resources*

For the Funeral of a Child:

I Samuel 1:27-28—*Dedicating a child to God.*
Isaiah 11:6—*A little child shall lead us.*
Isaiah 40:11—*The Good Shepherd.*
Matthew 18:1-4—*Who is the greatest?*
Matthew 19:14—*Jesus loves children.*

For the Funeral of a Young Adult:

Psalm 90:12—*The value of the years.*
Matthew 11:28-30—*For one who has faithfully served.*
Matthew 25—*The good and faithful servant.*
John 11:25-26—*The importance of faith.*
John 14:1-2—*The need to trust.*
I Corinthians 15:42-58—*The perishable and the imperishable body.*
Hebrews 11:13-15—*For someone whose death seems without meaning.*

For a Father:

I Kings 2:1-4—*A Father's leadership.*
Psalm 103:13—*God's love and a father's love.*
John 14—*The father is faithful.*

For a Mother:

Proverbs 31:28—*Her children shall call her blessed.*
Isaiah 66:13—*God's comfort and a mother's comfort.*
II Timothy 1:5—*A mother's faith.*

*"Scripture Resources" and "A Funeral Sermon" from *Preaching to Sufferers* by Kent D. Richmond. Copyright © 1988 by Abingdon Press. Used by permission.

For Those Who Have Grown Old:

Genesis 15:15—*A good old age.*
Psalm 90:5-6—*The naturalness of death.*
Ecclesiastes 3:2—*Death, a part of life.*
Luke 2:29-30—*A long life of faith.*
II Timothy 4:6-8—*Faith prepares us for dying.*

For Those Who Have Suffered Through a Long Illness:

Deuteronomy 33:27—*Rest from suffering.*
Psalm 23—*Even in pain, the Lord is present.*
Romans 8:18—*Suffering compared to glory.*
II Corinthians 4:7-12—*In pain, but not in despair.*

Sample Sermons and Namings

A Funeral Sermon*

This sermon is for Jean. She was born with a rare illness and lived six weeks before she died, much longer than the doctors predicted. Her parents were both members of a medical profession and were able to give much of the daily care that Jean required. I had never met her parents before they were referred to me by one of our church members. Her parents, feeling that death was imminent, wanted to have her baptized, but did not have a relationship with a pastor.

Jean was a beautiful child. Her death was hard for all concerned, though her parents were enabled to do much anticipatory grieving in the weeks that they cared for her with the knowledge that she could not survive her illness.

A SERMON FOR JEAN

Text: "*Let the children come to me . . . for to such belongs the kingdom of heaven.*" (Matthew 19:14)

There is no more difficult event in all of life than the death of a child. It violates everything that we have grown up believing to be right and just. It intrudes upon all of the hopes and dreams that we had built for our children as we awaited their coming. It leaves us feeling empty, devoid of hope.

Death, when it comes to those who are old, who have lived a long and a full life, can be accepted as a reasonable part of living. Though it hurts to lose those we love, there is yet a sense that life must be that way.

However when it comes to an infant like Jean, then we are left wondering, "If death can happen to her, then what is left? Is there anything on which we can place our trust?"

Hard on those kinds of questions are the nagging doubts that are shoved, almost brutally, into the middle of our faith. Where is God in the midst of our pain? Does God even care? Is there really any reason for believing in God, if this is all that it comes to? In the midst of our tears and our pain, we struggle to find anything that makes any sense at all.

Dick and Jane (parents), heaven knows I know how you feel, for I have been there. I know your pain. I have cried your tears. I still do. And yet, fifteen years down the road from my own son's death, I have learned some things that have been helpful for me, and I would like to share them with you.

It is common at times like this to hear people say, "Well, it's God will." Such people mean well, but I do not believe that it is God's will that any child die, any more than it was God's will that his own Son die. God's will? No, for if that is God's will, then I want nothing to do with such a God.

There are those who would say that it is from experiences such as Jean's illness and death that we are enabled to live stronger lives, that we are made better able to cope with life's troubles. Again, I believe such suggestions are offered in the hope that they will be helpful, but I find that I have more in common with Professor Dorothee Soelle, who sees in such experiences a God who may be "insensitive to human misery."[1]

What do I believe? I believe most firmly that God hurts just as much as we do, that our faith was never given to us with a promise that we would be protected from pain, but that faith does provide us with a means of handling the pain and even of finding meaning in the midst of it. And I believe that life's meaning has very little to do with its length and very much to do with its quality. What's more, I find a basis for that belief in the faith given to us by Jesus Christ.

When the prophet Isaiah spoke of hope to an exiled nation, he said "a little child shall lead" you (11:6). When asked who would get into the kingdom of heaven, Jesus called to his side a child and said to that crowd of self-satisfied people that unless we become as children, we shall not enter the kingdom of heaven (see Matt. 18:1-5). When the disciples would have held them back, Jesus said, "Let the children come to me . . . for to such belongs the kingdom of heaven" (Matt. 19:13-14).

When God decided once and for all to show the world how he intended for people to live, he didn't do it with brass bands and banners. Rather, as preacher Paul Scherer put it, "he came down the stairs of heaven with a child in his arms."[2] Why? Because children teach us so much that older people cannot.

A young mother who lost her daughter to leukemia put it this way:

> We felt privileged to have been her parents, for she had taught us so much. I read somewhere that "suffering ceases to be suffering when it has meaning," and I feel that this is what happened inside me when I first heard that she would not be with us for long. I saw her as a teacher. . . . We are constantly reminded of the lessons that she taught us.[3]

That is exactly the way I feel about Jean. Just take a look at the gifts of learning that she shared with us.

To her grandparents: You have seen your children confront one of the most painful events of life, do battle with it, and come through it. They are hurt, yes, but they have come through it whole. If ever you had any doubts about their ability to deal with the stresses of life (and what parent does not?), then you should have no such questions now. That was Jean's gift to you.

To Dick and Jane: I would be reluctant to say that God picks certain people to be parents of children like Jean, but how fortunate she was to have had the two of you. Your training enabled you to care for her in her illness and, as you ministered to her hurt, she showed you a determination and dedication to live in a way that you will never forget. You will recognize and engender it in others.

You have experienced depths of emotion, love, and compassion given only to those who have walked through "the valley of the shadow." And you will better minister to those who come to you with hurting hearts.

You have been brought much closer to each other, as you have shared the heights and depths of each other's feelings in a way not given to all. Those are just a few of the things that Jean shared with you.

To the members of the medical staff who treated Jean: She had something for you, too. She so touched your hearts by her desire to live that you came back after work hours were done, just to sit and hold her. You shook your heads in amazement at her determination, and, in the midst of that, she helped renew your sense of the worth of what you do.

In short, we have all learned something and have become better persons for Jean's having been among us.

Questions? Oh yes, there are all kinds of them, but there is no question as to meaning. Life is never meaningless, however short it may be. Jean's life was filled with meaning and purpose.

Jesus knew that. "Let the children come unto me . . . for of such is the kingdom of heaven." He knew what a gift children are to us, and that kingdom has become his gift to Jean. Thanks be to God!

Notes

1. Dorothee Soelle, *Suffering*, trans. Everett R. Kalin (Philadelphia: Fortress Press, 1975), p. 26.
2. Paul Scherer, exposition on the book of Job, in *The Interpreter's Bible*, vol. III, ed. Nolan B. Harmon (New York: Abingdon Press, 1954), p. 1173.
3. Bernard Schoenberg et al., *Anticipatory Grief* (New York: Columbia University Press, 1974), p. 152.

A Funeral Naming

Some funeral services refer to the eulogy as a "naming." The following naming was delivered at Haymount United Methodist Church by Dr. John Bergland. It is offered here as an example.
Hubert
May 19, 1908–February 20, 1989

Soil and water conservationist, bird watcher, dogwood tree enthusiast, faithful Kiwanian, North Carolina State University alumnus, Democratic Party loyalist, confidante to his friends and family, and supporter of The United Methodist Church.

No one rendered more outstanding service to his community. He championed efforts to relieve poverty, fear, and ignorance. His leadership in the Kiwanis program to plant dogwoods resulted in the designation of Fayetteville, North Carolina, as the "City of Dogwoods."

His seventeen years of distinguished leadership on the Cumberland County Soil and Water District Board of Supervisors led to his receiving the Cumberland County Distinguished Service Award for outstanding conservation work, the Outstanding Service Award from the Soil Conservation Society of America, and the Outstanding Leadership and Support of Agriculture Award from the Fayetteville Area Chamber of Commerce.

His daily work as a Christian found expression in his roles as a Sunday school teacher, member of United Methodist Men, and officer of the Administrative Board in the Haymount United Methodist Church and the Board of Lay Activities of the North Carolina Conference of The United Methodist Church.

Hubert left a legacy of service to his community and to the future by the way he lived and the commitment he made.

Now, as we remember his life among us and mark his passing, how shall we name him? To be sure, he was a good servant of Jesus Christ, a faithful husband, a devoted father and grandfather. He was a loyal kinsman, a helpful friend, and a man who never met a stranger. How shall we name him?

At the ford of the Jabbok, Jacob wrestled with God. Jacob was renamed Israel because he had struggled with God and with men (Gen. 32:28).

On the road to Caesarea Philippi, Simon bar Jonah made the first confession of faith, "You are the Christ!" He was named Peter the rock (Matt. 16:18).

It could be said that our friend Hubert was like a rock: stalwart, steady, always the same. It could be said that he was like the light of the world: warm, bright, and belonging to vision.

But consider with me the rightness of this image. Hubert was like a tree, planted by the river of life. Psalm 1 says so well what I want to say today.

> Blessed is the man
> who walks not in the counsel of
>   the wicked,
> nor stands in the way of sinners,
>   nor sits in the seat of scoffers;
> but his delight is in the law of the
>   Lord,
>   and on his law he meditates day
>   and night.
> He is like a tree
>   planted by streams of water,
> that yields its fruit in its season,

and its leaf does not wither.
In all that he does, he prospers.

Now a great tree has fallen in the forest, and today it leaves an empty place against the sky. But we know Hubert's name, and we know the God who named him and the Shepherd who calls him by name. A sheep of his own fold, a son of his own household, a citizen of God's kingdom. He is like a tree that has born good fruit for the blessing and benefit of us all.

Thanks be God for the life and work and witness of this man. Thanks be to God who gives victory through our Lord, Jesus Christ.

BIBLICAL AUTHORITY AND PREACHING

□

The Interpretation of Scripture

Since the late nineteenth century, there has been a conflict between the interpretation of scripture as the authority for Christian faith and life and the interpretation of scripture as infallible. A clear understanding of this difference can be helpful for biblical interpreters.

Emphasis on the Bible as infallible or as the result of plenary inspiration or as inerrant has come principally through the Calvinist tradition in the United States, with particular shaping by theologians at Princeton Theological Seminary during the first half of the nineteenth century. This school of thought emphasized the written word, the actual text of scripture, and insisted that God has spoken in and through those precise words.

Emphasis on the authority of the Bible was characteristic of several other traditions, including the Wesleyan tradition in North America. Stress on authority sets a high priority on the internal witness of the Holy Spirit, who acts as interpreter of the written word. The word of the text is important but never stands alone and is always to be understood only as the text is interpreted through the inspiration of the Holy Spirit.

Additional emphases should be made in regard to this second position: (1) The Holy Spirit works to inspire both the writers of the scriptural texts and the interpretation of those texts and (2) the Holy Spirit works in and through the community of faith as well as in and through the individual interpreter. These two tensions must always be maintained, for it is the same Holy Spirit who speaks through both text and interpreter, and it is the same Holy Spirit who speaks through both the community of faith and the individual interpreter.

Biblical Authority

Biblical authority is primary in Protestant theological understanding. In most traditions, affirmation of the scripture as an authoritative guide to faith and life is required as a part of church membership. But what is meant by the "authority" of the Bible?

"Authority" is that which possesses the power to shape the life of individuals and communities; moreover, authority is that which is acknowledged as possessing the right and worth to shape life. There are three emphases in this statement. First, authority is an expression of power. Authority has the ability to order or structure human existence. But, second, authority is not pure power. Authority does not impose itself as an external, strange force, and it is not tyrannical or insensitively authoritarian. Rather, authority presents itself so as to invite acknowledgment, acceptance, and responsive obedience. Third, authority is the primary factor in the shaping or molding of human life. To be a person or to be a community is to have an organizing authority.

With this definition, it is possible to see that any number of authorities might be the organizing principle of human existence. Consequently, the authority one acknowledges determines the sort of person or community that is formed. This is the tension between the true God and false gods. Life sculpted around a false god is always deformed; life ordered around the true God is shaped in the image of God as the body of Christ.

The Bible is authoritative in an intermediary way. It communicates the living God through the power of the Holy Spirit, so as to bring life into communion with Jesus Christ. Scripture is not the final authority, but our Bible is a necessary and indispensable medium through which primary authority presents itself, invites acknowledgment, and functions to integrate life around this divine center.

To be even more specific, the authority of God is expressed through Jesus Christ, who encounters human life through the agency of the Holy Spirit and draws human life into conformity with himself. Jesus Christ is the authority of Christian life, and the formative power of Christ is made known through the witness of the Bible as this is made a vitalizing power by the Holy Spirit.

Scripture, by the inspiriting of God, becomes the medium by which Christ is presented to us and evokes our responsive worship. In this sense, the Bible is authoritative.

The Wesleyan tradition, especially, has remained sensitive to the person, role, and enlivening activity of the Holy Spirit. This awareness has not always been sharp or unalloyed; and, indeed, at times it has not been given due attention. Nevertheless, through the late nineteenth and twentieth centuries, central acknowledgment of the Holy Spirit kept alive the authority of scripture, prevented an exclusive attention to the written texts of the Bible, and celebrated the freedom of God to speak through the Holy Spirit by making use of the Old and New Testaments.

An awareness of the Holy Spirit will prevent the preacher from entering the raucous debate over detailed inerrancy, partial infallibility, ironic inerrancy, or complete infallibility. These arguments ensue when too much weight is placed on the nature of the text as such. The counterbalancing tension of the Holy Spirit, who is the primary inspirer of both the authors and the interpreters, challenges us to a more dynamic and historical understanding of the relation of God and human beings.

Preaching and Word

The role of the interpreter of the word, including the role of the preacher, is one that must be sensitively employed. The interpreter of the word stands immediately and thoroughly indebted to the permeative activity of the Holy Spirit. Through study and prayer, one must be sensitive to the Holy Spirit's inspiring of the words of scripture. Through openness and contribution, one must be sensitive to the Holy Spirit, who guides interpretation in the community of faithful believers. And, through receptive obedience, hearers must be responsive to enlightenment by the Holy Spirit.

The Bible is authority as the Bible actually functions to mediate Jesus Christ and to effect the formation of life in Christ. Authority shapes life; Jesus Christ shapes Christian life. This occurs as the Holy Spirit operates as a pervasive presence for writers, interpreters, and hearers.

Thomas A. Langford
Duke Divinity School

SERMON CONTRIBUTORS

□

The Rev. Dr. H. Pat Albright
Senior Pastor of Mt. Lebanon United Methodist Church
3319 West Liberty Avenue
Pittsburgh, Pennsylvania 14216

The Rev. Dr. Richard Andersen
Senior Pastor of St. Timothy's Lutheran Church
5100 Camden Avenue
San Jose, California 95124

The Rev. Dr. James H. Bailey
Senior Pastor of White Plains United Methodist Church
307 E. Maynard Road
Cary, N.C. 27511

The Rev. Robert T. Baldridge
Superintendent of the Rockingham District of the North Carolina
    Conference of the United Methodist Church
1304 W. Church Street
Laurinburg, N.C. 28352

The Rev. Dr. J. Daniel Bauman
Senior Pastor of College Avenue Baptist Church
4747 College Avenue
San Diego, California 92115

The Rev. Robert Eric Bergland
Pastor of Grace United Methodist Church
300 Fairfax Street
Clinton, N.C. 28328

The Rev. H. Michael Brewer
Pastor of Crescent Springs Presbyterian Church
710 Western Reserve Road
Crescent Springs, Kentucky 41017

The Rev. Dr. Eugene Wayne Brice
Senior Pastor of Country Club Christian Church
Kansas City, Missouri

The Rev. Dr. James C. Cammack
Pastor Emeritus of the Snyder Baptist Church
2805 Millbrook Road
Fayetteville, N.C. 28303

The Rev. Dr. Kenneth L. Carder
Senior Pastor of Church Street United Methodist Church
P. O. Box 1303
Knoxville, Tenn. 37901

The Rev. Ronald E. Dietrich
Minister of Christian Education and Nurture
Haymount United Methodist Church
1700 Ft. Bragg Road
Fayetteville, N.C. 28303

The Rev. Heather Murray Elkins
Chaplain at Drew University and Ph. D Candidate in Homiletics
and History of Worship
Drew University, Madison, N. J. 07940

The Rev. Dr. Wallace E. Fisher
Pastor Emeritus of The Lutheran Church of the Holy Trinity,
Lancaster, Pa.
85 Briarwood Circle
Pinehurst, N.C. 28374

Bishop Ernest A. Fitzgerald
Bishop of the Atlanta Area of the United Methodist Church
159 Ralph McGill Blvd. N.E.
Atlanta, Georgia 30365

The Rev. R. Carl Frazier, Jr.
Pastor of the Battleboro-Clark Street United Methodist Charge
P.O. Box 153
Battleboro, N.C. 27809

The Rev. Dr. C. Thomas Hilton
Senior Pastor of The First Presbyterian Church
2331 N. E. 26th Avenue
Pompano Beach, Florida 33062

The Rev. Dr. Thomas A. Langford
William Kellen Quick Professor of Theology and Methodist Studies
Duke Divinity School, Duke University
Durham, N.C. 27706

The Rev. Michael T. McEwen
An Episcopal Priest who is Rector of Emmanuel Episcopal Church
Shawnee, Oklahoma

Chaplain Milford Oxendine, Jr. LCDR, CHC, USN
A Native American Chaplain in the United States Marine Corps.
3rd Assault Amphibian Battalion
1st Marine Division (REIN), FMF
Camp Pendleton, California 92055-5522

The Rev. Kent D. Richmond
A hospital Chaplain and a member of the Wisconsin Annual Conference of The United Methodist Church

The Rev. Dr. Lucy Rose
A Ordained minister of the United Presbyterian Church who teaches homiletics at Columbia Theological Seminary in Decatur, Georgia
Columbia Theological Seminary; Decatur, Georgia 30031

The Rev. Dr. Ralph W. Sockman (DECEASED)
Distinguished preacher of the National Radio Pulpit and Minister of Christ Church in New York City

The Rev. H. Gray Southern
Minister of the West Nash United Methodist church
2106 West Nash Street; Wilson, N.C. 27893

W. C. Taylor, Jr.
Pastor of Grace United Methodist Church
101 West Avenue F; Copperas Cove, Texas 76522

The Rev. Robert M. Terhune
An ordained elder of The United Methodist Church who has served as Missionary to Japan for more than 25 years.
3-16-2 Naka Ochiana 3-Chrome
Shinjuku-ku; Tokyo 161, Japan

The Rev. Peter D. Weaver
Senior Minister of First United Methodist Church
Centre and Aiken Avenues; Pittsburgh, Pa. 15206

The Rev. Dr. William H. Willimon
Minister to the University and Professor of Christian Worship at Duke University
Duke Station
Durham, N.C. 27006

The Rev. Samuel Wynn
Minister of Calvary United Methodist Church and National Director of The Native American Caucus of the United Methodist Church
3636 Deaver Place
Hope Mills, N.C. 28348

The Rev. Dr. John K. Bergland (EDITOR)
Senior Minister of Haymount United Methodist Church
1700 Ft. Bragg Road
Fayetteville, N.C. 28303

Section III

□

INDEXES

SCRIPTURE INDEX

□

The abbreviation *ff.* following a page number indicates a sermon on this text.

SCRIPTURE INDEX

SCRIPTURE INDEX

General Index

□

Abel, 262
Abiathar, 148
Abraham, 61, 63, 113, 128, 244
Absalom, 215, 221
Adam, 272
Adonai, 253
Ahaz, 335
Ahimaz, 221
Allen, Nathan, 250
Anderson, Hugh, 49
Andrew, apostle, 30-34, 39
Anthony the Great, 244
Antiquities of the Jews (Josephus), 140-41
Apocalypse, 304-9, 317-23
Apocalypse Now, 308
Ark of the covenant, 172, 173
Augustine of Hippo, 124

Babylon, exile in, 42-46, 72, 327
Bacon, Francis, 262
Barth, Karl, 242
Bartimaeus, healing of, 285, 287-90
Bathsheba, 210
"Because He Lives," 308
Becker, Ernest, 127
Beecher, Henry Ward, 214
Bethlehem, 345, 346, 348-49
Biblical authority, 371-73
Blackwood, Andrew, 160
Boesak, Allan, 80-81
Bonhoeffer, Dietrich, 102-3
Borglum, Gutzar, 288
Bread of life, Jesus as, 211-13, 215-20, 221-26, 227-31
Brooks, Phillips, 152, 153
Brown, Capability, 72
Browne, Thomas, 222
Browning, Robert, 156
Brunner, Emil, 59
Buechner, Frederick, 306
Burch, Vacher, 91-92

Cain, 262
Calvin, John, 166
Calvinist biblical interpretation, 371
Carnegie, Dale, 255
Chardin, Teilhard de, 237-38
Charyn, Jerome, 149
Christ, the. See Messiah, the
A Christmas Carol (Dickens), 333
Christmas sermons, 332-50
Choctaw, Antoni (prayer), 296

Communion: mystery of 143-44; with God, 243-44
Confusion, 25-29
Congregation (Charyn), 149
Congreve, William, 340
"The Contribution of Marital Happiness to Global Happiness," 266-67
Cornelius, 91, 121
Covenant: new, 63-65, 78; with Abraham, 61, 63
Cox, Harvey, 247
Crain, George, 104
Creation, 143, 166, 168-71
Cromwell, Oliver, 166
The Culture of Narcissism (Lasch), 128
Cyrus the Persian, 72

Daniel, apocalypse in, 304, 306
David: and Absalom, 215, 221; and ark, 172, 173; death of, 227, 232; as king, 146-60, 165, 166, 180, 188, 244, 256, 262; sin of, 195, 202, 210
Deaf and dumb man, healing of, 240-45
Dear God, Where Are You? (Goodrich), 99
Death of a child, sermon for, 365-68
Dent, Enid, 72
Dickens, Charles, 333
Discipleship, 30-31, 37-41, 259-65
Divorce, 266-71
Doubt, 98-100

Efird, James, 269
Eli, prophet, 30, 33
Elijah, prophet, 48, 49, 51, 244, 298, 301
Eliot, T.S., 327
Elisha, prophet, 48
Elizabeth, 337-39
Emerson, Ralph Waldo, 232-33
Emmaus Road experience, 104-7
Empedocles, 92
Envy, 260-65
Ephesus, disciples at, 24
Epiphany, 17-23
The Escape from Evil (Becker), 127
Eucharist, the, 221, 224-25. See also Holy Communion
Eulogy, sample, 368-70
Eunuch, Ethiopian, 115
Evangelical Faith (Thielicke), 241
Eve, 272
The Exorcist, 43

Farber, Leslie H., 261

381

Naphtali (pseudepigraphical book), 55
Nathan, prophet, 180, 188, 202
Nathaniel, apostle, 30, 31
Nazareth, Jesus in, 180-86, 189
Nebuchadnezzar, 327
Nerken, Ira, 299-300
New Orleans, Battle of, 94
Nicodemus, 140
Nineveh, 37, 167
Noah, 55, 57

Obedience, 121-25
O God, Book II, 58
Oman, John, 191
Oppenheimer, Robert, 262
Othello, 263

Pandora, 57
Passover, 67
Paul, apostle: 17, 161, 202, 253; on discipleship, 260-61, 263; and the law, 291; suffering of, 147, 152, 159; visions of, 180
Peace, Jesus' words on, 321-22
Peck, M. Scott, 156
Pentecost, 133-39
People of the Lie (Peck), 156
Peter. *See* Simon Peter
Pharisees on marriage and divorce, 266, 268-69
Philip, apostle, 30, 31, 202-3
Philip, deacon, 115
Pilate, Pontius, 310, 321
Places in the Heart, 300
Potrosyan, Susan, 80
Prayer, 244, 254-57; of Jesus, 126-32
Princeton Theological Seminary, 271

Quakers, 213
The Quest for the Historical Jesus (Schweitzer), 106-7
Quoist, Michael, 212-13

Rainbow, 55, 56-57, 59-60
Realf, Richard, 60
Reconciliation with God, 165, 198-99
Rees, Wilbur, 278
"Religio Medici" (Browne), 222
Repentance, 37, 38, 102-3, 331-32
Resurrection, the, 91-96, 97-101, 102-8
Rich young ruler, 272-76
Rickenbacker, Eddie, 313
Rittenhouse, Jessie, 235
Rousseau, Jean Jacques, 263

Sabbath laws, 146-47
Sacrament, definition, 230
The Sacred Journey (Buechner), 306
Sagan, Carl, 320
Sanders, Carl, 58

Sangster, W. E., 141
Samuel: boyhood of, 30, 33, 34, 344; as prophet, 148-50, 155, 166
Sarah, 61
Satan, 56
"Saul" (Browning), 156
Saul, king, 149, 152-56, 159-60, 180, 262
Saul of Tarsus. *See* Paul, apostle
Sawyer, Tom, 62-63, 64
Scherer, Paul, 367
Schweitzer, Albert, 106-7
Scripture, interpretation of, 371-73
Scrooge, Ebenezer, 333
Service, 277-84
Shema, 291, 293, 294
Shepherd, the Good, 109-14, 196-201
Sighing for Eden (Willimon), 272-73
Simeon, 339
Simon Peter, apostle: 30, 31, 32, 33, 39, 49, 50, 51, 52, 61, 63, 64, 369; and Cornelius, 91, 121; and gift of the Spirit, 133; healing of lame man, 102, 109; recognition of Christ, 246-51, 287
Soelle, Dorothee, 366
Solomon, king, 232
Soweto, South Africa, 340, 341
Spirit of God. *See* Holy Spirit
Stern, Aaron, 128
Stone, Samuel, 345
Storm, Jesus' stilling of, 165-71
Struther, Jan, 315
Survival in the Rat Race (Valbrecht), 93
Swindoll, Charles, 277-78

The Tempest (Shakespeare), 176
Temple of Jerusalem, 43, 67-70, 73, 319
Ten Commandments, 76
Thanksgiving, 311-16
Thielicke, Helmut, 62, 241
Thomas, apostle, 97-100, 105
A Thousand Years of Indian Storytelling (Henry and Costo), 295
"The Three Wise Men" (Auden), 17
Tiberius Caesar, 324, 325, 332
Time, concept of, 304-9
Tom Brown's School Days (Hughes), 348
Transfiguration, the, 48-54
Trinity, the Holy, doctrine of, 140-45
Tsali, Cherokee brave, 295
Twelve, the, 189-94, 195, 347-48

Uzzah, 172, 173

Valbrecht, Lous, 93
"The Voortrekker," 211

Wallerstein, Judith, 268
Walter Reed Medical Center, 228-29
War, Jesus' words on, 321-22